Viewpoints

from Black America

edited by

Gladys J. Curry
Southern University
in New Orleans

VIEWPOINTS
FROM
BLACK AMERICA

PRENTICE-HALL, INC.
Englewood Cliffs, New Jersey

C 13-941963-2
P 13-941955-1
Library of Congress Catalog Card no.: 78-114008

Printed in the United States of America

PRENTICE-HALL INTERNATIONAL, INC., *London*
PRENTICE-HALL OF CANADA, LTD., *Toronto*
PRENTICE-HALL OF AUSTRALIA, PTY., LTD., *Sydney*
PRENTICE-HALL OF INDIA PRIVATE LTD., *New Delhi*
PRENTICE-HALL OF JAPAN, INC., *Tokyo*

Current printing (last digit):
10 9 8 7 6 5 4 3 2 1

To The Memory of My Mother

Anita Joseph

Preface

Viewpoints from Black America is a collection of prose pieces by black writers covering a fairly wide variety of topics. It is intended to make the reader aware of what has been the thinking of the Negro in several of the vital areas of American life. It is also intended to acquaint the reader with the contributions of the Negro to American life and culture. To this end, I have arranged the essays topically: "On Education," "On Assimilation," "On Literature and Language," "On the Arts," "On Religion," and "On Politics." Some of the authors included here are well-known writers, but others are not so well known. My intent is to present not only a variety of topics but a variety of writers who have made worthwhile contributions to American literature, especially in the area of prose writing.

As a reader for college composition courses, this book includes essays that are intended to stimulate the students' thinking and thereby provide ideas for their compositions. At the end of each essay, I have placed questions for discussion and writing. At the end of some of the essays, I have also included an "Identification" section, in the hope that the student might obtain at least a cursory knowledge of Negroes, other than the authors in this text, who have made significant contributions to American life and culture. For the identification section the following reference books may be helpful:

Davis, John P., *American Negro Reference Book*, Englewood Cliffs, New Jersey: Prentice-Hall, Inc., 1966.
Ebony Editors, *The Negro Handbook*. Chicago: Johnson Publishing Co., 1966.
Fleming, G. James and Christian Burchell (eds.), *Who's Who in Colored America*. Yonkers, N.Y.: C. E. Burchell and Associates, 1951.
Negro Heritage Library, (10 Vols.) Yonkers, N.Y.: Educational Heritage, Inc., 1966.

I have placed the questions at the end of the essays for those instructors who may find them useful in approaching the study of the essays. It is not my intention, however, that the instructor should feel restricted by these questions.

While this book is designed primarily as a reader for writers, I feel that it will serve as a basic or supplementary text for any introductory Afro-American Literature course. Aside from its use as a textbook, however, it should provide interesting and worthwhile reading for the general public—especially for those people who have an interest in or even some curiosity about the literary and cultural contribution of the American Negro.

I believe that a word need be said about the contents of this book, in that it includes only the writings of Negroes. While I feel that a work of this nature should include works by Americans in general, I believe that the exclusivity may be justified by the fact that Negro writers have been almost totally ignored in college reading texts as well as in general American literature anthologies. There are signs, however, that the Negro writer will soon be included in anthologies of American writing. Until that time comes, I trust that this book will help to close the gap which is so glaringly evident in the present college English readers and hasten the day of the ideal reader.

Finally, I am deeply indebted to many people who have helped in various ways to make this book a reality—to A. J., Sam, and Bill, who first saw the possible merit of such a work; to John Curry and the librarians at Southern University in New Orleans, to Helen Scott and Rosemary Ventress for the preparation of the manuscript, to Helen Evans for her faith in me, and to Paul, a constant source of strength, courage, and endurance.

New Orleans, Louisiana   G. J. C.

Acknowledgments

The author makes the following acknowledgments to persons and publishers for works reprinted in this book.

Dial Press for the excerpt from *The Fire Next Time*. Reprinted from *The Fire Next Time* by James Baldwin. Copyright © 1962, 1963 by James Baldwin and used by permission of the publishers, The Dial Press.

Harper and Row for the excerpt (pp. 119–126) from *Strength to Love* by Martin Luther King, Jr. Copyright © 1963 by Martin Luther King, Jr. For an excerpt (pp. 102–109) from *The Luminous Darkness* by Howard Thurman; for the excerpt from Saunders Redding's "The Negro Writer and American Literature" (pp. 1–5, 17–19) from *Anger and Beyond: The Negro Writer in The United States*. All reprinted by permission of Harper and Row, publishers.

Dodd, Mead, and Company for lines from "The Poet," from *The Complete Poems of Paul Laurence Dunbar*, by permission of the publisher.

Random House for an excerpt from Ralph Ellison's *Shadow and Act.* Copyright © 1964 by Ralph Ellison.

Beacon Press for an excerpt from James Baldwin's *Notes of a Native Son.* Reprinted by permission of the publisher.

Doubleday and Company for "The Psychological Reactions of Oppressed People" from *White Man Listen!*, by Richard Wright. Copyright © 1957 by Richard Wright; reprinted by permission of Doubleday and Company, Inc.

Marzani and Munsell for "The Exiles" from *Black-Anglo Saxons* by Nathan Hare. Reprinted by permission of Marzani and Munsell, Inc.

Porter Sargent for The Question of Power segment from "The Crisis that Bred Black Power" by Nathan Wright, Jr. from *Black Power Revolt* (Floyd B. Barbour, ed.) Boston: Porter Sargent, Publisher, 1968, pp. 114–118.

Random House for "Beating That Boy," copyright © 1945 by Ralph Ellison, and "Living with Music," copyright © 1955 by Ralph Ellison. Reprinted from *Shadow and Act*, by Ralph Ellison, by permission of Random House, Inc.

Alfred A. Knopf for "The Negro as Artist and in Art," copyright © 1956 by Margaret Butcher; reprinted by permission of the publisher.

John Hope Franklin for permission to reprint "The Dilemma of The American Negro Scholar" from *Soon One Morning*, edited by Herbert Hill.

Stephen J. Wright and *Saturday Review* for permission to reprint "The Promise of Equality" from *Saturday Review*, July 20, 1968. Copyright © *Saturday Review*, Inc., 1968.

Margaret Walker Alexander for permission to reprint "Religion, Poetry, and History: Foundations for a New Educational System." Originally printed in *Vital Speeches of the Day*, October, 1968.

Marian Musgrave for permission to reprint "Teaching English as a Foreign Language to Students with Sub-Standard Dialects" from the *CLA Journal*, September, 1963.

ASNCC for permission to reprint "Power and Racism" by Stokely Carmichael.

William Morrow for "Soul Food," copyright © 1962, 1966 by LeRoi Jones, and for "Myth of a Negro Literature" copyright © by LeRoi Jones. Both from *Home: Social Essays*. Also for "Classic Blues" from *Blues People, copyright* © 1963 by LeRoi Jones. All reprinted by permission of William Morrow and Company, Inc.

Contents

ON LITERATURE
AND LANGUAGE

ON THE ARTS

ON POLITICS

Viewpoints

from Black America

I sit with Shakespeare and he winces not. Across the color line I move arm in arm with Balzac and Dumas, where smiling men and welcoming women glide in gilded halls. From out the caves of evening that swing between the strong-limbed earth and the tracery of stars, I summon Aristotle and Aurelius and what soul I will, and they come all graciously with no scorn nor condescension. So, wed with Truth, I dwell above the veil. Is this the life you grudge me, O knightly America? Is this the life you long to change into the dull red hideousness of Georgia? Are you so afraid lest peering from this high Pisgah, between Philistine and Amalekite, we sight the promised land?

W.E.B. DuBois

ON EDUCATION

Booker T. Washington

Booker T. Washington, educator, and founder of Tuskegee Institute at Tuskegee, Alabama, was born the son of slaves and was largely self-educated. He managed, however, to obtain some formal training in night school; and after overcoming many obstacles, he entered Hampton Institute (Hampton, Virginia) in 1872. He later became an instructor at Hampton, and in 1881 he was selected to organize a normal school in Tuskegee, Alabama. He served as president of Tuskegee Institute until his death in 1915.

Washington made a significant contribution to the education of Negroes in the United States. He espoused the philosophy that the major aim of Negroes should be economic independence, which, he felt, could best be attained through a "practical" education. This philosophy, which suggested that Negroes were more suited for manual than mental tasks, earned for Washington the censure of some of his contemporaries and harsh criticism from black Americans of today's society.

Washington was an excellent public speaker and was frequently invited to give public addresses. Perhaps one of the most noteworthy is the following, which was delivered at the International Exposition at Atlanta, Georgia in 1893. In it, he expounds his philosophy of "practical" education for the Negro that evoked an immediate negative reaction from his contemporary, W. E. B. DuBois, and initiated one of the first major debates on the education of Negroes.

Booker T.
Washington

Cast Down Your Bucket

Where You Are . . .

(1) A ship lost at sea for many days suddenly sighted a friendly vessel. From the mast of the unfortunate vessel was seen the signal: "Water, water, we die of thirst." The answer from the friendly vessel at once came back, "Cast down your bucket where you are." A second time the signal, "Water, water, send us water," ran up from the distressed vessel and was answered, "Cast down your bucket where you are," and a third and fourth signal for water was answered, "Cast down your bucket where you are." The captain of the distressed vessel, at last heeding the injunction, cast down his bucket and it came up full of fresh, sparkling water from the mouth of the Amazon River. To those of my race who depend on bettering their condition in a foreign land, or who underestimate the importance of cultivating friendly relations with the southern white man who is their next door neighbor, I would say, cast down your bucket where you are, cast it down in making friends, in every manly way, of the people of all races by whom you are

surrounded. Cast it down in agriculture, in mechanics, in commerce, in domestic service, and in the professions. And in this connection it is well to bear in mind that, whatever other sins the South may be called upon to bear, when it comes to business pure and simple it is in the South that the Negro is given a man's chance in the commercial world; and in nothing is this Exposition more eloquent than in emphasizing this chance. Our greatest danger is that, in the great leap from slavery to freedom, we may overlook the fact that the masses of us are to live by productions of our hands, and fail to keep in mind that we shall prosper in the proportion as we learn to dignify and glorify common labor and put brains and skill into the common occupations of life; shall prosper in proportion as we learn to draw the line between the superficial and the substantial, the ornamental gewgaws of life and the useful. No race can prosper till it learns that there is as much dignity [in] tilling a field as in writing a poem. It is at the bottom of life we must begin and not the top. Nor should we permit our grievances to overshadow our opportunities.

(2) To those of the white race who look to the incoming of those of foreign birth and strange tongue and habits for the prosperity of the South, were I permitted, I would repeat what I say to my own race, "Cast down your bucket where you are." Cast it down among the 8,000,000 Negroes whose habits you know, whose loyalty and love you have tested in days when to have proved treacherous meant the ruin of your firesides. Cast it down among those people who have, without strikes and labor wars, tilled your fields, cleared your forests, builded your railroads and cities, and brought forth treasures from the bowels of the earth and helped make possible this magnificent representation of the progress of the South. Casting down your bucket among my people, helping and encouraging as you are doing on these grounds, and with education of head, hand and heart you will find that they will buy your surplus land, make blossom the waste places in your fields, and run your factories. While doing this you can be sure in the future, as you have been in the past, that you and your families will be surrounded by the most patient, faithful, law-abiding, and unresentful people that the world has seen. As we have proved our loyalty to you in the past, in nursing your children, watching by the sick beds of your mothers and fathers, and often following them with tear-dimmed eyes to their graves, so in the future, in our humble way, we shall stand by you with a devotion that no foreigner can approach, ready to lay down our lives, if need be, in defense of yours; interlacing our industrial, commercial, civil and religious life with yours in a way that shall make the interests of both races one. In all things that are purely social we can be as separate as the fingers, yet one as the hand in all things essential to mutual progress.

(3) There is no defense or security for any of us except in the highest intelligence and development of all. If anywhere there are efforts tending

to curtail the fullest growth of the Negro, let these efforts be turned into stimulation, encouraging and making him the most useful and intelligent citizen. Effort or means so invested will pay a thousand per cent interest. These efforts will be twice blessed—"blessing him that gives and him that takes."

(4) There is no escape, through law of man or God, from the inevitable:

> The laws of changeless justice bind
> Oppressor with oppressed,
> And close as sin and suffering joined
> We march to fate abreast.

Nearly sixteen millions of hands will aid you pulling the load upwards, or they will pull against you the load downwards. We shall constitute one-third and much more of the ignorance and crime of the South, or one-third of its intelligence and progress; we shall contribute one-third to the business and industrial prosperity of the South, or we shall prove a veritable body of death, stagnating, depressing, retarding every effort to advance the body politic.

(5) The wisest among my race understand that the agitation of questions of social equality is the extremist folly, and the progress in the enjoyment of all the privileges that will come to us must be the result of severe and constant struggle, rather than of artificial forcing. No race that has anything to contribute to the markets of the world is long in any degree ostracized. It is important that we be prepared for the exercise of these privileges. The opportunity to earn a dollar in a factory just now is worth infinitely more than the opportunity to spend a dollar in an opera house.

(6) In conclusion, may I repeat, that nothing in thirty years has given us more hope and encouragement and drawn us so near to you of the white race as the opportunity offered by this Exposition; here bending, as it were, over the altar that represents the results of the struggles of your race and mine, both starting practically empty handed three decades ago, I pledge that, in your effort to work out the great and intricate problem which God has laid at the doors of the South, you will have at all times the patient, sympathetic help of my race. Only let this be constantly in mind, that while, from representations in these buildings of the products of field, of forest, of mine, of factory, letters and art, much good will come—yet, far above and beyond material benefit, will be that high good, that let us pray God will come, in a blotting out of sectional differences and racial animosities and suspicions, and in a determination, even in the remotest corner, to administer absolute justice; in a willing obedience

among all classes to the mandates of law, and a spirit that will tolerate nothing but the highest equity in the enforcement of law. This, this coupled with material prosperity, will bring into our beloved South new heaven and new earth.

Questions for Discussion and Writing

1. State the central idea of this essay.

2. Relate the anecdote in the introductory paragraph to the central idea. Is the significance of this anecdote clearly evident in the development of the essay? Explain.

3. Explain the figure of speech in the last sentence of paragraph 2: "In all things that are purely social we can be as separate as the fingers, yet one as the hand in all things essential to mutual progress." Do you believe this to be a valid concept for the society of Washington's day? For society today?

4. Considering the period in which Washington wrote, can you justify the following statement: "The opportunity to earn a dollar in a factory just now is worth more than the opportunity to spend a dollar in an opera house." Can it be justified in today's society? Why? Why not?

5. The author states: "There can be no defense or security for any of us except in the highest intelligence and development of all." Defend or criticize this idea.

6. Write a short paper in which you express your reaction to Washington's basic philosophy of the education of Negroes.

W. E. B. DuBois

William E. Burghardt DuBois, historian, sociologist, and novelist, was educated at Fisk University and at Harvard University. He also studied for two years in Germany at the University of Berlin. His writings include such sociological works as *The Suppression of the Slave Trade, The Philadelphia Negro, Color and Democracy*, and novels *Dark Princess* and *The Quest of the Golden Fleece*.

DuBois was a vociferous opponent of Booker T. Washington's philosophy of the education of the Negro in America. A major result of the Washington-DuBois conflict was the organization of the Niagara Movement out of which grew the National Association for the Advancement of Colored People. DuBois became the founder and editor of the *Crisis*, a national organ of the NAACP, and served as Public Relations Director of the organization for more than twenty years. In 1944, he went to Atlanta, Georgia to become the chairman of the NAACP's Special Research Department. In 1961, he immigrated to Africa where he served as editor of the *Encyclopedia Africana*. He died in 1963 at the age of ninety-five, having made many significant contributions to American civilization and culture.

W. E. B.
DuBois

From

An ABC of Color

(1) The men of the Niagara Movement* coming from the toil of the year's hard work and pausing a moment from the earning of their daily bread turn toward the nation and again ask in the name of ten million the privilege of a hearing. In the past year the work of the Negro hater has flourished in the land. Step by step the defenders of the rights of American citizens have retreated. The work of stealing the black man's ballot has progressed and the fifty and more representatives of stolen votes still sit in the nation's capital. Discrimination in travel and public accommodation has so spread that some of our weaker brethren are actually afraid to thunder against color discrimination as such and are simply whispering for ordinary decencies.

(2) Against this the Niagara Movement eternally protests. We will not be satisfied to take one jot or tittle less than our full manhood rights. We

*The Niagara Movement was a conference called by DuBois at Fort Erie, Canada near Niagara Falls. It consisted of men who were opposed to the Washington philosophy—men who believed in Negro freedom and growth.

claim for ourselves every single right that belongs to a freeborn American, political, civil and social; and until we get these rights we will never cease to protest and assail the ears of America. The battle we wage is not for ourselves alone but for all true Americans. It is a fight for ideals, lest this, our common fatherland, false to its founding, become in truth the land of the thief and the home of the Slave—a byword and a hissing among the nations for its sounding pretentions and pitiful accomplishment.

(3) Never before in the modern age has a great and civilized folk threatened to adopt so cowardly a creed in the treatment of its fellow citizens born and bred on its soil. Stripped of verbiage and subterfuge and in its naked nastiness the new American creed says: Fear to let black men even try to rise lest they become the equals of the white. And this is the land that professes to follow Jesus Christ. The blasphemy of such a course is only matched by its cowardice.

(4) In detail our demands are clear and unequivocal.

First, we would vote; with the right to vote goes everything: freedom, manhood, the honor of your wives, the chastity of your daughters, the right to work, and the chance to rise, and let no man listen to those who deny this.

(5) We want full manhood suffrage, and we want it now, henceforth and forever.

(6) Second, we want discrimination in public accommodation to cease. Separation in railway and street cars, based simply on race and color, is un-American, undemocratic, and silly. We protest against all such discrimination.

(7) Third, we claim the right of freemen to walk, talk, and be with them that wish to be with us. No man has a right to chose another man's friends, and to attempt to do so is an impudent interference with the most fundamental human privilege.

(8) Fourth, we want the laws enforced against rich as well as poor; against Capitalist as well as Laborer; against white as well as black. We are not more lawless than the white race, [but] we are more often arrested, convicted and mobbed. We want justice even for criminals and outlaws. We want the Constitution of the country enforced. We want Congress to take charge of Congressional elections. We want the Fourteenth Amendment carried out to the letter and every State disfranchised in Congress which attempts to disfranchise its rightful voters. We want the Fifteenth Amendment enforced and no State allowed to base its franchise simply on color.

(9) The failure of the Republican Party in Congress at the session just closed to redeem its pledge of 1904 with reference to suffrage conditions [in] the South seems a plain, deliberate, and premeditated breach of promise, and stamps that party as guilty of obtaining votes under false pretense.

(10) Fifth, we want our children educated. The school system in the country districts of the South is a disgrace and in few towns and cities are the Negro schools what they ought to be. We want the national government to step in and wipe out illiteracy in the South. Either the United States will destroy ignorance or ignorance will destroy the United States.

(11) And when we call for education we mean real education. We believe in work. We ourselves are workers, but work is not necessarily education. Education is the development of power and ideal. We want our children trained as intelligent human beings should be, and we will fight for all time against any proposal to educate black boys and girls simply as servants and underlings, or simply for the use of other people. They have a right to know, to think, to aspire.

(12) These are some of the chief things which we want. How shall we get them? By voting where we may vote, by persistent, unceasing agitation, by hammering at the truth, by sacrifice and work.

(13) We do not believe in violence, neither in the despised violence of the raid nor the lauded violence of the soldier, nor the barbarous violence of the mob, but we do believe in John Brown, in that incarnate spirit of justice, that hatred of a lie, that willingness to sacrifice money, reputation, and life itself on the altar of right. And here on the scene of John Brown's martyrdom we reconsecrate ourselves, our honor, our property, to the final emancipation of the race which John Brown died to make free.

(14) Our enemies, triumphant for the present, are fighting the stars in their courses. Justice and humanity must prevail. We live to tell these dark brothers of ours—scattered in counsel, wavering and weak–that no bribe of money or notoriety, no promise of wealth or fame, is worth the surrender of a people's manhood or the loss of a man's self-respect. We refuse to surrender the leadership of this race to cowards and trucklers. We are men; we will be treated as men. On this rock we have planted our banners. We will never give up, though the trump of doom find us still fighting.

(15) And we shall win. The past promised it, the present foretells it. Thank God for John Brown; thank God for Garrison and Douglass!, Sumner and Phillips, Nat Turner and Robert Gould Shaw, and all the hallowed dead who died for freedom! Thank God for all those today, few though their voices be, who have not forgotten the divine brotherhood of all men, white and black, rich and poor, fortunate and unfortunate.

(16) We appeal to the young men and women of this nation, to those whose nostrils are not yet befouled by greed and snobbery and racial narrowness: Stand up for the right; prove yourselves worthy of your heritage and whether born north or south dare to treat men as men. Cannot the nation that has absorbed ten million foreigners into its political life without catastrophe absorb ten million Negro Americans into that same

political life at less cost than their unjust and illegal exclusion will involve?

(17) Courage, brothers! The battle for humanity is not lost or losing. All across the skies sit signs of promise. The Slave is rising in his might, the yellow millions are tasting liberty, the black Africans are writhing toward the lights, and everywhere the laborer, with ballot in his hand, is voting open the gates of Opportunity and Peace. The morning breaks over blood-stained hills. We must not falter, we may not shrink. Above are the ever-lasting stars.

Questions for Discussion and Writing

1. State the central idea of this essay. Compare and/or contrast it with that of Booker T. Washington's essay.

2. In what ways are the demands stated by DuBois in this essay similar to the demands of the Negro in American society today? Is there evidence that some of these demands are being met or that there have been attempts to meet them? To what extent?

3. What methods does the author suggest that the Negro use to achieve his goals? Are these methods being used today? Are other methods also being used? What are they? Of the various methods, which ones, in your opinion are, or have been, most successful?

4. Read carefully paragraph 11. In this paragraph DuBois disagrees with Washington's philosophy of education for black men. State briefly the essence of his disagreement.

5. In the final paragraph of the essay, the author makes the following statement: "The battle for humanity is not lost or losing. All across the skies sit signs of promise . . . the black Africans are writhing toward the lights, and everywhere the laborer, with ballot in hand, is voting open the gates of Opportunity and Peace." Has the history of America from the time of the writing of this essay to the present proved DuBois to be right or wrong? Use examples to support your answer.

Stephen Wright, educator and scholar, has served as president of two universities (Bluefield State and Fisk University) and as president of the Association of Colleges and Secondary Schools for Negroes. Having received the Ph.D. degree from New York University, Dr. Wright has been the recipient of several honorary degrees including the Doctor of Laws degree from New York University, Michigan State, and the University of Notre Dame. His other honors include his election to Phi Beta Kappa both at New York University and at Pomona College. He also attended the inauguration of President William V. S. Tubman in Liberia, Africa as a special ambassador from the United States.

Dr. Wright has made many outstanding contributions to American life and culture, particularly in the areas of civic and educational affairs. He has been a regular contributor to such journals as the *Harvard Educational Review*, *Educational Abstracts*, and the *Journal of Educational Soci-*

ology. In the following essay, taken from *Saturday Review,* Dr. Wright focuses upon the function of the black university in twentieth-century society. Despite much controversy about the place of the Negro university in America today, the author expresses the belief that the Negro university still has a very vital role to play in American society today.

Stephen J.
Wright

The Promise
of Equality

(1) The principal
task of the Negro colleges and universities for the next decade or two, as
it has been for more than a hundred years, is to take the Negro students
as they are, with all their disadvantages, and prepare them for effective
roles in American society. This involves, and will continue to involve, considerable remedial and compensatory education, as well as massive finan-
cial aid. This is because at least 40 per cent of the Negro families in the
United States live in or near poverty by federal definition. Last year, for
example, the 36 private colleges of the United Negro College Fund (UNCF)
provided more than $17,000,000 in loans, scholarships, grants-in-aid, and
work opportunities.

(2) The educational task confronting these institutions is the most

Reprinted from Stephen J. Wright, "The Promise of Equality," Saturday Review,
July 20, 1968. Copyright © 1968 by Saturday Review, Inc.; *used by permission.*

formidable in higher education, and when this fact is taken into account, it is no exaggeration to assert that they have performed a near miracle in rendering both the Negro community and the nation a tremendous service.

(3) We know that the overwhelming majority of the students they serve are "prepared," generally, in the nation's poorest, most overcrowded, understaffed, and underequipped schools. Any group of institutions that seeks to be responsive to the needs of such students, irrespective of race, would confront special problems. The number of qualified Negroes has been insufficient to staff these institutions at the optimum level. And while the number of well-trained Negroes has increased dramatically during the past decade, new and emerging opportunities—including teaching and administrative positions—in predominantly white institutions have prevented the elimination of the deficit. White teachers have helped to reduce the deficit in some institutions, but the number of qualified, mature white teachers is also in short supply—particularly at the salaries these colleges can offer.

(4) The continuing assumption that every Negro or predominantly Negro institution is inferior has limited the support for public institutions from state legislatures and for private institutions from private philanthropy. Probably it has also retarded efforts to integrate student bodies. This image may, indeed, be the most difficult of all the problems, because the ability to compete for faculty, to provide the necessary depth in administrative staffs, to strengthen libraries, to purchase modern teaching equipment, and to introduce new and relevant curricula is contingent upon adequate budgets. As a president of one of the colleges put it: "It isn't the *love* of money that is the root of all evil where the Negro colleges are concerned; it is the lack of money and all that this implies."

(5) The new competition from predominantly white institutions for the top ten per cent of Negro high school graduates—sometimes with special foundation grants—is both a problem and a blessing. It is a problem because it deprives the Negro colleges of some of the bright, provocative minds that tend to accelerate and deepen the educative process. It is a great blessing, in the larger sense, because it represents the widening of opportunities for Negro youth. Furthermore, the number of Negro youngsters who need to be educated is so staggeringly large—at least three times the present number—that the problem becomes not one of fewer students, but more students with more problems to be met.

(6) We need to devise curricula content and raise expenditures to help young Negroes in their search for identity and, at the same time, avoid their becoming racists. We must expand the curricula to include more preparation for careers in business and industry. For realistic and understandable reasons, the past emphasis has been on preparation for the professions of teaching, medicine, the ministry, social work, and the law—

fields historically open to Negroes. Curricula changes should be responsive to positions which have opened almost dramatically during the past seven years. A number of predominantly Negro institutions that were scarcely visited as late as 1961 had more recruiters from government, business, and industry during the past year than they had graduating seniors!

(7) The learning experience for Negro students can be made richer by the new trend of exchanging expertise between Negro and predominantly white colleges in a given city. This division of labor or merging is suggested by the fact that two state institutions—one predominantly Negro and one predominantly white—often exist in the same city. Examples include Florida State and Florida A & M Universities in Tallahassee; the University of Houston and Texas Southern, also in Houston; the University of North Carolina at Greensboro and A & T University, also in Greensboro.

(8) The possibilities and future role of the predominantly Negro colleges and universities are contingent, in the main, upon their ability to solve their special problems. According to Sir Eric Ashby, "An institution is the embodiment of an ideal. In order to survive, it must fulfill two conditions: It must be sufficiently stable to sustain the ideal which gave it birth and sufficiently responsive to remain relevant to the society which supports it." Against enormous odds, the predominantly Negro colleges and universities have demonstrated unusual stability. Several have already celebrated their centennial years. Except for the very weak and marginal, the private colleges and universities appear to be gaining strength and stability. During the year 1966–1967, for example, the member colleges of the UNCF completed new and renovated construction worth some $28,-000,000. And while some graduate and professional work may be discontinued and some division of responsibility decided upon in cities where public institutions are clearly involved in wasteful duplication, the state institutions appear to be stable. They will doubtless also become increasingly integrated. Thus Ashby's first condition of survival appears to be in no jeopardy.

(9) The real question, however, turns on his second condition—remaining responsive and relevant to the society which supports it. The stronger predominantly Negro colleges are not on trial as American institutions of higher learning. They have produced the great majority of Negro leaders at all levels, perhaps 85 per cent of the physicians and dentists, the great majority of the teachers, lawyers, ministers, and trained businessmen. Such leaders as Justice Thurgood Marshall, Senator Edward Brooke, Congressmen William L. Dawson and Charles C. Diggs, Whitney M. Young, Jr., the late Martin Luther King, Jr., and at least four federal judges are the proud products of Negro higher education. Writers such as Frank Yerby, Ralph Ellison, and John Killens were educated in Negro colleges; singers such as Mattwilda Dobbs and Leontyne Price, and social psychologist

Dr. Kenneth B. Clark are prominent alumni. Of equal importance are the literally thousands of physicians, lawyers, professors, librarians, social workers, and enlightened ministers who are the leaders and movers of their communities. These institutions can, without doubt, continue to develop such people—and they are the ultimate test of relevance and quality.

(10) Whatever else may be done as a temporary expedient in the Negro's long search for equality in America, it will never come until he has equal education—a fact too seldom emphasized in the "noise and strife" of the revolution. With adequate support, the predominantly Negro colleges and universities will play a vital, if not the decisive role in providing the education required. And certainly the education will not be secured without them, for they, without adequate means, have demonstrated more know-how in dealing with the disadvantaged than any other group of institutions. It will be these colleges and universities that will assume the formidable task of educating "high risk" students—those not being recruited vigorously on any appreciable scale by any other group of institutions.

(11) If given the support they deserve, not only will they bear the burden of equipping their full share of young Negroes for their place in American society, but they will be made stronger in the process for their ultimate role—serving as American colleges and universities without regard to race, serving as microcosms of the world as it ought to be.

Questions for Discussion and Writing

1. State the central idea of the essay.

2. What, according to the author, is the central purpose of the Negro university? What are the circumstances that serve to make the task of the Negro university more difficult than it would otherwise be?

Identification

Briefly identify each of the following persons:

1. Thurgood Marshall

2. Charles C. Diggs

3. Whitney Young

4. Mattwilda Dobbs

5. Leontyne Price

6. Frank Yerby

3. Do you feel that there should be remedial or compensatory programs in the university? Why? Does your university have such a program? If so, what is its nature and function? Write a brief discussion of this program.

4. The author suggests that the image of the Negro colleges as inferior has hindered their effectiveness in several ways. List and discuss some of these. Do you feel that his reasons are valid? Is there such evidence in your community or state?

5. In what ways has competition from predominantly white colleges served to compound the problems of the black university? In light of these problems, do you think that such competition should be discontinued? Why? Why not?

6. Read again the quotation in paragraph 8 of this essay: "An institution is the embodiment of an ideal. In order to survive, it must fulfill two conditions: It must be sufficiently stable to sustain the ideal that gave it birth and sufficiently responsive to remain relevant to the society which supports it." Criticize this idea. Support your argument with examples from today's society, focusing especially on the universities and recent student unrest.

John
Hope
Franklin

John Hope Franklin, renowned American historian, received his undergraduate training at Fisk University. He also attended Harvard University from which he received both the M.A. and Ph.D. degrees. He has held the Edward Austin Fellowship from Harvard as well as a fellowship from the Julius Rosenwald Fund.

Dr. Franklin has served as teacher and lecturer in several American and foreign universities. Having taught at Fisk and Howard universities, he has also served as chairman of the History Department at Brooklyn College. He has been a guest lecturer at such universities as Harvard, Cornell, the University of Wisconsin, and Cambridge University in England. In 1947, Dr. Franklin represented the American Council of Learned Societies at the centennial observance of Calcutta, Madras, and Bombay.

Dr. Franklin has contributed to many leading journals both in America and in Europe. Some of his major publications include *The Negro in North Carolina 1790–1860, The Militant South,* and *From Slavery to*

Freedom. Of the latter work, Margaret Butcher has commented: "Franklin's book is very unprecedented as a first rate history—ostensibly of the Negro, but really of America with the Negro's share in it."

The following essay was first published in *Soon One Morning*, an anthology of Negro literature edited by Herbert Hill. In the essay, Dr. Franklin sees the American Negro scholar as having to decide "whether he should turn his back on the world, concede that he is the Invisible Man, and lick the wounds that come from isolation, or whether he should use his training, talents and resources to beat down the barriers that keep him out of the mainstream of American life and scholarship."

John
Hope
Franklin

The Dilemma of the
American Negro Scholar

(1) The problems of
the scholar who belongs to a particular group, ethnic or otherwise, must
be considered in the context of the general problem of the scholar in the
United States. In America the scholar's role in the community and the
nation has always been limited. Indeed, his role has been rather carefully
defined by the history of the country. Questions have often been raised
about the effective use of the scholar in a society whose fundamental
preoccupation has been with problems that have little or nothing to do
with the life of the mind. Intellectual prowess and mental acumen, it was
argued almost from the beginning, could make no substantial contribution
to the tasks of clearing the forests, cutting pathways to the frontier, and
making a living in the wilderness. The intellectual life was reserved for

those whose task it was to preserve and promote the moral and religious life of the community. In the early days of the nation there was a widespread feeling, moreover, that these aspects of life could be kept separate from the other aspects. Meanwhile, the rest of the community could live in blissful ignorance, with little or no concern for the great world of scholarship and learning that might be flourishing as far away as London and Paris or as close as the nearest county seat.

(2) This was a mere fiction, but Americans liked to believe in it. In the final analysis, however, those who devoted themselves to intellectual pursuits became forces in the community in spite of the community itself. The lack of respect for learning or the lack of concern for it melted before the exigencies of conflict, when ideological justifications and rationalizations were needed for actions that had already been taken. Thus, when the patriots were fighting for independence, the scholars came to the rescue of the polemicists and agitators, and Locke and Hume and Dickinson and Jefferson became household words among groups considerably larger than those who could be described as learned. It was at this juncture that the peculiar ambivalence that was to characterize American attitudes became evident. On the one hand, there was little regard, if not downright contempt, for the scholar and the serious thinker. On the other hand, there was the acknowledged need for the talents and resources of the man who was devoted to the intellectual life; and there was a willingness to call upon him to strengthen the hand of those who had decided upon a particular course of action.

(3) There has always been some acknowledgment, from that day to this, of the importance of the role of the scholar and intellectual in American life. Too often it has been begrudgingly conceded and too often the pervasive influence of scholarship in policy making and decision making is wholly unrecognized. We have been inclined to discount this influence and to insist that theorizing is the pastime of less practical-minded people. As for ourselves, we move, we act, we get things done, we have no time for indulging in the fantasies that emanate from the ivory tower. We do not seem to care that for this attitude we may be branded unintellectual or even anti-intellectual. We prefer to be known and recognized as practical-minded, down-to-earth. After all, our Constitution is a practical, workable document. Our economy reflects our hardheaded approach to exploiting our resources and developing effective and efficient means of production. Even our social order and our institutions are evidence of our pragmatic orientation. I would suspect, however, that the more generous and broadminded among us would recognize the fact that an untold amount of scholarship went into the writing of our constitution; that theoretical scientists as well as technicians and businessmen helped to make our economy what it has become; and that many scholarly hands contributed

to the formulation of our social order and the institutions of which we boast.

(4) The point is that, whether he wanted to or not, the American scholar has been drawn irresistibly into the main stream of American life, and has contributed his knowledge and his ingenuity to the solution of the major problems that the country has faced. Jonathan Edwards's *Freedom of the Will*, with all its scholarship, good and bad, was primarily an effort to preserve the unity of the older religious institutions in the face of powerful currents of change. Thomas Jefferson was a close student of eighteenth-century political theory, but the most significant manifestation of his scholarship in this area is to be found in the Declaration of Independence, whose practical-mindedness can hardly be surpassed. Even Ralph Waldo Emerson's "American Scholar," while embodying some remarkable generalizations about the intellectual resources and powers of mankind, was in truth a declaration of American intellectual independence, calling the American scholar to arms in the war against ignorance and in behalf of the integrity of American intellectual life.

(5) In recent years the story has been essentially the same. It was Woodrow Wilson, the former professor at Princeton, testing his theories of congressional government while President of the United States. It was James MacGregor Burns, of Williams College, adding scholarship and a new dimension to the traditional campaign biography with his life of John F. Kennedy. It was John Kenneth Galbraith descending from the insulation of a Harvard economics chair to make searching and stimulating observations on the industrial and business community of the nation. If these and scores of other scholars were faced with dilemmas—of whether to satisfy themselves in attacking the theoretical problems of their fields or to grapple with the fundamental problems of mankind—they resolved them fearlessly and unequivocally by applying their disciplines to the tasks from which they felt that they could not escape. In that way they gave meaning, substance, and significance to American scholarship.

(6) It is in such a setting and context that we must examine the position of the American Negro scholar. The dilemmas and problems of the Negro scholar are numerous and complex. He has been forced, first of all, to establish his claim to being a scholar, and he has had somehow to seek recognition in the general world of scholarship. This has not been an easy or simple task for, at the very time when American scholarship in general was making its claim to recognition, it was denying that Negroes were capable of being scholars. Few Americans, even those who advocated a measure of political equality, subscribed to the view that Negroes—any Negroes—had the ability to think either abstractly or concretely or to assimilate ideas that had been formulated by others. As late as the closing years of the nineteenth century it was difficult to find any white persons

in the labor or business community, in the pulpit or on the platform, in the field of letters or in the field of scholarship who thought it possible that a Negro could join the select company of scholars in America.

(7) The Negro, then, first of all, had to struggle against the forces and personalities in American life that insisted that he could never rise in the intellectual sphere. Thomas Nelson Page, the champion of the plantation tradition and the defender of the superiority of the white race, insisted that, "The Negro has not progressed, not because he was a slave, but because he does not possess the faculties to raise himself above slavery. He has not yet exhibited the qualities of any race which has advanced civilization or shown capacity to be greatly advanced." In 1895, a future President of the United States, Theodore Roosevelt, argued that "A perfectly stupid race can never rise to a very high place; the Negro, for instance, has been kept down as much by lack of intellectual development as anything else." If one were to thumb through the pages of the most respectable journals of the early years of this century—*Atlantic, Harper's, Scribner's, Century, North American Review*—he would find the same spirit pervading the articles published there. Industrial and vocational education, they contended, was peculiarly suitable for the Negro. Negroes, they argued, were childish, simple, irresponsible, and mentally inferior. It was the same wherever one looked.

(8) The Negro who aspired to be a scholar in the closing years of the nineteenth century and the opening years of this century must have experienced the most shattering and disturbing sensations as he looked about him in an attempt to discover one indication of confidence, one expression of faith in him and his abilities. If he doubted himself, it would be understandable, for he had been brainwashed, completely and almost irrevocably, by assertions of Caucasian superiority, endorsements of social Darwinism, with its justifications for the degradation of the Negro, and political and legal maneuverings that lowered the Negro still further on the social and intellectual scale. But the aspiring Negro scholar did not doubt himself, and he turned on his detractors with all the resources he could summon in the effort to refute those who claimed he was inferior. In 1888, a Negro, William T. Alexander, published a whole volume to support the claim that the Negro was the intellectual equal of others. "By the closest analysis of the blood of each race," he argued with eloquence, and futility, considering the times, "the slightest difference cannot be detected; and so, in the aspirations of the mind, or the impulses of the heart, we are all one common family, with nothing but the development of the mind through the channel of education to raise one man, or one people above another. . . . So far as noble characteristics are concerned, the colored race possess those traits to fully as great a degree as do the white."

(9) Alexander and numerous contemporaries of his had faced their dilemma, and they had made their choice. They had to combat the contentions of Negro inferiority. They had to demonstrate that Negroes were capable of assimilating ideas and of contributing to mankind's store of knowledge. They made their argument simply and directly. It was as though whites had said they could not count, and Negroes then counted from one to ten to prove that they could. There were subtle, more sophisticated ways of proving their mental acumen, but if Negroes thought of them, they must have been convinced that such methods would have no effect on those whose arguments were not based on fact of reason in the first place.

(10) It must have been a most unrewarding experience for the Negro scholar to answer those who said that he was inferior by declaring: "I am indeed not inferior." For such a dialogue left little or no time for the pursuit of knowledge as one really desired to pursue it. Imagine, if you can, what it meant to a competent Negro student of Greek literature, W. H. Crogman, to desert his chosen field and write a book entitled *The Progress of a Race*. Think of the frustration of the distinguished Negro physician C. V. Roman, who abandoned his medical research and practice, temporarily at least, to write *The Negro in American Civilization*. What must have been the feeling of the Negro student of English literature Benjamin Brawley, who forsook his field to write *The Negro Genius* and other works that underscored the intellectual powers of the Negro? How much poorer is the field of the biological sciences because an extremely able and well-trained Negro scientist, Julian Lewis, felt compelled to spend years of his productive life writing a book entitled *The Biology of the Negro*?

(11) Many Negro scholars, moreover, never entered any of the standard branches of learning. Perhaps they would have been chemists, geologists, essayists, critics, musicologists, sociologists, historians. But they never were. From the moment of their intellectual awakening they were drawn inexorably, irresistibly into the field that became Negro studies. Here they were insulated from the assaults of the white scholars, who could be as vicious and intolerant in their attacks and in their attitudes as the out-and-out racists were. Here, too, they would work relatively unmolested in a field where they could meet, head on, the assaults of those who would malign them and their race. In a sense, they could establish not only a professional standing by dealing objectively and in a scholarly fashion with the problems related to them and their race, but also the value and integrity of the field of Negro studies itself, which they had brought into being.

(12) The careers of three Negro scholars—W. E. B. DuBois, Carter G. Woodson, and Alain L. Locke—epitomize the history of Negro scholar-

ship in the first half of the twentieth century. All three were carefully trained and held degrees of doctor of philosophy from Harvard University. After writing a doctoral dissertation that became Volume I in the Harvard Historical Studies, DuBois moved on from his path-breaking work on the suppression of the African slave trade to a series of studies that not only treated many aspects of the Negro problem but also covered a number of areas in the social sciences and humanities. He produced *The Philadelphia Negro*, a modern sociological study; he was the editor of the Atlanta University *Studies of the Negro Problem*, called a pioneering work in the field of the social sciences; he wrote *The Souls of Black Folk*, a critique of approaches to the solution of the race problem, *Black Folk Then and Now*, a history of the Negro in Africa and the New World; *Black Reconstruction*, a study of the Negro's part in the years following the Civil War, and literally dozens of other works. In his ninety-fourth year, he has recently completed an epic three-volume novel of the Negro, *The Ordeal of Mansard*, and is now planning an encyclopedia of the Negro.

(13) Woodson's first scholarly work, *The Disruption of Virginia*, was a rather general study. He soon settled down to a systematic study of the Negro, however. Successively, he produced his *Education of the Negro Prior to 1860*, his studies of the free Negro, his *Century of Negro Migration, The History of the Negro Church, The Negro in Our History, African Background Outlined*, and many others. In 1915 he organized the Association for the Study of Negro Life and History, and shortly thereafter became editor of the *Journal of Negro History*, which today is one of the major historical publications in the United States.

(14) Alain Locke's career was, in several important respects, different from that of DuBois and Woodson. He was an honor graduate of Harvard College, where he was elected to Phi Beta Kappa. He was a Rhodes Scholar at Oxford and later studied at the University of Berlin. Trained in philosophy, he soon became involved in the literary activity that was later called "The Negro Renaissance." Although he maintained his interest in the theory of value and cultural pluralism, he became a powerful force in articulating the position and aspirations of the new Negro. Thus, his *The New Negro: An Interpretation, The Negro in Art,* and *Plays of Negro Life* eclipsed his "Values and Imperatives," "Ethics and Culture," and "Three Corollaries of Cultural Relativism." After 1925 he never gave very much attention to purely philosophical problems.

(15) Under the shadow and influence of these three figures and others, there emerged a large number of Negro scholars who devoted themselves almost exclusively to the study of some aspect of the Negro. Soon recognized fields emerged: the history of the Negro, the anthropology of the Negro, the sociology of the Negro, the poetry of the Negro, the Negro novel, the Negro short story, and so on.

(16) In moving forthrightly in this direction, what had the Negro scholar done? He had, alas, made an institution of the field of Negro studies. He had become the victim of segregation in the field of scholarship in the same way that Negroes in other fields had become victims of segregation. There were the Negro press, the Negro church, Negro business, Negro education, and now Negro scholarship. Unhappily, Negro scholars had to face a situation, not entirely their own creation, in the perpetuation of which their stake was very real indeed. In the field of American scholarship, it was all they had. It grew in respectability not only because the impeccable scholarship of many of the Negroes commanded it, but also because many of the whites conceded that Negroes had peculiar talents that fitted them to study themselves and their problems. To the extent that this concession was made, it defeated a basic principle of scholarship—namely, that given the materials and techniques of scholarship and given the mental capacity, any person could engage in the study of any particular field.

(17) This was a tragedy. Negro scholarship had foundered on the rocks of racism. It had been devoured by principles of separatism, of segregation. It had become the victim of the view that there was some "mystique" about Negro spirituals which required that a person possess a black skin in order to sing them. This was not scholarship; it was folklore, it was voodoo.

(18) The Negro scholar can hardly be held responsible for this sad turn of events. He had acted in good faith, and had proceeded in the best traditions of American scholarship. American scholarship had always been pragmatic, always firmly based on need. DuBois and Woodson and Locke were in the same tradition as Jonathan Edwards and Thomas Jefferson. Here was a vast field that was unexplored. Here was an urgent need to explore it in order to complete the picture of American life and institutions. Here was an opportunity to bring to bear on a problem the best and most competent resources that could be commandeered. That the field was the Negro and that the resources were also Negroes are typical irrelevancies of which objective scholarship can take no cognizance. One wonders what would have happened had their been no DuBois, no Woodson, no Locke, just as one wonders what would have happened had there been no Jonathan Edwards, no Thomas Jefferson. DuBois could have moved toward imperial or colonial history or toward literary criticism; and Woodson could have moved toward political history or economic geography. Locke could have become a leading authority in values and aesthetics. Perhaps they would have been accepted in the main stream of American scholarship; perhaps not. Their dilemma lay before them, and their choice is evident. It is not for us to say that American scholarship suffered as a result of the choice they made. We can say, however, that it is tragic

indeed, and a commentary on the condition of American society, that these Negro scholars felt compelled to make the choice they did make. Had conditions been different, had they been free Americans functioning in a free intellectual and social climate, they might well have made another choice. Nothing, however, can degrade or successfully detract from the contributions they made, once they had chosen.

(19) There were other Negro scholars, however, who did not take the road to Negro studies, who preferred to make their mark, if they were to make one at all, in what may be termed the main stream of American scholarship. When W. S. Scarborough graduated from Oberlin in 1875 with a degree in Greek and Latin, it was widely thought that the only suitable pursuit for Negroes was in the area of vocational studies. Scarborough neither followed such a course nor yielded to the temptation to become a student of Negro life. In 1881 he published his *First Lessons in Greek*, and *Theory of Interpretation*. Then he translated the twenty-first and twenty-second books of Livy, published other works in Latin and Greek, and became a competent student of Sanskrit, Gothic, Lithuanian, and Old Slavonic. But there was no place for him in American scholarly circles, not even at the predominantly Negro Howard University, where the white members of the Board of Trustees took the position that the chair in classical languages could be filled only by a Caucasian. Three generations later, the fate of William A. Hinton, one of America's most distinguished syphilologists, whose discoveries revolutionized the techniques for the detection and cure of dread social diseases, was almost the same. Despite his signal accomplishments, Harvard University Medical School kept him on for many years as a non-teaching clinical instructor. Not until he neared retirement and not until the position of the Negro in American society had significantly changed after World War II was Hinton elevated to a professional rank. Scarborough and Hinton wore down their knuckles rapping at the door of the mainstream of American scholarship. Whenever the door was opened, it was done grudgingly and the opening was so slight that it was still almost impossible to enter.

(20) The wide gap that separates the white world from the Negro world in this country has not been bridged by the work of scholarship, black or white. Indeed, the world of scholarship has, for the most part, remained almost as partitioned as other worlds. The Negro scholars that have become a part of the general world of American scholarship can still be counted on the fingers of a few hands. The number of Negro scholars on the faculties of non-Negro American colleges and universities is still pitifully small. The lines of communication between the two worlds are few and are sparingly used. Thus, the world of scholarship in America is a mirror of the state of race relations generally. Perhaps the world scholarship is a step or two ahead of the general community; but the vigor and

the pragmatism that characterize the American approach to other problems are missing in this all-important area. The Negro scholar is in a position not unlike that of Ralph Ellison's Invisible Man; he is a "fantasy," as James Baldwin puts it, "in the mind of the republic." When he is remembered at all he is all too often an afterthought. When his work is recognized it is usually pointed to as the work of a Negro. He is a competent *Negro* sociologist, an able *Negro* economist, and outstanding *Negro* historian. Such recognition is as much the product of the racist mentality as the Negro rest rooms in the Montgomery airport are. It was this knowledge of racism in American scholarship, this feeling of isolation, that fifty years ago drew from DuBois this comment: "I sit with Shakespeare and he winces not. Across the color line I move arm in arm with Balzac and Dumas, where smiling men and welcoming women glide in gilded halls. From out the caves of evening that swing between the strong-limbed earth and the tracery of the stars, I summon Aristotle and Aurelius and what soul I will, and they come all graciously with no scorn nor condescension. So, wed with Truth, I dwell above the Veil. Is this the life you grudge us, O knightly America? Is this the life you long to change into the dull red hideousness of Georgia? Are you so afraid lest peering from this high Pisgah, between Philistine and Amalekite, we sight the Promised Land?"

(21) It is, of course, asking too much of the Negro scholar to demand he remain impervious and insensitive to the forces that seek to destroy his dignity and self-respect. He must, therefore, be permitted to function as vigorously as his energies and resources permit, in order to elevate himself and those of his group to a position where they will be accepted and respected in the American social order. This involves a recognition of the difference between scholarship and advocacy. On the one hand, the Negro scholar must use his scholarship to correct the findings of pseudo psychologists and sociologists regarding Negro intelligence, Negro traits, and the alleged Negro propensity for crime. He must rewrite the history of this country and correct the misrepresentation and falsifications in connection with the Negro's role in our history. He must provide the social engineers with the facts of the Negro ghetto, the overt and the subtle discriminations inflicted on the Negro in almost every aspect of existence, the uses and misuses of political and economic power to keep the Negro in a subordinate position in American life. There is also a place for advocacy, so long as the Negro scholar understands the difference. Recognizing the importance of the use of objective data in the passionate advocacy of the rectification of injustice, the Negro can assume this additional role for his own sake and for the sake of the community. When I wrote the first working paper to be used in the briefs of the National Association for the Advancement of Colored People in their school desegregation arguments, I was flattered when the chief counsel, Thurgood Marshall, told me that

the paper sounded very much like a lawyer's brief. I had deliberately transformed the objective data provided by historical research into an urgent plea for justice; and I hoped that my scholarship did not suffer.

(22) When such an opportunity does not present itself, there is still another way to keep one's scholarly work from being polluted by passion —namely, by blowing off steam in literary efforts. . . . Several years ago, while waiting in the segregated Atlanta railway station, I was so mortified and touched by the barbaric treatment of Negro passengers by officials and city policemen that I immediately sat down and wrote a piece called "DP's in Atlanta," in which I drew some comparisons between the treatment of these Negroes and the treatment of displaced refugees in Nazi-occupied countries during World War II. After that, I was able to go out to Atlanta University and give the series of lectures that I had been invited to deliver.
. . .

(23) I suspect that such a repression of one's true feelings would not be satisfying to some, and it may even be lacking in courage. I do not commend it; I merely confess it. It is doubtless a temporary escape from the painful experience of facing the dilemma and making the choice that every Negro scholar must sooner or later make. For the major choice for the Negro scholar is whether he should turn his back on the world, concede that he is the Invisible Man, and lick the wounds that come from cruel isolation, or whether he should use his training, talents, and resources to beat down the barriers that keep him out of the main stream of American life and scholarship. The posing of the question, it seems, provides the setting for the answer. I have said that the American scholar has been drawn irresistibly into the main stream of American life, and has contributed his knowledge and ingenuity to the solution of the major problems his country has faced. I now assert that the proper choice for the American Negro scholar is to use his knowledge and ingenuity, his resources and talents, to combat the forces that isolate him and his people and, like the true patriot that he is, to contribute to the solution of the problems that all Americans face in common.

Questions for Discussion and Writing

1. What ambivalent attitudes characterized the thinking of Americans regarding the scholar during the early days of this country? Are there evidences in today's society that this ambivalence, in some measure, still exists?

2. The author states that, ". . . whether he wanted to or not, the American scholar has been drawn irresistibly into the mainstream of American life." What examples does he use to support this idea?

3. The author asserts that the scholar has had to struggle for acceptance as a "practical-minded, down-to-earth" individual. What are the circumstances that have made the struggle of the Negro scholar even more difficult?

4. Was the field of Negro studies created out of choice or necessity? Who were some of the major figures instrumental in its creation?

5. According to Franklin, what two things contributed to the growth of Negro studies as a respectable field?

6. Franklin suggests that the foundering of Negro scholarship on "the rocks of racism" has fostered the idea that there is some "mystique" about Negro studies. Can you point to examples in today's society that indicate that this idea still persists?

7. What does Franklin believe to be the solution to the dilemma faced by the American Negro scholar?

8. What was the fate of the two Negro scholars mentioned by Franklin who rejected Negro studies as their life work?

9. Read Ralph W. Emerson's "The American Scholar." Compare and contrast the ideas of Emerson with those of Franklin.

Margaret
Walker
Alexander

Margaret Walker Alexander, poet and novelist, received the A.B. degree from Northwestern University and the Ph.D. degree from the University of Iowa. Aside from writing, she has taught at several colleges and universities, including Jackson State College, where she is presently professor of English. Not only has Mrs. Alexander lectured at many colleges, she has also spoken for numerous organizations.

Mrs. Alexander has contributed to such magazines as *Poetry, A Magazine of Verse; Opportunity, A Journal of Negro Life;* and *Creative Writing.* She has been the recipient of many honors, both for her work as an educator and for her achievements in the area of creative writing. Her major poems have been published in a volume entitled *For My People,* a work for which she won the Yale Series of Younger Poets award. Her novel, *Jubilee,* the story of the slavery period in America, has been translated into several foreign languages.

The following essay was originally presented as a speech at the National Conference of the Urban League and was later published in *Vital Speeches of the Day*. In it, the author argues for a new educational system —one structured to serve more adequately the needs of American society. She suggests that this new system will revitalize a society that is gradually but surely deteriorating.

Margaret
Walker
Alexander

Religion, Poetry
and History:
Foundations for a
New Educational System

(1) Why do we need a new educational system? We stand today in the throes of cataclysmic social change. We are caught in a world-wide societal revolution that breeds ideological and military conflict between nations. We are impaled on a cross of constant economic problems such as automation and cybernation have brought us with the electronic revolution. We are deeply distressed by the conditions of our inner cities. We are equally concerned with the confusing drama on our college campuses which reflects the search of our young people for values different from our own.

(2) Our young people seem to be seething in a boiling caldron of

From a speech delivered at the National Urban League Conference in New Orleans, Louisiana, July 29, 1968 and printed in Vital Speeches of the Day *(October, 1968). Reprinted by permission of the author.*

discontent. Like the youth of every generation they want to know and they demand to be heard. Like youth in every age they are the vanguard of our revolutionary age. They are the natural leaders of revolution whether that revolution be of race, class, or caste; whether it is sexual or academic, whether it is political or intellectual. Today the revolutions we are witnessing encompass all of these, for the violence or revolution not only threatens but definitely promises to sweep out every corner of our outmoded existence. Violence today is more than the tool of tyranny, as it has always been, it is also the tool of revolution.

(3) We are not only shedding the old ways of the past. We are overwhelmed by the problems of a new universe. Here in this decade of the 1960's we stand under the watershed of the twentieth century totally unprepared for the innovations of the twenty-first century already rushing headlong among us. The historical process, of which we are a part, does not necessarily mark off the cycles of man's progress with the man-made dates or hours we have set for change. The life of the twenty-first century has already begun while the debris of the structures in a dying twentieth century crashes all around us.

(4) Our basic institutions of the home, the school, and the church are threatened by the same violent destruction undermining our socio-economic and political system, for they are part and parcel of the whole. Three hundred and fifty years ago, when the American colonies were not yet a nation, a set of built-in values were superimposed upon the American continent and people by European powers. These values were composed of three basic philosophies: (a) a religious body of belief containing the Protestant work ethic with duty and work as a moral imperative, with the puritanical and Calvinistic aversion to pleasure of secular play, song and dance, coupled with (b) the economic theories of a commonwealth only groping for the rising industrialism and capitalism that did not fully emerge until a century later, but which were hidden under (c) the American political dream of democracy. This democracy was based on the idealism of Christianity which declared all men are brothers and the children of God. Except for the facts of chattel slavery and inhuman segregation the ideal dream might have become a reality. Slavery and segregation as institutions contradicted the ideal dream and America developed instead a defensive philosophy or rationale of racism, the fruits of which we are reaping today.

(5) Black people in America have so long born the stigma of slavery and segregation that every community, black and white, has been warped by this wanton subjugation. For a very long time after slavery, almost a century in time, the federal government gave tacit consent to Jim Crow and segregation was supported boldly by law which of course became

custom. Now it has been outlawed, but the mark of Cain is still on the land. White America has educated black and white children with a set of monstrous lies—half truths and twisted facts—about race. Both black and white children, as a result, have been stunted in their mental growth and poisoned in their world outlook. The American white child in the north and south is just as distorted in this thinking as the black child although the expressed manifestations are not the same. The white child has been taught to value race more than humanity. He has been taught to overestimate his intelligence and human worth because of race, and at the same time to underestimate the human worth and intelligence of anyone who is not of his race. The white American is therefore basically ignorant of the new cultures of other people and has no appreciation for any other language, art, religion, history or ethical system save his own. He is in no way prepared to live in a multi-racial society without hostility, bigotry and intolerance. He believes that he must convert all people to his way of thinking because he cannot possibly conceive that his way of thinking may not always be right for everyone else. Everyone must dress, think, pray and amuse himself as he does. Every socio-economic and political system must emphasize or epitomize the values of his mechanistic and materialistic society. He falsely assumes that his values are idealistic and altruistic, and that he is democratic and Christian while all others are totalitarian and pagan, yet in all his actions he contradicts his preaching. His every waking hour is spent getting and spending for himself, while denying his brother any and all of the same rights he claims for himself. Self-righteous and self-centered he thanks God daily that he is not as other men (meaning other races) are.

(6) On the other hand, our black children have been taught to hate themselves, to imitate people whom they have been taught to believe are superior. Everyday they read in the schoolbooks, the newspapers, the movies, and the television the monstrous lies that deny their existence and denigrate their world. They have been led to believe that we have no black history, no black culture, no black beauty, nor anything black that has value or worth or meaning that is good. They have been told that our world is white and western with a cultural heritage that is Graeco-Roman, Christian in religion, Protestant in ethic and democratic in politics; that all these things are right and of necessity good and civilized while all the opposites of these are wrong and of necessity evil and savage. The non-western or Oriental world which is colored is therefore primitive in culture, heathen in religion, pagan in ethics, communistic in economics and totalitarian in politics. This of necessity is evil, anti-Christian, and anti-white and therefore anti-American. Ancient civilizations and empires of Ethiopia, Karnak, Ghana, Mali, and Songhai, to say nothing of that famous city of Carthage which the Roman orator, Cato, constantly declared must be destroyed—

these ancient names are not recited in our history books nor is the fact that both Asians and Africans and all the Arab world enjoyed their great Renaissance eras before the Europeans and the Christians. Thus our world has been divided into East and West, into black and white, and given the separate connotations of good and evil. For the most part our people have been gullible and believed the half-lies and the half-truths denying our blackness and wishfully affirming their whiteness by seeking to become carbon copies of white people. But the fact remains that we are living in a multi-racial world in which there are varying cultures, religious beliefs and socio-economic or political systems, and whether we like or dislike it our children must be educated to live in such a world. They must learn to live in a world that is four-fifths color, nine-tenths poor and in most cases neither Christian in religion nor democratic in ideals.

(7) The struggle of black people in America in this decade of societal revolution must therefore re-emphasize the battle for intellectual emancipation. A new self-concept must be instilled in the black and a new perspective must be developed in the white child. Moreover, it becomes the awesome task of every well-meaning, clear-thinking American, black and white alike to rectify the wrongs caused by racism, to change the basic attitudes and twisted facts still erroneously held by segregationist America, by racists who are white and black. All America must move toward a new humanism with a preoccupation of providing a full measure of human dignity for everyone. We must create a new ethic that is neither Protestant, Catholic, Jewish, Moslem, Buddhist nor any other ethic narrowed by creed but liberated into respect for the human rights of all men. Our ethic will then become a universal blessing of mutual respect and concern for every living spirit. We need a new educational philosophy in order to achieve this. A knowledge of world religions, world cultures, and all the racial and nationalistic strains that make up the human family will make such an ethic possible. The appreciation of other people and their cultures is predicated upon an understanding of them and understanding is predicated purely upon genuine knowledge. We *need* a new educational system. The recent revolution in teaching has been largely electronic; an intellectual revolution is of necessity a revolution in basic ideas.

(8) Our present-day system of education began in the nineteenth century when the scientific revolutions of the eighteenth and nineteenth centuries were charting a new universe with Newtonian physics. The Einsteinian revolution has outmoded such thinking. We no longer live in the nineteenth century. Even the twentieth century is largely behind us. Yet our religion is still that of the Middle Ages and the Protestant Reformation. What should a creative and spiritually vital religion do for our society? Why is the Christian Church in America today derelict in its duty and slow to move its feet toward full integration of all Americans into the main-

stream of American life? All America knows that institutionalized religion has lost its basic meaning because it has too long been in the employ of racism that has viciously used the Church and the Christian religion for selfish ends and vested interests. Segregationists such as the Ku Klux Klan and the Americans for the Preservation of the White Race have so long declared themselves as the true representatives of Christianity, the true American patriots, and the standard bearers of such nonsense as racial purity and integrity that they have whipped the truth of Christianity—the truth of the brotherhood of man and the fatherhood of God, whipped it senseless beyond recognition. Their lynch ropes, their high explosives, boxes of dynamite, long-range rifles and burning crosses are all used in the name of Christ and the Christian religion. Our burned churches are quite symbolic of racial hatred and spiritual decay. Our people deserve something better than a begging ministry in the employ of a powerful and wealthy hierarchy. The pages of history that tell the true story of slavery and segregation are stained with the blood of black men who were crucified by white Christians. No hypocritical whitewashings of moribund congregations that are stinking with moral decay will deliver us today. Perhaps it is time for a new Avatar. Violently shaken by class, caste, and racial disturbances the church in America craves a new awakening in which the spiritual meaning is reborn and revitalized. Religion in a society should be the underlying philosophy of the people. It is part of the aesthetic or cultural heritage of the people which undergirds the basic institutions of that society. When the religion of the people is dead, they are without vision without moral imperatives, and without all their aesthetic or cultural values. Anything false that is used in the name of religion is then the opiate or drug by which men lull themselves into a false consciousness, into deadly apathy and supine complacency. A vital and dynamic religion is necessary to take the cultural advancement of all people. Religious faith is personal, but religious institutions are of necessity social. As such they must serve all the people or they have no value.

(9) Black men, before they came to America, had a religion and ethic that was tribal or communal and that was based on their group participation in rites and ceremonies that gave impetus to their living and moral order to their community. White Puritan Americans at home and abroad as missionaries frowned on this as superstitious nonsense. In America black people lost their ties with Mother Africa but they have neither lost religious faith nor mystical charisma. We are still a people of spirit and soul. We are still fighting in the midst of white American racism for the overwhelming truth of the primacy of human personality and the spiritual destiny of all mankind. We fight for freedom and peace because we know these are spiritual entities and have nothing to do with guns and money and houses

and land. Contrary to the prevailing belief of racist society all black men do not necessarily believe that a guaranteed employment of all the people is the highest essence and accomplishment of a society. Artists and the religious of all nations know this is not so. Wise men are not all bankers and soldiers. Some are philosophers and poets and they too make their religious contribution to society. Some men therefore serve their society with the creative gifts of themselves neither for money nor fame but for the cause of righteousness and with human integrity for the advancement of all mankind. Whether we remain the test of democracy, the soul of the nation, the consciousness of America, the redemptive suffering people of the world, or the tragic black heroes of a dying society, we know that the essence of life is in spirit, not in cars, whiskey, houses, money and all the trappings of an affluent society. Call it soul if you wish, but it is our great gift and a part of our black heritage. We declare it worthy to offer on the altars of the world toward the enduring philosophy of a new and necessary humanism.

(10) Our music, and art, our literature born out of our folkways and folk beliefs are also part and parcel of the cultural gift and heritage. Like religion, the poetry of a people, their art, songs, and literature, come from the deep recesses of the unconscious, the irrational and the collective body of our ancestral memories. They are indeed the truth of our living, the meaning and the beauty of our lives, and the knowledge of this heritage is not only fundamental to complete understanding of us as a people, it is a fundamental ingredient in the development of our world consciousness. Black people today in America are more than ever before socially conscious, aware of the damage that racism has done to our psyche, the traumatic injury to our children's morale and mental growth. We know the effects of the brutalizing, stigmatizing, dehumanizing systems of slavery and segregation under which we have existed in America for three hundred and fifty years.

(11) A new awareness of this black history has taken hold of us in the way of the Riot Commission's report that white racism is the creeping sickness destroying America. How, then, shall we diagnose this racism and prescribe for its cure? Will more jobs, better housing, more ballots, and [fewer] guns cure racism? Hardly. This is a battle for the minds of men. In the words of one of our greatest thinkers who predicted that the problem of the color line would be the problem of the twentieth century, in the words of that classic, *The Souls of Black Folk*, let us remember that we have three great gifts, a gift of song, a gift of labor or brawn with which we have helped to build a nation, and a gift of spirit or soul. Let us stir up the gift of God that is within us and let us create a new world for all Americans. Let us use our heritage of religion, poetry and history as founda-

tions for a new educational system. Let us teach our children that we are a great people, that they have a great heritage, and that their destiny is even greater.

(12) It must come as a shock to many of our people living in the inner cities of America when they read about the deplorable conditions in our ghettoes, to discover that all this abuse directed against criminals, against dope addicts, against looters and conspirators, all this abuse and condemnation directed against those of us who live in subhuman conditions of black colonies of the white power structure, all of this is a blanket condemnation of us as a race and as a people. What, then, is a ghetto and how did it come into existence? Must we be blamed for this too, on top of all the other racist hatred and injustice vented upon us? Who values all their property more than they value our lives? Is this why they send the police to protect their property while only God protects our lives? Is it not true that the ghetto is a black colony of the white power structure in which we are exploited with no representation in the political and economic system? Do the people in the ghettos control their economic and political lives? Is the money spent in the ghetto returned to the ghetto? Do the people living in the inner cities run the governments of those municipalities? Somewhere we must truly place the blame where it belongs. Poor black people can no longer be the scapegoats who bear the blame for everything in our society. We not only must build economic and political power in the ghettoes, we must change the thinking in the ghettoes as we must change the thinking of all America. We must create a new mental climate.

(13) Fortunately for many of our people, all of us have not been blighted by ignorance of our heritage. Some of us have come from homes where all our lives this positive healing process has existed. While we were simultaneously reading the lies in the history books at school we were learning our true history at home from our parents. We have neither the segregationists' views of the South nor the racist views of the North about slavery, the Civil War, and Reconstruction. Some of us grew up reading *Opportunity* and *Crisis* magazines, reading the *Louisiana Weekly*, the *Chicago Defender*, and the *Pittsburgh Courrier* [sic] or whatever our local newspaper was. We heard the poetry of DuBois and James Weldon Johnson and Langston Hughes, and the music of Roland Hayes, Paul Robeson, and Marian Anderson. We learned the names of our leaders such as Harriet Tubman, Sojurner Truth, and Mary McCleod Bethune. We knew our great Blues singers and Broadway stars and prizefighters and Olympic winners. I was delighted to hear Dr. Sam Proctor say at Commencement that he did not need Stokely to tell him he was beautiful, his mother told him that. That is what mothers are supposed to do. But all our children do not know how beautiful they are for all of them have not been so fortunate. All of

them do not know that physical beauty is relative according to man-made standards and that what we believe in our minds and hearts is what we are; that we need not become what our enemies wish us to become. We can be what we want to be and most of all we want to be ourselves, and not an imitation of other people.

(14) Contrary to what some of our black brothers believe, this new educational system must not be one of racial exclusion or this will become another face for racism. This learning must be all inclusive. Any notions that a wider cleavage in the American people based on race, class, caste, sex or age—any such notion is unrealistic, naive, negative, and detrimental. Whether black and white Americans are divided by yellow men, red men, or the little green men of Mars, the result can mean nothing but chaos. Shall we divide and conquer? Who will conquer, and who stands to benefit from such cleavage? If any foreign nation can divide us by indoctrination it can also completely destroy us. Some of our black brothers seem confused by the conflict, and the tactics of the struggle seem to cloud the issues. When we were subjected to segregation by law we sought to become assimilated into the mainstream of American life. We regarded this as a worthy and positive goal. Now some of us seem to have some extreme thinking in the opposite direction. These seem to be appalled with the apparent failure of integration, and disappointed with the slow business of desegregation. Shocked and stung by the ugly face of white racism, they now declare that the sickness of America makes segregation and apartheid more to be desired than either desegregation or integration. This is not a clear incentive toward building power in the ghettoes nor rebuilding the moral fibre of America. Whatever we have learned from our struggles in the past, at least a few facts should be clear: We fight with faith in the goodness of the future. No matter how troubled we have been, we have not lost our perspective. Our sense of history tells us that our human personality is potentially divine, hence our destiny must be spiritual. These may not seem much but they are enough, if in terms of these truths we teach our children the worth of their human personality, a pride in their heritage, a love for all people in the recognition of our common humanity, and a sense of dignity and purpose in living. They help us realize that freedom like peace is spiritual. It is with such tools that we must build our houses for tomorrow.

(15) Just as we minister to the physical needs that are human we must minister to our mental needs that are also human. We must recognize the worth of every living person. All America is crying for this new humanism, for a new educational system, for a new creative ministry from a new and spiritually vital religion, meaningful and with a genuine moral imperative. A new Space Age of the twenty-first century craves a vital and new religion to usher in the millenium. A new century promises to erase the color line. A new humanism must prevail. We must find the strength and

the courage to build this new and better world for our children. Many of us will die trying in these last years of a dying century but in the twenty-first century our progeny will raise their eyes to more than a vision of a brave new world. They will occupy the citadel. There truth will be honored and freedom understood and enjoyed by everyone. Racial justice and understanding will be a prelude to international peace and good will. But we must begin now to destroy the lies, to attack the half truths, to give our children something in which they can believe, to build faith in themselves, love for mankind, and hope for the future. Most of all we must teach them that righteousness is more to be desired than money; for the great possession of money without guiding principles, without judgment, without pride and integrity, such possession is nothing . . . that cars and houses and whiskey and clothes and all the trappings of an affluent society do not dress up empty minds, and ugly hearts, and loveless lives; that meaningless living is without immortality and that it does not give us heroes to honor. Our martyred dead are great because they died for freedom. Our list of heroes is three centuries long, but they are deathless and forever with us. Wisdom and understanding cannot be bought in the Vanity Fairs of the world. Justice and freedom are prizes to be sought and our martyred men of goodwill have already proven they are well worth dying to obtain.

(16) Teach then, our children, that their heritage is great and their destiny is greater. That we are a great people with a great faith who have always fought and died for freedom. Teach them that life and love are for sharing and above all they are never to forget that we are all a part of the mainland, involved with humanity. We are not alone in our beauty and our strength. We are part of all mankind who throughout all recorded time have bravely fought and nobly died in order to be free.

(17) Our religion, poetry, and history—they are our folk heritage; they are our challenge today to social commitment; they are the foundations of a new education, a new moral imperative, a new humanism on which we base our cultural hope for a free world tomorrow morning in the twenty-first century.

These things shall be:

> A nobler race than e'er the world hath known shall rise
> With flame of freedom in their souls
> And light of knowledge in their eyes.
> They shall be gentle, brave, and strong
> To spill no drop of blood, but dare
> All that may plant man's lordship firm
> On earth and fire and sea and air
> Nation with nation, land with land
> Unarmed shall live as comrades free
> In every heart and brain shall throb

The pulse of one fraternity
New arts shall bloom of loftier mold
And mightier music thrill the skies
And every life shall be a song
When all the earth is paradise.

Questions for Discussion and Writing

1. In paragraph 3, the author states: "The life of the twenty-first century has already begun while the debris of the structures in a dying twentieth century crash all around us." Does this statement seem to reflect the attitudes of the younger generation? Discuss.

2. According to the author, the mental growth of both black and white children in America has been stunted. She gives several reasons to support this statement. Do you agree with her contention? Do you agree with her reasons? Totally or in part? Discuss.

3. The question "Why do we need a new educational system?" is answered specifically by the author in paragraph 7. State the essence of her answer. Write a defense of the present educational system or an argument in favor of a new system.

4. The author suggests that the Christian Church is not relevant to American society today. How does she support this idea? Read Howard Thurman's essay from *The Luminous Darkness*. Compare and contrast the ideas of the two authors about the Christian Church.

5. What are the three great gifts with which black Americans have been endowed? Are there evidences in today's society that black Americans have contributed these gifts to America? Try to find specific instances to support your answer.

6. Do you believe that the real answer to the problems of the ghetto lies not so much in economic or political power but rather in the "creation of a new mental climate" in America? Explain.

7. In paragraph 14, the author concludes that the new educational system must not be racially exclusive. Does this conclusion arise logically from the development of the essay? Do you agree or disagree with this conclusion? Support your position.

8. In the concluding paragraphs of the essay, the author draws up a kind of blueprint for this new educational system. What would be its characteristics, its aims and purpose?

ON ASSIMILATION

Frederick Douglass

Frederick Douglass, born a slave in Maryland in 1817, escaped from his second master at the age of twenty-one and gained his freedom legally some eight years later. While still a slave, however, he had the desire to learn to read. This desire was fulfilled when the wife of his second master taught him to read despite the objections of her husband.

Having escaped to New York, Douglass began to tell the story of slavery wherever he could gain an audience. He was an orator of such passion and force that he was noticed by an abolitionist group led by William Lloyd Garrison, and he eventually became the chief spokesman for that group. Douglass gained distinction as an antislavery orator and writer, speaking out for emancipation and enfranchisement of the Negro as well as for other civil rights.

Douglass' fame as orator and writer spread, and in 1845 he traveled to Europe where, according to Douglass, his time and labors were divided among England, Scotland, Ireland, and Wales. He was very well received in Great Britain where he spent nearly two years. When he left, the British donated money for him to establish his own newspaper, which, despite some setbacks, he finally did.

During his lifetime, Frederick Douglass served as Recorder of Deeds in Washington and as Minister Resident and Consul General to Haiti. His major works include *Narrative of the Life of Frederick Douglass, The Life and Times of Frederick Douglass* and *My Bondage and My Freedom*. The following essay is taken from the latter work and is especially typical of Douglass' antislavery ideas and his oratorical technique.

Frederick
Douglass

Inhumanity of Slavery

(1) The relation of
master and slave has been called *patriarchal*, and only second in *benignity*
and tenderness to that of the parent and child. This representation is doubtless believed by many northern people; and this may account, in part, for
the lack of interest which we find among persons whom we are bound to
believe to be honest and humane. What, then, are the facts? Here I will not
quote my own experience in slavery; for this you might call one-sided testi-
mony. I will not cite the declarations of abolitionists; for these you might
pronounce exaggerations. I will not rely upon advertisements cut from
newspapers; for these you might call isolated cases. But I will refer you to
the laws adopted by the legislatures of the slave states. I give you such evidence, because it cannot be *invalidated* nor denied. I hold in my hand
sundry extracts from the slave codes of our country, from which I will
quote.

* * *

(2) Now, if the foregoing be an indication of kindness, *what is*

cruelty? If this be parental affection, *what is bitter malignity?* A more atrocious and blood-thirsty string of laws could not well be conceived of. And yet I am bound to say that they fall short of indicating the horrible cruelties constantly practiced in the slave states.

(3) I admit that there are individual slaveholders less cruel and barbarous than is allowed by law; but these form the exception. The majority of slaveholders find it necessary, to insure obedience, at times, to avail themselves of the utmost extent of the law, and many go beyond it. If kindness were the rule, we should not see advertisements filling the columns of almost every southern newspaper, offering large rewards for fugitive slaves, and describing them as being branded with irons, loaded with chains, and scarred by the whip. One of the most telling testimonies against the pretended kindness of slaveholders, is the fact that uncounted numbers of fugitives are now inhabiting the Dismal Swamp preferring the untamed wilderness to their cultivated homes—choosing rather to encounter hunger and thirst, and to roam with the wild beasts of the forest, running the hazard of being hunted and shot down, than to submit to the authority of *kind* masters.

(4) I tell you, my friends, humanity is never driven to such an unnatural course of life, without great wrong. The slave finds more of the milk of human kindness in the bosom of the savage Indian, than in the heart of his *christian* master. He leaves the man of the *bible*, and takes refuge with the man of the *tomahawk*. He rushes from the praying slaveholder into the paws of the bear. He quits the homes of men for the haunts of wolves. He prefers to encounter a life of trial, however bitter, or death, however terrible, to dragging out his existence under the dominion of these *kind* masters.

(5) The apologists for slavery often speak of the abuses of slavery; and they tell us that they are as much opposed to those abuses as we are; and that they would go as far to correct those abuses and to ameliorate the condition of the slave as anybody. The answer to that view is, that slavery is *itself* an abuse; grant that the relation of master and slave may innocently exist; and there is not a single outrage which was ever committed against the slave but what finds an apology in the very necessity of the case. As was said by a slaveholder (the Rev. A. G. Few) to the Methodist conference, "If the relation be right the means to maintain it are also right;" for without those means slavery could not exist. Remove the dreadful *scourge* —the plaited thong—the galling fetter—the accursed chain—and let the slaveholder rely solely upon moral and religious power, by which to secure obedience to his orders, and how long do you suppose a slave would remain on his plantation? The case only needs to be stated; it carries its own refutation with it.

(6) Absolute and arbitrary power can never be maintained by one

man over the body and soul of another man, without brutal chastisement and enormous cruelty.

(7) To talk of *kindness* entering into a relation in which one party is robbed of wife, of children, of his hard earnings, of home, of friends, of society, of knowledge, and of all that makes this life desirable, is most absurd, wicked, and preposterous.

(8) I have shown that slavery is wicked—wicked, in that it violates the great law of liberty, written on every human heart—wicked, in that it violates the first command of the *decalogue*—wicked, in that it fosters the most disgusting *licentiousness*—wicked, in that it mars and defaces the image of God by cruel and barbarous inflictions—wicked, in that it *contravenes* the laws of eternal justice, and tramples in the dust all the humane and heavenly *precepts* of the New Testament.

(9) The evils resulting from this huge system of iniquity are not confined to the states south of Mason and Dixon's [line]. Its noxious influence can easily be traced throughout our northern borders. It comes even as far north as the state of New York. Traces of it may be seen even in Rochester; and travelers have told me it casts its gloomy shadows across the lake, approaching the very shores of Queen Victoria's dominions.

(10) The presence of slavery may be explained by—as it is the explanation of—the mobocratic violence which lately disgraced New York, and which still more recently disgraced the city of Boston. These violent demonstrations, these outrageous invasions of human rights, faintly indicate the presence and power of slavery here. It is a significant fact, that while meetings for almost any purpose under heaven may be held unmolested in the city of Boston, that in the same city, a meeting cannot be peaceably held for the purpose of preaching the doctrine of the American Declaration of Independence, "that all men are created equal." The *pestiferous* breath of slavery taints the whole moral atmosphere of the north, and *enervates* the moral energies of the whole people.

(11) The moment a foreigner ventures upon our soil, and utters a natural repugnance to oppression, that moment he is made to feel that there is little sympathy in this land for him. If he were greeted with smiles before, he meets with frowns now; and it shall go well with him if he be not subjected to that peculiarly fitting method of showing *fealty* to slavery, the assaults of a mob.

(12) Now, will any man tell me that such a state of things is natural, and that such conduct on the part of the people of the north, springs from a consciousness of *rectitude*? No! Every fibre of the human heart unites in detestation of tyranny, and it is only when the human mind has become familiarized with slavery, is accustomed to its injustice, and corrupted by its selfishness, that it fails to record its abhorrence of slavery, and does not exult in the triumphs of liberty.

(13) The northern people have been long connected with slavery; they have been linked to a decaying corpse, which has destroyed the moral health. The union of the government; the union of the north and south, in the political parties; the union in the religious organizations of the land, have all served to deaden the moral sense of the northern people, and to impregnate them with sentiments and ideas forever in conflict with what as a nation we call *genius of American institutions.* Rightly viewed, this is an alarming fact, and ought to rally all that is pure, just, and holy in one determined effort to crush the monster of corruption, and to scatter "its guilty profits" to the winds. In a high moral sense, as well as a national sense, the whole American people are responsible for slavery, and must share, in its guilt and shame, with the most obdurate men-stealers of the south.

(14) While slavery exists, and the union of these states endures, every American citizen must bear the chagrin of hearing his country branded before the world as a nation of liars and hyprocrites; and behold his cherished national flag pointed at with the utmost scorn and derision. Even now an American abroad is pointed out in the crowd, as coming from a land where men gain their fortunes by "the blood of souls," from a land of slave markets of blood-hounds, and slave-hunters; and, in some circles, such a man is shunned altogether, as a moral pest. Is it now time, then, for every American to awake, and inquire into his duty with respect to this subject?

(15) Wendell Phillips—the eloquent New England orator—on his return from Europe, in 1842, said, "As I stood upon the shores of Genoa, and saw floating on the placid waters of the Mediterranean, the beautiful American warship Ohio, with her masts tapering proportionately aloft, and an eastern sun reflecting her noble form upon the sparkling waters, attracting the gaze of the multitude, my first impulse was of pride, to think myself an American; but when I thought that the first time that gallant ship would gird on her gorgeous apparel, and wake from beneath her sides her dormant thunders, it would be in defense of the African slave trade, I blushed in utter shame for my country."

(16) Let me say again, *slavery is alike the sin and the shame of the American people*; it is a blot upon the American name, and the only national reproach which need make an American hang his head in shame, in the presence of monarchical governments.

(17) With this gigantic evil in the land, we are constantly told to look *at home*; if we say ought against crowned heads, we are pointed to our enslaved millions; if we talk of sending missionaries and bibles abroad, we are pointed to three millions now lying in worse than heathen darkness; if we express a word of sympathy for Kossuth and his Hungarian fugitive brethren, we are pointed to that horrible and hell-black enactment, "the fugitive slave bill."

(18) Slavery blunts the edge of all our rebukes of tyranny abroad—

the criticisms that we make upon other nations, only call forth ridicule, contempt, and scorn. In a word, we are made a reproach and a by-word to a mocking earth, and we must continue to be made, so long as slavery continues to pollute our soil.

Questions for Discussion and Writing

1. The author points out that the slave master often assumed a parental attitude toward his slaves which was interpreted as a special type of kindness shown to the slaves. How does Mr. Douglass refute this idea? Compare the parental concept expressed here with the "father image" idea referred to in "Psychological Reactions of an Oppressed People." Is there evidence that such ideas still exist in black-white relations in American society today?

2. The author develops his idea in paragraph 4, largely by a series of ironic antitheses. Does he gain any special effect or force by employing this method?

3. In paragraph 5, Mr. Douglass begins the development of his argument against the "apologists for slavery." What is his major premise? How is it developed? In your opinion, is his argument relevant to his thesis? Is it valid?

4. In paragraph 8, the author utilizes the rhetorical device of repetition. What effect does he achieve? Has each of the assertions made here been supported in the essay?

5. The author recognized that in his day there was little difference in the attitudes of the northern and southern white man toward the Negro. Have there been incidents in contemporary society that would suggest that this situation still exists? Are attitudes of white Americans toward black Americans undergoing change? Support your answer by specific examples.

6. Read paragraph 17 again. Mr. Douglass points out several ironies of American democracy. What are some of these? Do such ironies still exist? If so, what effect have they had on the American image abroad?

Richard
Wright

Richard Wright was
primarily a novelist and short story writer. Born in Mississippi, he moved
to Chicago as a youth in 1927. There he began his literary career, first publishing his essays and poems in various journals and later becoming editor
of his own magazine. With the publication of *Uncle Tom's Children* and
Native Son, he gained recognition as a major literary talent; the latter work,
published in 1940, set the standard for a whole generation of black prose
fiction writers.

In 1947, Wright moved to Paris where he continued writing both
fiction and nonfiction until his death in 1960. *White Man, Listen!*, the work
from which the following essay is taken, was written three years before his
death and was published posthumously in 1963. The book treats the problems of race and oppression as they exist in America and abroad. He concludes that the problem will never be solved until the oppressor recognizes
the problem and accepts his responsibility for having created it. In this

essay, the author examines some of the causes of oppression and the effect that it has had on the black peoples of the world and especially on black men in America.

Richard
Wright

Psychological Reactions
of Oppressed People

(1) Buttressed by their belief that their God had entrusted the earth into their keeping, drunk with power and possibility, waxing rich through trade in commodities, human and non-human, with awesome naval and merchant marines at their disposal, their countries filled with human debris anxious for any adventures, psychologically armed with new facts, white Western Christian civilization during the fourteenth, fifteenth, sixteenth, and seventeenth centuries, with a long, slow, and bloody explosion, hurled itself upon the sprawling masses of colored humanity in Asia and Africa.

(2) I say to you white man of the West: Don't be too proud of how easily you conquered and plundered those Asians and Africans. You had unwitting allies in your campaigns; you had Fifth Columns in the form of

Reprinted from White Man Listen!, *by Richard Wright. Copyright © 1957 by Richard Wright. Reprinted by permission of Doubleday & Company, Inc.*

indigenous cultures to facilitate your military, missionary, and mercenary efforts. Your collaborators in those regions consisted of the mental habits of the people, habits for which they were in no way responsible, no more than you were responsible for yours. Those habits constituted corps of saboteurs, of spies, if you will, that worked in the interests of European aggression. You must realize that it was not your courage or racial superiority that made you win, nor was it the racial inferiority or cowardice of the Asians and Africans that made them lose. This is an important point that you must grasp, or your concern with this problem will be forever wide of the facts. How, then, did the West, numerically the minority, achieve, during the last four centuries, so many dazzling victories over the body of colored mankind? Frankly, it took you centuries to do a job that could have been done in fifty years! You had the motive, the fire power, the will, the religious spur, the superior organization, but you dallied. Why? You were not aware exactly of what you were doing. You didn't suspect your impersonal strength, or the impersonal weakness on the other side. You were as unconscious, at bottom, as were your victims about what was really taking place.

(3) Your world of culture clashed with the culture-worlds of colored mankind, and the ensuing destruction of traditional beliefs among a billion and a half of black, brown, and yellow men has set off a tide of social, cultural, political, and economic revolution that grips the world today. That revolution is assuming many forms, absolutistic, communistic, fascistic, theocratistic, etc.—all marked by unrest, violence, and an astounding emotional thrashing about as men seek new objects about which they can center their loyalties.

(4) It is of the reactions, tortured and turbulent, of those Asians and Africans, in the New and Old World, that I wish to speak to you. Naturally I cannot speak for those Asians and Africans who are still locked in their mystical or ancestor-worshiping traditions. They are the voiceless ones, the silent ones. Indeed, I think that they are the doomed ones, men in a tragic trap. Any attempt on their part to wage a battle to protect their outmoded traditions and religions is a battle that is lost before it starts. And I say frankly that I suspect any white man who loves to dote upon those "naked nobles," who wants to leave them as they are, who finds them "primitive and pure," for such mystical hankering is, in my opinion, the last refuge of reactionary racists and psychological cripples tired of their own civilization. My remarks will, of necessity, be confined to those Asians and Africans who, having been partly Westernized, have a quarrel with the West. They are the ones who feel that they are oppressed. In a sense, this is a fight of the West with *itself*, a fight that the West blundering began, and the West does not to this day realize that it is the sole responsible agent, the sole instigator. For the West to disclaim responsibility for what it so clearly did

is to make every white man alive on earth today a criminal. In history as in law, men must be held strictly responsible for the consequences of their historic actions, whether they intended those consequences or not. For the West to accept its responsibility is to create the means by which white men can liberate themselves from their fears, panic, and terror while they confront the world's colored majority of men who are also striving for liberation from the irrational ties which the West prompted them to disown—ties of which the West has partially robbed them.

(5) Let's imagine a mammoth flying saucer from Mars landing, say, in a peasant Swiss village and debouching swarms of fierce-looking men whose red eyes flash lightning bolts that deal instant death. Those inhabitants are all the more terrified because the arrival of these men had been predicted. The religious myths of the Western world—the Second Coming of Christ, the Last Judgment, etc., have conditioned Europeans for just such an improbable event. Hence, those Swiss natives will feel that resistance is useless for a while. As long as the blue strangers are casually kind, they are obeyed and served. They become Fathers of the people. Is this a fragment of paperback science fiction? No. It's more prosaic than that. The image I've sketched above is the manner, by and large, in which white Europe over-ran Asia and Africa. (Remember the Cortes-Montezuma drama!)

(6) But why did Europe do this? Did it only want gold, power, women, raw materials? It was more complicated than that.

(7) The fifteenth-, sixteenth-, and seventeenth-century neurotic European, sick of his thwarted instincts, restless, filled with self-disgust, was looking for not only spices and gold and slaves when he set out; he was looking for an Arcadia, a Land's End, a Shangri-la, a world peopled by shadow men, a world that would permit free play for his repressed instincts. Stripped of tradition, these misfits, adventurers, indentured servants, convicts and freebooters were the most advanced individualists of their time. Rendered socially superfluous by the stifling weight of the Church and nobility, buttressed by the influence of the ideas of Hume and Descartes, they had been brutally molded toward attitudes of emotional independence and could doff the cloying ties of custom, tradition, and family. The Asian-African native anchored in family-dependence systems of life, could not imagine why or how these men had left their homelands, could not conceive of the cold arid emotions sustaining them. . . . Emotional independence was a state of mind not only utterly inconceivable, but an attitude toward life downright evil to the Asian-African native—something to be avoided at all costs. Bound by a charged array of humble objects that made up an emotionally satisfying and exciting world, they, trapped by their limited mental horizon, could not help thinking that the white men invading their lands had been driven forcibly from their homes!

(8) Living in a waking dream, generations of emotionally impover-

ished colonial European whites wallowed in the quick gratification of greed, reveled in the cheap superiority of racial domination, slaked their sensual thirst in illicit sexuality, draining off the dammed-up libido that European morality had condemned, amassing through trade a vast reservoir of economic fat, thereby establishing vast accumulations of capital which spurred the industrialization of the West. Asia and Africa thus became a neurotic habit that Europeans could forgo only at the cost of a powerful psychic wound, for this emotionally crippled Europe had, through the centuries, grown used to leaning upon this black crutch.

(9) But what of the impact of those white faces upon the personalities of the native? Steeped in dependence systems of family life and anchored in ancestor-worshipping religions, the native was prone to identify those powerful white faces falling athwart his existence with the potency of his dead father who had sustained him in the past. Temporarily accepting the invasion, he transferred his loyalties to those white faces, but, because of the psychological, racial, and economic luxury which those faces derived from their domination, the native was kept at bay.

(10) Today, as the tide of white domination of the land mass of Asia and Africa recedes, there lies exposed to view a procession of shattered cultures, disintegrated societies, and a writhing sweep of more aggressive, irrational religion than the world has known for centuries. And, as scientific research, partially freed from the blight of colonial control, advances, we are witnessing the rise of a new genre of academic literature dealing with colonial and post-colonial facts from a wider angle of vision than ever possible before. The personality distortions of hundreds of millions of black, brown, and yellow people that are being revealed by this literature are confounding and will necessitate drastic alteration of past evaluations of colonial rule. In this new literature one enters a universe of menacing shadows where disparate images coalesce—white turning into black, the dead coming to life, the top becoming the bottom—until you think you are seeing Biblical beasts with seven heads and ten horns rising out of the sea. Imperialism turns out to have been much more morally foul a piece of business than even Marx and Lenin imagined!

(11) An agony was induced into the native heart, rotting and pulverizing it as it tried to live under a white domination with which it could not identify in any real sense, a white domination that mocked it. The more Westernized that native heart became, the more anti-Western it had to be, for that heart was now weighing itself in terms of white Western values that made it feel degraded. Vainly attempting to embrace the world of white faces that rejected it, it recoiled and sought refuge in the ruins of moldering tradition. But it was too late; it was trapped; it found haven in neither. This is the psychological stance of the elite of the populations, free or still in a state of subjection, of present-day Asia and Africa; this is

the profound revolution that the white man cast into the world; this is the revolution (a large part of which has been successfully captured by the Communists) that the white man confronts today with fear and paralysis.

Frog Perspectives

(12) I've now reached that point where I can begin a direct descent into the psychological reactions of the people across whose lives the white shadow of the West has fallen. Let me commence by presenting to you concept number one: "Frog Perspective."

(13) This is a phrase I've borrowed from Nietzche to describe some-one looking from below upward, a sense of someone who feels himself lower than others. The concept of distance involved here is not physical; it is psychological. It involves a situation in which, for moral or social reasons, a person or a group feels that there is another person or group above it. Yet, physically, they all live on the same general material plane. A certain degree of hate combined with love (ambivalence) is always involved in this looking from below upward and the object against which the subject is measuring himself undergoes constant change. He loves the object because his chances of resembling it are remote, slight.

(14) Proof of this psychological reality can be readily found in the ex-pressions of oppressed people. If you ask an American Negro to describe his situation, he will almost always tell you: "We are rising."

(15) Against what or whom is he measuring his "rising?" It is beyond doubt his hostile white neighbor.

(16) At Bandung, Carlos Romulo of the Philippines said:

"I think that over the generations the deepest source of our own confidence in ourselves had to come from the deeply rooted knowledge that the white man was wrong, that in proclaiming the superiority of his race, *qua race*, he stamped himself with his own weakness and confirmed all the rest of us in our dogged conviction that we could and would re-assert ourselves as men. . . ."

(17) That "we" that Romulo speaks of here are the so-called "col-ored" peoples of the world. It is quite clear here that it is against the dominance of the white man that Romulo measures the concept of man-hood. Implied in his statement is the feeling or belief that the white man has, by his presence or acts, robbed the colored peoples of a feeling of self-respect, of manhood. Once more we are confronted with the problem of distance, a psychological distance, a feeling that one must regain some-thing lost.

(18) At Bandung, in 1955, President Sukarno of Indonesia spoke as follows: "The peoples of Asia and Africa wield little physical power. Even

their economic strength is dispersed and slight. We cannot indulge in power politics. Diplomacy for us is not a matter of the big stick. Our statesmen, by and large, are not backed up with serried ranks of jet bombers."

(19) Listen to the above words with a "third ear" and you will catch echoes of psychological distance; every sentence implies a measuring of well-being, of power, of manners, of attitudes, of differences between Asia and Africa and the white West. . . . The core of reality today for hundreds of millions resides in how unlike the West they are and how much and quickly they must resemble the West.

(20) This "frog perspective" prevails not only among Asians and Africans who live under colonial conditions, but among American Negroes as well. Hence, the physical nearness or remoteness of the American or European white has little or nothing to do with the feeling of distance that is engendered. We are here dealing with values evoked by social systems or colonial regimes which make men feel that they are dominated by powers stronger than they are.

Questions for Discussion and Writing

1. State the central idea of the essay.

2. The author states that the clash of the culture of the Western world with that of colored mankind has had serious repercussions—social, economic, political, and cultural—that manifest themselves even in today's society. Can you find examples that would support this idea? That would refute this idea?

3. The author suggests that the clash of the culture worlds, the traditional beliefs of colored peoples were destroyed. What evidences in American society today would suggest that black people are attempting in some manner to recapture some of their traditional beliefs?

4. Do you believe that people should be held responsible for the consequences of the deeds of their forebears? If so, to what extent? If not, why not? Explain your position.

5. In paragraph 2, Mr. Wright suggests that the destruction of traditional beliefs of colored peoples was an evil; in paragraph 4, he states that those who still maintain their "ancestor-worshiping traditions are "the doomed ones, men in a tragic trap." Are those ideas incongruous? Can you reconcile them?

6. Explain Mr. Wright's use of the term "frog perspective." In your opinion, does this term accurately describe the attitude of the Negro in today's society?

Saunders
Redding

J. Saunders Redding, scholar and lecturer, has attained some stature in the world of American letters. Redding received his graduate training at Brown University, to which he later returned as a visiting professor. He has also served as guest lecturer at Bowdoin College, Lake Forest College (Illinois), and the University of Virginia.

His major publications are books concerned primarily with Negro life and culture. Among these is *No Day of Triumph*, a work for which he won the Mayflower Award for distinguished writing in 1944. His shorter works have appeared in such journals as *American Mercury*, *Antioch Review*, and *The American Scholar*. Saunders Redding has received the Rockefeller Foundation Fellowship and has twice been appointed a Guggenheim Fellow, his second appointment coming in 1959.

The following essay is taken from Mr. Redding's book entitled *On Being Negro in America*, a work in which the author, in re-examining his feelings as a Negro in America, strikes at the core of the black experience in America.

Saunders
Redding

On Being Negro
in America

(1) While I am in a
petulant mood, let me say that I am race-conscious enough to be shocked
and irritated frequently by what even professed white friends do not know,
on both the personal and historical level, about Negroes. There is a glaring
case in point.

(2) During her husband's administration, Mrs. Eleanor Roosevelt became acquainted with a black, bosomy and intensely dynamic woman
named Mrs. Mary McLeod Bethune. The Negro woman was then Deputy
Administrator of NYA, and through her the President's wife, a sincere and
fearless woman, got closely involved with the race problem. The white
South fretted over the spectacle of Mrs. Roosevelt being shepherded
through the intricate mazes of racial and interracial affairs. It was alleged
(and the South, as did Negroes everywhere, took it for truth) that Mrs.

Bethune, through Mrs. Roosevelt, had special rights to the ear of F.D.R. More than one photograph shows the two women in earnest conversation in what seem to be intimate circumstances.

(3) Mrs. Bethune is very much alive. She is frequently mentioned and pictured in the colored press. She is ex-president of the National Federation of Colored Women. She took a dominant part in a conference on old age at the Shoreham Hotel in Washington in 1950. She spoke at perhaps a half dozen major college commencements in 1951. But in her book *This I Remember*, written in 1949, Mrs. Roosevelt, after words of heartening warmth for the black woman, refers to her as "the late [dead, deceased!] Mrs. Mary McLeod Bethune." Mrs. Roosevelt's reputation (earned at the cost of great personal criticism) for knowledge about and interest in Negroes, for liberalism, for social intelligence and tact is as a broad pen stroke underscoring the pattern of false belief and cavalier know-nothing-about-the-Negro attitude to which the majority conforms. Yet even she could make this error!

(4) As an ideal, of course, I am all for the deletion of racial designations in newspaper stories and the like. But the ideal is nowhere near attainment. It seems that it is still a general practice in newsrooms in a large part of the country to specify race when Negroes are involved in crime, and it is still usual to omit, except from feature stories and special articles, racial designation in news copy that would reflect credit on the colored people. When Ralph Bunche stepped in as mediator of the Jewish-Arab dispute, the fact that he was an American Negro first broke in the foreign press. In spite of hundreds of front-page news stories from competent war correspondents, it is even now not generally known that the 24th Infantry, which fought so hard and bought with its life (it was almost totally destroyed) the time General MacArthur needed in the early fighting in Korea, was a Negro outfit in the segregated United States Army.

(5) Personally, as matters stand, I would settle for something less than the ideal. Seldom does one see the minority-group designations "Italian," "Greek," "Jewish," "Irish" and the like attached to crime stories involving persons of these groups. But neither, it is replied, do you see them attached to other stories. True, and this is all very well. It is a matter of nomenclature. Negro names being what they generally are—as indigenous to America as "hot dog," or as unmistakably Anglo-Saxon-derived as "Gudger"—Ralph Bunche and Charles Drew, William Hastie and George Dows Cannon might belong to any Anglo-Saxon, Protestant or Catholic. But no one of reading intelligence would mistake Bernard Baruch or Sholem Asch as of other than Jewish heritage, or Fiorello LaGuardia and Vincent Impellitteri as of other than Italian ancestry, or George Skouras of other than Greek, or Roosevelt and Vanderbilt as other than Dutch, or William Cardinal O'Connell as other than Irish. We make these associa-

tions automatically, and there passes into the communal intelligence some sense of the contributions these groups make to American life. On the other hand, diffused throughout our national life and thought is the fallacy that the Negro has contributed nothing substantial.

(6) Not to know the Negro on the group and historical level is to rob him of his pride and of his rightful share in the American heritage. He cannot claim what is his, except in an intorted and psychologically unhealthy way. The Negro on the lower levels saves himself from complete madness by following a pattern of neurotic expression that is patent in his lazy-lipped and mumbling speech, in his gaybird dress, and in his prowlike walk. The Negro on the upper level turns back upon himself with a voracity of egocentrism that bewilders the casual observer. "What a self-conscious people your Negroes are!" a recent French visitor exclaimed. He was right. The Negro lives constantly on two planes of awareness. Watching the telecast of a boxing match between Ezzard Charles, the Negro who happened to be heavyweight champion, and a white challenger, a friend of mine said, "I don't like Charles as a person [one level] but I've got to root for him to beat this white boy—and good [second level]."

(7) One's heart is sickened at the realization of the primal energy that goes undeflected and unrefined into the sheer business of living as a Negro in the United States—in any one of the United States. Negroness is a kind of superconsciousness that directs thinking, that dictates action, and that perverts the expression of instinctual drives which are salutary and humanitarian—the civic drive, for instance, so that in general Negroes are cynically indifferent to politics; the societal drive so that ordinarily the Negro's concern is only with himself as an individual; and even the sex and love drive, so that many Negro couples refuse to bear children who will "inevitably grow under a burden of obloquy and shame that would daunt and degrade a race of angels." It is impossible to believe with Lillian Smith that the psychological damage caused by the race situation in America is greater to whites than Negroes. "Every one of us knows," an internationally known Negro said recently "that there is no 'normal' American Negro." Public asylums for the mentally deranged offer a telling statistic. Though Negroes are something less than ten per cent of the country's population, they are eleven per cent of the total population of public institutions for the insane.

(8) Compulsively dissociated from the American tradition, the Negro on the upper level has had to maintain the pretense of possessing what he is in fact denied. He has had no choice but this. He has not been free to realize his ideals or to strive to be what the American tradition has made him wish to be. Paul Laurence Dunbar, probably the most popular American poet at the turn of the century, did not wish to write "jingles in a broken tongue," but he was Negro and as a Negro he had to write dialect

or else have no hearing as a poet. James Weldon Johnson did not wish to compose those "darky" lyrics and "coon songs" for Williams and Walker's and his own brother Rosamond's shows—nor did Williams and Walker and Rosamond Johnson wish to sing and caper to them. But how else were they to find outlets for their creative urges, when all of the more congenial and less particularized were dammed up against them? DuBois had ideas for a career other than the one he was compelled to follow. "Had it not been for the race problem early thrust upon me and enveloping me," he wrote in *Dusk and Dawn*, "I should have probably been an unquestioning worshiper at the shrine of the social order and economic development into which I was born. . . . What was wrong was that I and people like me and thousands of others who might have my ability and aspiration were refused permission to be a part of this world. It was as though moving on a rushing express, my main thought was as to the relations I had to other passengers on the express, and not to its rate of speed and its destination. . . . My attention from the first was focused . . . upon the problem of the admission of my people into the freedom of democracy."*

(9) The dissociation of the Negro from the American tradition and the lack of knowledge of the Negro on the historical level are certainly in part the fault of social commentators and historians and social scholars. The historians particularly have been guilty of almost complete silence, like William A. Dunning; or of faulty investigation, like James Ford Rhodes; or of misinterpretation of the facts, like Ulrich Philips and W. E. Woodward; or of propaganda, like William E. Dodd and Jesse Carpenter; or of frank and anti-Negro bias, like dozens, major and minor, including Claude Bowers, James Truslow Adams, and John W. Burgess—the last of whom, by his prestige as a faculty member at Columbia University, gave scholarly sanction to prejudice. He wrote as follows:

(10) "The claim that there is nothing in the color of the skin from the point of view of political ethics is a great sophism. A black skin means membership in a race of men which has never of itself succeeded in subjecting passion to reason, has never, therefore, created any civilization of any kind. To put such a race of men in possession of a 'state' government in a system of federal government is to trust them with the development of political and legal civilization upon the most important subjects of human life. . . . There is something natural in the subordination of an inferior race to a superior race, even to the point of the enslavement of the inferior race. . . . It is the white man's mission, his duty and his right, to hold the reins of political power in his own hands for the civilization of the world and the welfare of mankind."†

*W. E. B. DuBois, *Dusk of Dawn* (New York: Harcourt, Brace and World, Inc., 1940), pp. 27–28. Reprinted by permission of the publishers.

†John W. Burgess, *Reconstruction and the Constitution* (New York: Charles Scribner's Sons, 1903), p. 133. Reprinted by permission of the publishers.

(11) Ignorance and willful distortion of the facts of American life and history in regard to the Negro's role have set the Negro scholar what up to now has been a thankless task. In pure self-defense he has had to try to set the record straight. The first Negro professional writer in America, William Wells Brown, was primarily a historian. Negro scholars have written thousands of dissertations, theses, monographs, articles, essays, and books in a gigantic effort to correct the multiple injuries done the race by white writers. Five great collections—at Howard, Hampton, Fisk, Yale and the Harlem Branch of the New York Public Library—house thousands of volumes and hundreds of magazine and newspaper files, but few except Negroes bother to disturb their dust. Whites show little interest in this Negroana. They seem to feel that they do not need to know about the Negro; they seem to feel that the basic truths about him were established long ago. Even the primary source material on him whom white America calls the greatest Negro American, him whom they have enshrined in the Hall of Fame and about whom they have written ten million words—even the primary source material on Booker Washington—some twenty thousand letters and other papers—remain scarcely touched and certainly unexplored in the Library of Congress, though the Harvard University Press published an erudite and "definitive biography" of the man in 1949.

(12) Negro writers remain generally unrepresented in anthologies of American literature, though in the light of the cultural history of America, the slave biographies (and there are some "literary" ones among them) are at least as important as anything Seba Smith, Charles Augustus Davis, John P. Kennedy and William Gilmore Simms ever wrote. Paul Laurence Dunbar was a better poet, and, in the opinion of William Dean Howells, a more popular poet and, by the very standard of indigenousness which some anthologists claim to follow, a more important poet than James Whitcomb Riley. James Weldon Johnson and Claude McKay enjoyed international reputations as writers, but they are absent from the best-known American anthologies. Richard Wright has been translated into a dozen languages, including the Chinese, and is rated by Europeans with Steinbeck, Hemingway and Faulkner, but American anthologies neglect him. Gwendolyn Brooks has won the Pulitzer prize for poetry, which is more than Jesse Stuart and William Carlos Williams have done, but her work is not in the collections of American writing.

(13) Nor is the most representative work by whites who have written about Negroes with some regard for justice and truth. Editors use Faulkner's "A Rose for Emily," "The Bear" and chapters from Sartoris and Told by an Idiot, but not "Evening Sun Go Down," or excerpts from Light in August and Intruder in the Dust. Chapters from Huckleberry Finn are used, but not those which show Nigger Jim to be much like other human beings, nor those which excoriate the institution of slavery and express Huck's hatred of it. George W. Cable is generally represented by selections from Old

Creole Days and innocuous passages from *The Grandissimes*, but never by *Madame Delphine* (certainly one of his best books), *The Silent South* or *The Negro Question*.

(14) The result of this arrogant neglect has been to render American cultural history less effective as an instrument of diagnosis and evaluation. What we have as history reflects little credit upon American historians as scholars. There work makes pleasant reading and inflates the national ego, but it does not tell those sometimes hard and shameful truths that might now be helpful for the world to know. What Lillian Smith calls "the old conspiracy of silence" needs to be broken, and the "maze of fantasy and falsehood that [has] little resemblance to the actual world" needs to be dissolved. The psychopathic resistance to self knowledge that the American mind has developed must be broken down. What we have got to know are the things that actually happened—and are still happening—in America. With these things clear before us, perhaps we can use our knowledge and experience for the guidance of mankind.

Identification

Briefly identify each of the following:

1. Mary McLeod Bethune

2. Ralph Bunche

3. Charles Drew

4. William Hastie

5. Claude McKay

6. Gwendolyn Brooks

Questions for Discussion and Writing

1. In the introductory paragraph of this essay, the author uses an anecdote. Can you relate it to the title and thesis of the essay?

2. Read paragraph 4 in which the author discusses the news media's handling of stories and articles concerning Negroes. Does this situation exist to any great extent in the United States today?

3. Comment on the statement: "The Negro lives constantly on two planes of awareness."

4. Redding states that "Negroness is a superconsciousness . . . that perverts the expression of instinctual drives." How does he explain this? Do you agree with the author?

5. Can you find justification for the assertion that there is no "normal American Negro"? If so, what reasons would you give for this.

6. Mr. Redding suggests that the dissociation of the Negro from the American mainstream has thwarted the creative genius of the Negro. As a case in point, he mentions the Negro historian. Compare his idea with that of John Hope Franklin in "The Dilemma of the American Negro Scholar."

Nathan
Hare

Nathan Hare, a sociologist, received the B.A. degree from Langston University (Langston, Oklahoma) and the Ph.D. degree from the University of Chicago. He has served as professor of sociology at Virginia State College, Howard University and San Francisco State College. As an educator, Professor Hare recognized early the void existing in American education—a void created by an almost total neglect of the contributions of black people to American culture. Because of this recognition, he has been very active in the movement to incorporate Black Studies Programs into university curriculums.

Although Nathan Hare has contributed articles to such magazines as the *Negro Digest* and *Saturday Review*, his major work to date is *The Black Anglo-Saxons*, from which the following essay is taken. According to the author, *The Black Anglo-Saxons* is "an exposé of Black Anglo-Saxons . . . [and] the white norms they so blindly and eagerly ape," and "a search for white persons . . . with enough sense of 'humanhood' to feel moved by what race prejudice and discrimination have done to those Negroes driven to the Black Anglo-Saxon frame of mind."

Nathan
Hare

The Exiles

(1) Bounced against the wall of segregation, the Negro Anglo-Saxon Exile compensates by seeking to remove himself from the Negro world. His separation is both spatial and social. If wealthy, he will purchase exclusive property, such as a seaside home, putting up fences and locked gates to keep out other Negroes.

(2) To offset any feeling of similarity to lower-class Negroes, Exiles label these high-class residential sections "Gold Coast," even though the nearest body of water may be miles away. Those who have moved from low-income Negro districts will return periodically on "slumming" trips, to reinforce their self-fantasies, contemptuously referring to the "loose, no-account ways" of the slum inhabitants. Some will boost their egos by traveling through white slums and skid rows, remarking that they are so much "better than a whole lot of whites," who "had every chance in the world to get ahead." In this way, they seek to place themselves with the "better class of whites."

Reprinted from Nathan Hare, The Black Anglo-Saxons, by permission of Marzani and Munsell, Inc., publishers.

(3) Like many whites, the Exile gains a sense of exclusivity from having an unlisted telephone number. With such a number, he "doesn't have to be bothered with so many niggers." He repeatedly affirms, for the benefit of white ears, that a "nigger," simply means "a niggardly individual" and that anybody can be a "nigger," regardless of color; in the same breath, he will turn around and declare that "there is nothing in the world wrong with the Negro race, except that it has too many damned 'niggers' in it." Another oft-repeated saying is: "Deliver me from the average Negro."

(4) Other Exiles resort to a curious form of escalator-switching in their religious lives, as a means of evading their Negro identities. This is especially true of middle-class Exiles, who have grown uncomfortable within the confines of lower class church life. Professor Frazier has aptly described them as "running from the Baptists to the Congregationalists and the Bahai, trying to find some place where folks don't know they're colored."

(5) The present vogue for Catholicism stems, in part, from a quest for kinship with the late President Kennedy; it also affords the Black Anglo-Saxon parishioner the chance to say that he "just got through singing high mass in Latin" (which seems to him a distinctly non-Negro undertaking), or that he just came from confession. A Catholic marriage ceremony, presided over by a white priest, is regarded as the apex of honor.

(6) Many simply cannot accept the fact, as they sit in all-Negro flocks, that they are on the "right road to Glory"; heaven—they feel certain —is integrated. Others, more worldly in their escape, enjoy commuting between the two different neighborhoods. This intensifies their sense of separation from the Negro ghetto.

(7) Many Exiles, in their efforts to escape their true identity, seek to disassociate themselves from Africa. Their contact with Africans is often limited to those who can secure invitations to embassy affairs. Although officials from Africa flood Washington's embassies, the presence of one at an Exile social affair is as rare (as one commentator put it) as "a fly in a glass of milk." One Exile social studies supervisor, in Washington, D.C., ordered her teachers to instruct their Negro pupils in the history of North Africa, rather than that of South Africa. With a few exceptions (such as Howard), few Negro institutions either offer or require courses in Negro history and other matters pertaining to Africa. The Negro seeking such knowledge must generally attend a white college. Even at Howard, Exile scholars prefer emerging as authorities on ancient and medieval eras in European, Greek and Roman history.

(8) Exiles regard themselves as above Africa and its history. Many exhibit actual hostility toward visiting Africans, according to some African students in the U.S. They delight in questioning these students as to the

incidence of nakedness on that continent, or on how many lions they have seen and wrestled with. This view of Africans as barbarians (as perceived through white-directed vision), explains the delight of the Black Anglo-Saxon when he is afforded the prospect of visiting "the dark continent," to "help civilize"—and missionize—Africans. Huge sums are collected for this purpose, in Black Anglo-Saxon churches.

(9) Upon their arrival, however, these people often find themselves unwanted and shunned by the Africans. The latter feel that the American Negroes themselves have a far greater need of missionary aid, as well as divine intervention, just as their white sponsors need lessons in civility.

(10) Those individuals displaying the least interest in Africa are, according to Lloyd General, Exiles of the "middle and upper class, the educated and the traveled." In a piece entitled "Has the U.S. Negro Any Real Ties to Africa?" (published in a December 1962 issue of the Chicago Defender) he speaks of a professional worker in Chicago. She had traveled to every continent in the world except Africa and confessed: "I have never had a desire to visit Africa, especially the areas known as 'Negro Africa.' I might like to visit North Africa and the Holy Land, but I don't think I would like to visit Liberia or Ghana."

(11) Another society lady related what "a most wonderful time" she had in Rome, Paris, Monte Carlo and London the year before, but stated that the "very thought of living in Africa" was something of a shock to her. Said the Exile: "They have all those Mau-Mau and other people. I would probably die of fright just thinking about it."

(12) A famous Negro college professor and writer was sent to Africa by an organization made up predominantly of Negro scholars and fine artists, to speak on "American literature in general." He found, however, that his African audiences expressly preferred to hear about literature written by and concerning Negroes. Yet, novelists James Baldwin and John O. Killens, and playwright Ossie Davis, have complained of Exiles who approach them at informal gatherings to soberly inquire why they don't "just write about people"—as if Negroes weren't people! Other authors and social scientists, including this writer, have encountered this same query over and over again. Exiles are continually calling upon Negro scholars and writers to "resist the impulse to write from [their own] narrow lives of racial protest" and go in more for "pure entertainment values."

(13) While white authors receive no special consideration for their ability to write convincingly about Negroes, Exiles proudly acclaim the ability to write about white people (in the manner of Frank Yerby) as a special "credit to Negroes." They are forever trumpeting the fact that so-and-so "has won pre-eminence in a general field, without regard to his race."

(14) Not infrequently, Exiles themselves become men (and women)

of letters. One poetess, featured in a leading Negro weekly, gave this explanation of her disdain for Negro themes: "I write the way I feel." Her poetry is free of the color or racial theme, she continued, "because I don't have that 'oppressed Negro' feeling. This comes from being raised in the Northwest. It's only been in the last few years that I've been acquainted with Negro history.[The know-nothing attitude again.] I prefer to write to everybody. People are just people to me." (If only everyone in these United States felt this way!) In fact, these Exiles are merely escaping responsibility to the Negro's cause, by striving to turn out "non-Negro" work: to write, paint and, in the case of actors, play white (pun intended).

(15) So intense is this escapist desire that one woman Exile was outraged at the sight of a sign on a display, advertising "Books Written by Negroes"; it had been placed there by a group of Negro high-school and college students. Said the woman: "I was so offended by it that I took it upon myself to stand up in front of these young people and tell them so. I felt that the sign should indicate simply a display of current literature."

(16) Exiles maintain that Negro publications "hold back racial progress" by their protests and elaborations of "discord" between the races. They propose, therefore, a conspiracy of silence. (However, many whites, including "liberals," confess that they thought Negroes were more or less content before the recent outbursts of racial unrest.) Exiles rationalize this by saying that these publications make Negroes "more race-conscious," rather than less so. The development of the Negro's self-respect is as undesirable, to the Exiles, as it is to the white who originated this line of reasoning. . . .

(17) Exiles, in short, have accepted the white evaluation of the Negro as lowly and inferior. Consequently, they feel superior to Negroes as a group and search for a helping hand "up" into the white world. But they are not welcomed into this world; instead, they are cruelly thrust back, again and again, into the milieu they hate with such white-hot passion (pun intended) and contempt. If the Exiles were to succeed in their goal of divorcing themselves from their race, it would not matter to them if whites were finally to accept Negroes; they would still be excluded. Because they have failed to gain equality as members of a certain race, they seek to abolish that race; integration becomes synonymous, in their minds, with the disintegration of the Negro. They operate on the pathetic assumption that the sooner they forget that they are Negroes, the sooner the whites will also.

Identification

Briefly identify each of the following persons:

1. John O. Killens
2. Lloyd General

Questions for Discussion and Writing

1. To what group does the author ascribe the term "Exiles"? From your reading of the essay, does this term accurately describe the group? Why? Why not?

2. The author asserts that the Exiles place labels on "high-class residential sections," calling them " 'Gold Coast,' even though the nearest body of water may be miles away." Does Mr. Hare's characterization of the Exiles suggest any possible reason or reasons for such labeling?

3. Mr. Hare indicates that the Exiles endeavor to escape their true identity by disassociating themselves from Africa. What are some of the examples that he uses to support this idea? Is there any indication in society today that this attitude on the part of the Exiles is changing?

4. Try to state briefly the central idea of the essay. What is the principal method of development used throughout the essay?

5. The author seems to suggest that black writers should restrict themselves to writing about the black experience and that those who "turn out 'non-Negro' work" are merely escapists. Do you agree with this point of view? Give reasons to support your position.

6. Read carefully paragraph 15. Do you feel that accomplishments of Negroes should be designated by "color labels"? Why? Why not? Should the accomplishments of people of other races be labeled?

James
Baldwin

James Baldwin, a
novelist and essayist, was born and educated in New York City. He developed an interest in writing during his years as editor of his high school paper. Three years after his graduation from high school, Baldwin received the Eugene Saxton Fellowship, which allowed him to devote full time to his writing.

Mr. Baldwin's essays and interviews have appeared in several periodicals, including *Harper's Magazine* and the *New York Herald Tribune*. The collection of essays, *Nobody Knows My Name*, and the novel, *Another Country*, won for him a prominent place in the world of American letters. *The Fire Next Time*, considered to be one of the most brilliant works in the history of Negro protest, is the book from which the following essay is taken. The central theme of the book is that a world holocaust can be averted only if men learn to have mutual respect for each other.

James
Baldwin

From

The Fire Next Time

(1) The American Negro has the great advantage of having never believed that collection of myths to which white Americans cling: that their ancestors were all freedom-loving heroes, that they were born in the greatest country the world has ever seen, or that Americans are invincible in battle and wise in peace, that Americans have always dealt honorably with Mexicans and Indians and all other neighbors or inferiors, that American men are the world's most direct and virile, that American women are pure. Negroes know far more about white Americans than that; it can almost be said, in fact, that they know about white Americans what parents—or, anyway, mothers—know about their children, and that they very often regard white Americans that way. And perhaps this attitude, held in spite of what they know and

have endured, helps to explain why Negroes, on the whole, and until lately, have allowed themselves to feel so little hatred. The tendency has really been, insofar as this was possible, to dismiss white people as the slightly mad victims of their own brainwashing. One watched the lives they led. One could not be fooled about that; one watched the things they did and the excuses that they gave themselves, and if a white man was really in trouble, deep trouble, it was to the Negro's door that he came. And one felt that if one had had that white man's worldly advantages, one would have never become as bewildered and as joyless and as thoughtlessly cruel as he is. The Negro came to the white man for a roof or for a letter to the judge; the white man came to the Negro for love. But he was not often able to give what he came seeking. The price was too high; he had too much to lose. And the Negro knew this, too. When one knows this about a man, it is impossible for one to hate him, but unless he becomes a man —becomes equal—it is also impossible for one to love him. Ultimately, one tends to avoid him, for the universal characteristic of children is to assume that they have a monopoly on trouble, and therefore a monopoly on you. (Ask any Negro what he knows about the white people with whom he works. And then ask the white people with whom he works what they know about *him*.)

(2) How can the American Negro past be used? It is entirely possible that this dishonored past will rise up soon to smite all of us. There are some wars, for example (if anyone on the globe is still mad enough to go to war), that the American Negro will not support, however many of his people may be coerced—and there is a limit to the number of people any government can put in prison, and a rigid limit indeed to the practicality of such a course. A bill is coming in that I fear America is not prepared to pay. "The problem of the twentieth century," wrote W. E. B. DuBois around sixty years ago, "is the problem of the color line." A fearful and delicate problem, which compromises, when it does not corrupt, all the American efforts to build a better world—here, there, or anywhere. It is for this reason that everything white Americans think they believe in must now be re-examined. What one would not like to see again is the consolidation of peoples on the basis of their color. But as long as we in the West place on color the value that we do, we make it impossible for the great unwashed to consolidate themselves according to any other principle. Color is not a human or a personal reality; it is a political reality. But this is a distinction so extremely hard to make that the West has not been able to make it yet. And at the center of this dreadful storm, this vast confusion, stand the black people of this nation, who must now share the fate of a nation that has never accepted them, to which they were brought in chains. Well, if this is so, one has no choice but to do all in one's power to change that fate, and at no matter what risk—eviction, imprisonment, torture, death. For the sake of one's children, in order to minimize the bill

that they must pay, one must be careful not to take refuge in any delusion —and the value placed on the color of the skin is always and everywhere and forever a delusion. I know that what I am asking is impossible. But in our time, as in every time, the impossible is the least that one can demand —and one is, after all, emboldened by the spectacle of human history in particular, for it testifies to nothing less than the perpetual achievement of the impossible. And here we are, at the center of the arc, trapped in the gaudiest, most valuable, and most improbable water wheel the world has ever seen. Everything now, we must assume, is in our hands; we have no right to assume otherwise. If we—and now I mean the relatively conscious whites and the relatively conscious blacks, who must, like lovers, insist on, or create, the consciousness of the others—do not falter in our duty now, we may be able, handful that we are, to end the racial nightmare, and achieve our country, and change the history of the world. If we do not dare everything, the fulfillment of that prophecy, re-created from the Bible in song by a slave, is upon us: *God gave Noah the rainbow sign, No more water, the fire next time!*

Questions for Discussion and Writing

1. A recurrent complaint of blacks is the paternalistic attitude of whites toward them. In Paragraph 1 of this essay, Baldwin suggests that blacks have a paternalistic attitude toward whites. Is the nature of this paternalism the same as that of whites for blacks? Does each type arise out of a different set of circumstances? Explain.

2. Baldwin voices an opinion that is and has been held by many blacks that they know whites much better than whites know them. Can you find examples within today's society that would support this position? If possible, test Baldwin's suggestion in the last sentence of paragraph 2. What are your findings?

3. Comment on the author's statement: "Color is not . . . a personal reality; it is a political reality."

4. Despite Baldwin's sometimes harsh indictment of America for its treatment of its black citizens, he has often stated that he has never lost faith in America. Are there passages in this essay that reveal the truth of this statement?

5. Many critics see in Baldwin's work a philosophy of hate; some, however, see the philosophy of love. Read the entire essay, "My Dungeon Shook" in *The Fire Next Time*. With which point of view do you agree? Write a brief paper supporting your position.

6. Explain the author's statement "A bill is coming that I'm afraid America is not prepared to pay." Compare the statement with this excerpt from Martin Luther King's, "I have a Dream"*: "We've come to our nation's capital to cash a check. When the architects of our republic wrote the . . . Constitution and the Declaration of Independence, they were signing a promissory note. . . ." Write a brief commentary on these ideas and their relevance to American society.

*Speech delivered at March on Washington, 1963.

LeRoi Jones

LeRoi Jones, poet and dramatist, was educated at the Newark branch of Rutgers University and at Harvard University. He also studied at Columbia University and the New School for Social Research where, following his return from military service, he taught poetry and writing.

Mr. Jones' poetry has appeared in such publications as *The Nation, Poetry, Harper's* and *The Negro Digest.* He has served as a jazz writer for *Downbeat, Metronome,* and *Jazz Review.* His contributions to American drama include *The Slave* and *The Dutchman.* A production of the latter play won for him the Off-Broadway "Obie" Award. His other works include *Blues People, The Dead Lecturer, The System of Dante's Hell,* and *Preface to a Twenty Volume Suicide Note.* Mr. Jones has also made a significant contribution to black theater in establishing the Black Arts Repertory Theatre in Harlem and later in associating himself with The Spirit House Movers and Players in Newark, New Jersey.

Although the writings of LeRoi Jones are usually very serious, indeed, often harsh and bitter—the following essay, "Soul Food," reveals a lighter side of Jones' personality.

LeRoi
Jones

Soul Food

(1) Recently a young Negro novelist writing in *Esquire* about the beauties of America mentioned that one of the things wrong with Negroes was that, unlike the Chinese, boots have neither a language of their own nor a characteristic cuisine. And this to me is the deepest stroke, the unkindest cut, of oppression, especially as it has distorted Black Americans. America, where the suppliant, far from rebelling or even disagreeing with the forces that have caused him to suffer, readily backs them up and finally tries to become an honorary oppressor himself.

(2) No language? No characteristic food? Oh, man, come on.

(3) Maws are things ofays seldom get to peck, nor are you ever likely to hear about Charlie eating a chitterling. Sweet potatoe pies, a good friend

Reprinted from LeRoi Jones, Home: Social Essays, *by permission of William Morrow and Company, Inc. Copyright © 1962, 1966 by LeRoi Jones.*

of mine asked recently, "Do they taste anything like pumpkin?" Negative. They taste more like memory, if you're not uptown.

(4) All those different kinds of greens (now quick frozen for everyone) once were all Sam got to eat. (Plus the potlikker, into which one slipped some throwed away meat.) Collards and turnips and kale and mustards were not fit for anybody but the woogies. So they found a way to make them taste like something somebody would want to freeze and sell to a Negro going to Harvard as exotic European spinach.

(5) The watermelon, friend, was imported from Africa (by whom?) where it had been growing many centuries before it was necessary for some people to deny that they had ever tasted one.

(6) Did you ever taste a black-eyed pea? (Whitey used it for forage, but some folks couldn't.) And all those weird parts of the hog? (After the pig was stripped of its choicest parts, the feet, snouts, tails, intestines, stomach, etc., were all left for the "members" who treated them mercilessly.) Is it mere myth that shades are death on chickens? (Deep fat frying, the Dutch found out in seventeenth century New Amsterdam was an African specialty: and if you get hold of a fried chicken leg, or a fried porgie, you can find out what happened to that tradition.)

(7) I had to go to Rutgers before I found people who thought grits were meant to be eaten with milk and sugar, instead of gravy and pork sausage . . . and that's one of the reasons I left.

(8) Away from home, you must take the trip uptown to get really straight as far as a good grease is concerned. People kill chickens all over the world, but chasing them through the dark on somebody else's property would probably insure once they were in the big bag, that you'd find some really beautiful way to eat them. I mean, after all the risk involved. The fruit of that tradition unfolds everywhere above 100th Street. There are probably more restaurants in Harlem whose staple is fried chicken, or chicken in the basket, than any other place in the world. Ditto, barbequed ribs—also straight out of the South with the West Indians, i.e., Africans from farther south in the West, having developed the best sauce for roasting whole oxen and hogs, spicy and extremely hot.

(9) Hoppin' John (black-eyed peas and rice), hushpuppies (crusty cornmeal bread cooked in fish grease and best with fried fish, especially fried salty fish, which ought to soak overnight unless you're over fifty and can take all that salt), hoecake (pan bread), buttermilk, biscuits and pancakes, fatback, i.e., streak's alean-streak' afat, dumplings, neckbones, knuckles (both good for seasoning limas or stringbeans), okra (another African importation, other name gumbo), pork chops—some more staples of the Harlem cuisine. Most of the food came North when the people did.

(10) There are hundreds of tiny restaurants, food shops, rib joints, shrimp shacks, chicken shacks, "rotisseries" throughout Harlem that serve

"soul food"—say, a breakfast of grits, eggs and sausage, pancakes, and Alaga syrup—and even tiny booths where it's at least possible to get a good piece of barbeque, hot enough to make you whistle, or chicken wing on a piece of greasy bread. You can always find a fish sandwich: a fish sandwich is something you walk with, or "Two of those small sweet potato pies to go." The Muslim temple serves bean pies which are really separate. It is never necessary to go to some big place to get a good filling grease. You can go to the Red Rooster, or Wells, or Jochs and get a good meal, but Jennylin's place on 135th near Lenox, is more filling, or some place like the A&A food shop in a basement up in the 140's, and you can really get away. I guess a square is somebody who's in Harlem and eats at Nedicks.

Questions for Discussion and Writing

1. What is the tone of this essay? Do you feel that Jones is absolutely serious or is there an element of tongue-in-cheek? Point out specific passages, words, or phrases which for you set the tone of the essay.

2. Commensurate with the title of the essay "Soul Food," the author uses many terms that have come to be known as "soul" words. Some of these terms refer to food: potlikker, maws, fatback, porgies, knuckles, etc.; some refer to people: boots, shades, woogies, ofays, Sam, Charlie, etc. If you are not acquainted with these terms, see if you can find out what they mean. Do you find other "soul" expressions in this essay that are unfamiliar to you?

3. In paragraph 4, Jones discusses the derivation of soul food and its place in "respectable" society. Several articles have been written on the origin or derivation of "soul." Try to find information on the subject, and write a brief paper on some aspect of it.

4. Comment on the following statements: "a fish sandwich is something that you walk with," and "a square is somebody who's in Harlem and eats at Nedicks."

ON LITERATURE
AND LANGUAGE

Saunders
Redding*

The Negro Writer and

American Literature

(1) **Of the several**
current assumptions regarding the Negro writer in the United States, one,
I think, stands out as primary. It is the assumption that there is a distinction
between writings by American Negroes and writings by other Americans.
It is an old assumption, and one that heretofore has been accepted blindly
as a truism, and if it is now possible to call it into question, it is not before
it has had a still more questionable consequence. It has led to the diversion
of writing by Negroes from the main channel of American expressiveness,
and to setting it off—to change the figure abruptly—as belonging, like por-
nography, to that class of literary works called curiosa. The critical treatment
of this body of writing has also been set apart, and the standards by which

*For a biographical sketch of the author, see the introductory material on p. 64.
From Saunders Redding, Anger and Beyond: The Negro Writer in the United
States, ed. Herbert Hill. Copyright © 1966 by Herbert Hill. Reprinted by permission of
Harper & Row, Publishers.

so much of it—indeed, most of it—has been judged have only rarely been aesthetic and literary.

(2) As questionable and detrusive as these consequences are, the assumption itself has validity. Of course writing by Negroes is different. The difference stems from the fact of their distinctive group experience in America. The cultural dualism of the American Negro is very real, and nearly all the Negro writers of more than local reputation have expressed it in one way or another, sometimes unconsciously—as, for instance, Phyllis Wheatley did way back in the 1770's, when, in her poetic epistle to the Earl of Dartmouth, she wrote:

> Should you, my lord, while you peruse my song,
> Wonder from whence my love of Freedom spring,
> Whence flow these wishes for the common good,
> By feeling hearts alone best understood,
> I, young in life, by seeming cruel fate
> Was snatched from Afric's fancied happy seat:
> What sorrows labor in my parent's breast!
> Steeled was that soul, and by no misery moved,
> That from a father seized his babe beloved:
> Such, such my case. And can I then but pray
> Others may never feel tyrannic sway?

(3) And just as real and as often expressed—also sometimes unconsciously—is a psychological dualism. In the autobiographical notes that are the introduction to his first collection of essays, *Notes of a Native Son*, James Baldwin is quite explicit and quite aware of both the psychological and cultural dualism:

> I know [he writes] . . . that the most crucial time in my own development came when I was forced to recognize that I was a kind of bastard of the West; when I followed the line of my past I did not find myself in Europe but in Africa. And this meant that in some subtle way, in a really profound way, I brought to Shakespeare, Bach, Rembrandt, to the stones of Paris, to the cathedral at Chartres, and to the Empire State Building, a special attitude. These were not really my creations, they did not contain my history, I might search in them in vain forever for any reflection of myself. . . . At the same time I had no other heritage which I could possibly hope to use. . . . I would have to appropriate these white centuries, I would have to make them mine—I would have to accept my special attitude, my special place in this scheme—otherwise I would have no place in *any* scheme. What was the most difficult was the fact that I was forced to admit something I had always hidden from myself, which the American Negro has had to hide from himself as the price of his public progress; that I hated and feared white people.

This did not mean that I loved black people; on the contrary, I despised them. . . .*

(4) And I take it also that this dualism is the principal thematic burden of a group of brilliant essays entitled *Shadow and Act*, by Ralph Ellison, who reminds us that when he began writing in earnest:

> I was forced to relate myself consciously and imaginatively to my mixed background as American, as Negro American, and as a Negro from what in its own belated way was a pioneer background. More important, and inseparable from this particular effort, was the necessity of determining my true relationship to that body of American literature . . . through which, aided by what I could learn from the literatures of Europe, I would find my own voice, and to which I was challenged, by way of achieving myself, to make some small contribution, and to whose composite picture of reality I was obligated to offer some necessary modifications.†

(5) Measured in psychological, sociological and raw cultural terms, the distinction and the differences between writing by American Negroes and other Americans are justified. But for all that, it is only the distinction between trunk and branch. The writing of Negroes is fed by the same roots sunk in the same cultural soil as writing by white Americans. Nevertheless, both academic and popular criticism has exaggerated the distinction into a dichotomy that has been the source of grave critical injustice to Negro writing on the one hand, and that has until recently at any rate—tended to vitiate its effectiveness as an instrument of social and cultural diagnosis and as a body of American experience through which we are enabled to understand the cultural psychology of the American world and, indeed—I think —the whole Western world. Three times within this century, writing by Negroes has been done nearly to death: once by indifference, once by opposition, and once by the enthusiasm of misguided friends.

(6) By 1906, Charles Waddell Chestnutt, the best writer of prose fiction the race had produced, was virtually silent; Paul Laurence Dunbar, the most popular poet, was dead. Booker T. Washington had published *Up from Slavery*, but Washington, who gave disastrous social dimensions to a literary tradition, was no writer. Though DuBois had written *The Souls of Black Folk*, he had not yet found an audience. The polemicists and propagandists like Monroe Trotter, Kelly Miller and George Forbes were faint whispers in a lonesome mood. Indifference had stopped the ears of all but

---

*Reprinted from James Baldwin, *Notes of a Native Son*, by special permission of Beacon Press.

†Reprinted from Ralph Ellison, *Shadow and Act*, by permission of Random House, Inc.

the most enlightened liberals, who, as often as not, were derided as "nigger lovers."

(7) But this indifference had threatened even before the turn of the century. It choked off and made bitter the purest stream of Dunbar's lyricism. Yearning for the recognition of his talent as it expressed itself in traditional poetry in conventional English, he had to content himself with being represented by what he considered to be third-rate. His literary sponsor, William Dean Howells, at that time the most influential critic in America, passed over Dunbar's verse in pure English with scarcely a glance, but went on to say that:

> . . . there is a precious difference of temperament between the two races which it would be a great pity ever to lose, and . . . this is best preserved and most charmingly suggested by Mr. Dunbar in those pieces of his where he studies the moods and traits of his own race. . . . We call these pieces dialect pieces . . . but they are really not dialect so much as delightful personal attempts and failures for the written and spoken language. In nothing is Mr. Dunbar's art so well shown as in these pieces, which . . . describe the range between appetite and emotion . . . which is the range of the race. He reveals in these a finely ironic perception of the Negro's limitations. I should say perhaps that it was this humorous quality which Mr. Dunbar has added to our literature, and it would be this which would most distinguish him, now and hereafter. . . .

(8) Dunbar's non-dialect verses appeared more or less on sufferance. The very format of *Lyrics of the Hearthside*, the book in which most of his non-dialect verses appeared, suggests this. No fancy binding, no fine paper, no charming photographs such as one finds in his other books. *Lyrics of the Hearthside* was the least publicized of all his works, and four lines from his poem "The Poet" tells why.

> He sang of love when earth was young
> And Love itself was in his lays
> But ah, the world, it turned to praise
> A jingle in a broken tongue.*

(9) The indifference was due to the fact that poetry written in pure English by a Negro contradicted the Negro stereotypes, which were effective in America's thinking about the Negro. According to them, the Negro was either—and sometimes both—a buffoon, a minstrel, and a harmless child of nature or an irresponsible beast of devilish cunning, soulless and

*Reprinted from "The Poet" by Paul Laurence Dunbar, by permission of Dodd, Mead & Company. (Paul Laurence Dunbar, *The Complete Poems of Paul Laurence Dunbar*.)

depraved. In either case, the Negro was a species of creature that was not quite man.

The influence of these concepts upon writing by American Negroes— and, of course, about American Negroes—had been and continued to be tremendous. Sterling Brown, one of the more searching scholars, had this to say as late as 1942:

> The market for Negro writers, then, is definitely limited . . . and the more truthfully we write about ourselves, the more limited the market. Those novels about Negroes that sell best . . . touch very lightly upon the realities of Negro life, books that make our black ghettos in big cities seem very happy places indeed. . . .

(10) Alain Locke complained that the Negro was "a stock figure perpetuated as an historical fiction partly in innocent sentimentalism, partly in deliberate reactionism. "The Negro himself," Locke wrote, "has contributed his share to this through a sort of protective mimicry . . . forced upon him through the adverse circumstances of dependence. Through having had to appeal from the unjust stereotypes of his oppressors and traducers to those of his liberators, friends and benefactors he has had to subscribe to traditional positions from which his case has been viewed."

(11) That the stereotypes were powerful there can be no doubt, and the Negro writer reacted to them in one of two ways. Either he bowed to them, and produced work that would do them no violence and offer them no contradiction, or he went to the opposite extreme and wrote for the purpose of correcting or denying the stereotypes. Dunbar did the former. Not only his dialect poetry but his short stories depicted Negroes as folksy, not-too-bright souls, all of whose concerns are minor, and all of whose problems can be solved by the emotional and spiritual equivalents of sticks of red peppermint candy.

(12) Charles Chestnutt's experience was both confoundingly unlike and strikingly similar to Dunbar's. When his stories began appearing in the *Atlantic Monthly* in 1887, it was not generally known that Chestnutt was a Negro. The editor of the *Atlantic*, Walter Hines Page, fearing that revealing the author's race would do harm to the reception of the author's work, kept his race a closely guarded secret for a decade. It was this same fear that led to the initial rejection of Chestnutt's first novel, *The House Behind the Cedars*, and publication in its stead of a collection of the stories that had appeared in the *Atlantic*. "At that time," Chestnutt wrote some years afterward, "a literary work by an American of acknowledged color was a doubtful experiment, both for the writer and for the publisher, entirely apart from its intrinsic merit. Indeed, my race was never mentioned by the publishers in announcing or advertising the book. . . ."

(13) Chestnutt's later books, published after his race became known, were doomed to failure, so far as reception and sales were concerned, on another count. They were honest; they probed the problem of race; they overrode the concepts and contradicted the stereotypes that supported the folk-dialect tradition.

(14) The indifference to the work of culture-conscious, race-conscious Negro writers seeking honest answers to real questions began to crystallize into opposition in the first decade of this century. It was opposition to the Negro's ambitions. It was opposition to the Negro writer who was honest and sincere. . . .

(15) Writing by Negroes beginning with this period [directly after the end of World War I] and continuing into the early Thirties had two distinct phases, which combined to mark the start of a psychological and artistic development that is now come to complete realization. The first of these phases was experimental, and it was a reflection of what was happening in all of American literature—of what T.S. Eliot and e. e. cummings were doing in poetry; of what Dos Passos, Anderson and Hemingway were doing in prose; of what Maxwell Anderson and Eugene O'Neill were doing in drama. That Negro writers could now afford to be touched by these influences was in itself a good sign.

(16) But the second phase is the one that is best remembered. One searches in vain for a term to characterize it, and for the exact impulses behind it. It was chock-full of many contradictory things. It showed itself naive and sophisticated, elemental and overwrought, hysterical and sober, frivolous and worthwhile, joyously free and yet hopelessly enslaved. It is simple enough to attribute this to the effects of the just-ended war, which were many and deep, but the atavistic release at this time of certain aberrant tendencies in writing by Negroes can nowhere be matched in contemporary literature. It seems to have been at once a period of catharsis—indeed of complete abreaction—and of ingurgitation. It produced the poignant, simple beauty of Johnson's *The Creation* and the depressing futility of Wallace Thurman's *The Blacker The Berry*. In the same period, Claude McKay could write the wholesome, picaresque *Banjo* and the utterly inexcusable filth in *Banana Bottom*. The same Hughes who wrote "I've Known Rivers" and "Mother to Son" could also find satisfaction in creating the bizarre "The Cat and the Saxophone."

(17) In general the mind of white America fastened upon the bizarre, the exotic and the atavistic elements of the second phase and turned them into a commercialized fad. Anyone who examines, even in a cursory fashion, the social history of the Twenties is immediately struck by the influence of Harlem upon it. That this Harlem was largely synthetic did not seem to matter. The well-advertised belief was that in Harlem gaiety was king. The revolters from Sauk Center, from Main Street and Winesburg,

from all the villages, found carnival in Harlem. Life, the dithyrambic said, had surge and sweep there—freedom, an honest savagery; and as Langston Hughes wrote in "To Midnight Man at Leroy's":

> Hear dat music . . .
> Jungle night.
> Hear dat music . . .
> And the moon was white.
> Jungle lover . . .
> Night black boy. . . .
> Two against the moon
> And the moon was joy.

The moon was also paper-maché.

(18) So vicious was the commercial angle that Negroes (represented as being the very gods and goddesses of unrestrained joy), who largely had no money anyway, could not—that is, were not permitted to—enter the best-known "Negro" night clubs in the world.

(19) Commercialism was the bane of the Negro renaissance of the Twenties. Jazz music, for instance, became no longer the uninhibited expression of unlearned music makers, but a highly sophisticated and stylized pattern of musical sounds. The Charleston, the Black Bottom, the Lindy Hop went down to Broadway and Park Avenue and were taught in Arthur Murray's dancing school. From being an authentic form, the blues became the torch song popularized by Ruth Etting and Helen Morgan. The stuff in which Negro writers were working passed into the less sincere hands of white writers, and Negro writers themselves, from a high pitch of creation, fell relatively (and pathetically) silent.

(20) Three times within this century writing by American Negroes has been done nearly to death, and yet today it is in an excellent state of health.

(21) When Richard Wright's *Uncle Tom's Children* was published in 1938, only the least aware did not realize that a powerful new pen was employing itself with stern and terrible material. Then, when *Native Son* appeared in 1940, even the least aware realized it. The first book, a collection of lengthy novelettes, is a clinical study of the social being under the cumulative effects of organized repression. The two books complement each other. The theme of both is prejudice—prejudgment, conceptual prejudgment. If one needs that expanded a little to make it crystal-clear, the theme is the effects of prejudice upon the human personality. For what Richard Wright deals with is only incidentally, for dramatic purposes, and because of the authenticity of empiricism, the subject of *Negro* and *white*. What he deals with is prejudice. ". . . Bigger Thomas was not black all the

time," he wrote in "How Bigger Was Born," "he was white, too, and there were literally millions of him, *everywhere.* . . . More than anything else, as a writer, I was fascinated by the similarity of the emotional tensions of Bigger in America and Bigger in Nazi Germany and Bigger in old Russia. All Bigger Thomases, white and black, felt tense, afraid, nervous, hysterical, and restless. . . . Certain modern experiences were creating types of personalities whose existence ignored racial and national lines of demarcation . . . these personalities carried with them a more universal drama-element than anything I'd ever encountered before; [and] these personalities were mainly consequent upon men and women living in a world whose fundamental assumptions could no longer be taken for granted. . . ."

(22) Because it was not in the truest sense particular and confined, because it was in the absolute sense universal, the stuff with which Wright employed his pen was stern and terrible.

(23) Some critics have said that the wide appeal of Wright's work is due to the sensationalism in it. But it is not this. One can have serious doubts that the girl Sue in *Bright and Morning Star* or Bessie in *Native Son* or the opening epistle in *Long Black Song* would come off very well in Chinese or in Swedish or some other tongue. What does come off well in any language is the total concept of the primary evil of prejudice. This the Chinese and the Russians and the Norwegians and the French and all other peoples would understand; and a delineation of its effects, particular though it be, interests them in the same way and for the same reason that love interests them.

(24) *Black Boy*, which does not prove the point—except perhaps very obliquely—does not deny it, either. Of course, this later book is autobiographical, which excuses it from the same kind of analysis that can be brought to bear upon the works of pure creation. But even here it may be argued, and not too incongruously, that Wright depicts, delineates, and skewers home the point that "To live habitually as a superior among inferiors, be the superiority intellectual or economic, is a temptation and hubris, inevitably deteriorating. . . ." And that, let it be averred, has nothing to do with the intrinsic particulars of race. It has an application as universal as "power corrupteth."

(25) So Richard Wright was a new kind of writer in the ranks of Negro writers. He had extricated himself from the dilemma, the horns of which are (1) to write exclusively for a Negro audience and thereby limit oneself to a monotypical, glorified and race-proud picture of Negro life, and (2) to write exclusively for a white audience and thereby be trapped in the old stereotypes, the fixed opinions, the stock situations that are as bulwarks against honest creation. Negro writers traditionally have been impaled upon one or the other horn of this dilemma, sometimes in spite of all their efforts to avoid it.

(26) Langston Hughes was undoubtedly sincere when he declared of young Negro artists and writers back in the Twenties: "If the white people are pleased, we are glad. If they aren't, it doesn't matter. . . . If colored people are pleased, we are glad. If they are not, their displeasure doesn't matter either. . . ." He was sincere, but mistaken.

(27) A writer writes for an audience. Consciously or unconsciously, he bears in mind the real or imagined peculiarities of the audience to whom he wishes to appeal. Until very recent years, Negro writers did not believe that a white audience and a colored audience were essentially alike because, in fact, they were not. They were kept apart by a wide socio-cultural gulf—by differences of concept, by deliberately cultivated fears, taboos, ignorance, and race and caste consciousness. Now that gulf is closed and the writer can write without being either false to the one audience or subservient to the other. The hope that James Weldon Johnson expressed many years ago is being fulfilled at last. "Standing on his racial foundation," the Negro author can create that which rises above race and reaches "out to the universal in truth and beauty."

(28) Thus Margaret Walker, writing for the two audiences now becoming one, can carry away an important poetry prize. Gwendolyn Brooks, in poetry such as her "Bronzefille" can do things with the language of imagery that appeal to all humanity. No longer fearing the ancient interdiction, Chester Himes in *If He Hollers* writes forcefully, even if somewhat irrelevantly, of the sexual attraction a white woman feels for a Negro man; and William Attaway, in *Let Me Breathe Thunder*, can concern himself almost entirely with white characters. On the purely romantic and escapist side, Frank Yerby can write *The Foxes of Harrow*, which sells over 600,000 copies and is bought by the movies. Thus the poetry of Gwendolyn Brooks, and Robert Hayden and Moses Carl Holman. Thus *The Street* by Ann Petry, *Invisible Man* by Ralph Ellison and *A Different Drummer* by William Melvin Kelley.

(29) Though what is happening seems very like a miracle, it has been a long, long time in preparation. Writing by American Negroes has never been in such a splendid state of health, nor with such a bright and shining future before it.

Identification

Briefly identify each of the following persons:

1. Phyllis Wheatley
2. Charles Chestnutt
3. Paul Laurence Dunbar

4. Monroe Trotter

5. Kelly Miller

6. George Forbes

7. Sterling Brown

8. James Weldon Johnson

Questions for Discussion and Writing

1. The author suggests, as have other Negro writers, that Negro literature is distinctively different from American literature in general. How does he support this argument? In your opinion, is this argument valid?

2. Mr. Redding points out that the distinction between the literature of black Americans and that of other Americans is "only the distinction between trunk and branch." Explain. Defend or criticize this idea, using, where possible, specific examples to support your argument.

3. The author states that three times within this century, the literature of black Americans has been "nearly done to death." By what means? Is the idea clearly and adequately developed in the essay?

4. As stereotypes of the Negro began to develop, the Negro writer reacted to these stereotypes in various ways. What were some of these reactions and the reasons that prompted them? Were these reactions valid?

5. What were the two distinctive phases of the revolution in Negro literature which began during the period directly after World War I?

6. What were the effects of commercialism on the Negro renaissance in literature and music?

7. The author sees the vogue of Negro literature as now being in "a splendid state of health." How does he account for this? Do you agree? Write a brief criticism of this idea, supporting your position with as many examples as you can.

Ralph
Ellison

Ralph Ellison, novelist and short story writer, attended Tuskegee Institute (Tuskegee, Alabama) where he studied music in the hope of becoming a professional musician. In the late 1930's however, he moved to New York where he turned first to sculpture and finally to writing. With the publication of his first novel, *Invisible Man* (1952), he emerged as one of the most important writers of this century. The book won for him the National Book Award for the best novel of that year.

Mr. Ellison has written articles, short stories, and book reviews for such magazines as *The Reporter, The Antioch Review, The New Republic,* and *Saturday Review.* He has received several awards and honors including the American Academy of Arts and Letters Fellowship to the American Academy in Rome (1955–57). Mr. Ellison has taught at Bard College and the University of Chicago and has served as guest lecturer at many American and foreign universities.

The two essays in this text, "Beating That Boy" and "Living with Music" are taken from his last published major work, *Shadow and Act* (1964). In the following essay, from "Beating That Boy," Ellison is concerned with the manner and degree to which the racial problem in America has influenced the nature and scope of American literature.

Ralph
Ellison

Beating That Boy

(1) During these post-military-phase-of-the-war days when a Negro is asked what occurs when he visits with white friends, he is likely to chuckle and drily reply, "Oh, we beat that boy," meaning to belabor in polite conversation what is commonly called the "Negro problem." Though Negroes laugh when the phrase is used, beneath its folksy surface there lies—like a booby trap in a music box of folk tunes—a disillusionment that only its attitude of detached participation saves from exploding into violent cynicism: its counterpart among those Negroes who know no whites as friends.

(2) For the racial situation has become like an irrational sea in which Americans flounder like convoyed ships in a gale. The phrase rotates like a gyroscope of irony of which the Negro maintains a hazardous stability as

the sea-tossed ship of his emotions whirls him willy-nilly along: lunging him toward the shoals of bitter rejection (of the ideology that makes him the sole sacrifice of America's tragedy); now away toward the mine-strewn shores of hopelessness (that despite the war democracy is still discussed on an infantile level and himself in pre-adult terms); now smashing him flush against waves of anger that threaten to burst his seams in revolt (that his condition is so outrageously flagrant); now teetering him clear on a brief, calm, sunlit swell of self-amusement (that he must cling to the convoy though he doubts its direction); now knocking him erect, like a whale on its tail, before plunging again into the still dark night of the one lone "rational" thing—the pounding irrational sea.

(3) This is a nightmarishly "absurd" situation, and perhaps no major problem affecting the destiny of a nation has ever received such superficial discussion. As Bucklin Moon knew when he conceived *Primer for White Folks*, a great deal of the superficiality comes from the general ignorance prevailing in our society of the historical and social condition of the black tenth of the population. He might have subtitled his anthology. *A Short Course on the American Negro for Those Who "Beat That Boy."*

(4) *Primer for White Folks* comes as a result of the long fight which Negroes have made to make their story known, and the aroused efforts of liberal whites, many of them Southerners, to chart more accurately that heart-lashing sea of irrationality called the "Negro problem." The fair-minded but uninformed should read the book to learn how much they have been humiliated, insulted and insured by the Rankins and Bilbos who speak in their name to the world.

(5) *Primer for White Folks* is something new in its genre. Unlike similar anthologies, it does not consist solely of Negro contributions, but of writings on the racial situation as seen by both white and Negro authors. The book, which presents such writers as Will W. Alexander, Kay Boyle, Sterling Brown, Henrietta Buckmaster, Fanny Kemble, Langston Hughes, Wendell Wilkie, Lillian Smith, Dorothy Parker, James T. Farrell and Richard Wright, divides into three major sections. The first, "Heritage," covers slavery, the Civil War and the end of Reconstruction in Negro disfranchisement, and presents unfamiliar information on Negro slave revolts and heroism; the second consists of short stories about the mores of our society and the relationships, "sometimes ludicrous, sometimes tragic, between Negroes and whites"; and the third, "Today and Tomorrow," presents the thoughts of contemporary white and Negro writers on the "Negro question" and their recommendations for its solution. This section is especially valuable and will bear repeated reference as the tense period we have just entered unfolds. Here are the most democratically informed discussions of the racial situation to appear in print since Pearl Harbor.

(6) But if you believe you have read many of these pieces before

then you're mistaken; even if you *have*, you haven't. For here, under Bucklin Moon's creative editing, they have been placed in a fresh context of meaning, where, like the subtle relationships of forms in a great painting, they ever reveal something new. Encountering some of them here, one wonders whether Moon's conception was not superior to even the best images which he found to give it articulation. What an astounding book this could have been had every piece been on a par with its conception! Since hardly any aspect of our culture escapes the blight of hypocrisy implicit in our social institutions, it is not surprising that many of the pieces mix appeal for fair play with double-talk; or that most are much too fearful of that absolute concept "democracy," circling above it like planes being forced to earth in a fog. They seemed concerned most often with patching up the merry-go-round-that-broke-down than with the projection of that oh, so urgently needed new American humanism. Here, too, the boy comes in for a bit of a beating.

(7) These negative criticisms of its parts do not, however, apply to the anthology as a whole. For the negative when piled up quantitatively often assumes a positive value; and certainly it is valuable to detect the cracks in the tones of our most Liberty Bell voices. Then, too, such studies inevitably reveal as much about the white American as about the American Negro— which lends them a value that is generally ignored. When viewed from a perspective which takes this circumstance into account, *Primer for White Folks* will be prized for the oblique light it throws upon an aspect of American writing which was not its immediate concern.

(8) One notices, for instance, that most of the fiction presented here, with the exception of stories by Dorothy Parker, Kay Boyle, Erskine Caldwell and William March, is by writers who have appeared since the Depression; and that most of the widely read authors of the between-wars period are, with the exceptions of James T. Farrell and Richard Wright, conspicuously missing. We are reminded that from 1776 to 1876 there was a conception of democracy current in this country that allowed the writer to identify himself with the Negro; and that had such an anthology been conceivable during the nineteenth century, it could have included such writers as Whitman, Emerson, Thoreau, Hawthorne, Melville and Mark Twain. For slavery (it was not termed a "Negro problem" then) was a vital issue in the American consciousness, symbolic of the condition of Man, and a valid aspect of the writer's reality. Only after the Emancipation and the return of the Southern ruling class to power in the counter-revolution of 1876, was the Negro issue pushed into the underground of the American conscience and ignored.

(9) To ignore, however, is not to nullify, and the fact that so many of our important writers are missing from *Primer for White Folks* raises the question whether the existence of the race problem in our culture has not

had an insidiously powerful effect upon twentieth-century writing that has not been generally suspected. Perhaps here, too, lies a partial explanation of why we have come to regard certain faults of this writing as excellences.

(10) But first let me hasten to say that I do not mean to imply that whites had any obligation to write of Negroes, nor that in the depiction of the racial situation lies any blueprint for a supreme fiction (if so, all Negro writers would rate with Tolstoy and Balzac, Shakespeare and Dostoievsky). Unfortunately, the connection between literature and society is seldom so naively direct. There is, nevertheless, an inescapable connection between the writer and the beliefs and attitudes current in his culture, and it is here exactly that the "Negro problem" begins to exert a powerful uncalculated influence.

(11) For since 1876 the race issue has been like a stave driven into the American system of values, a stave so deeply imbedded in the American *ethos* as to render America a nation of ethical schizophrenics. Believing truly in democracy on one side of their minds, they act on the other in violation of its most sacred principles; holding that all men are created equal, they treat thirteen million Americans as though they were not.

(12) There are, as always, political and economic motives for this rending of values, but in terms of the ethical and psychological, what was opportunistically labeled the "Negro problem" is actually a guilt problem charged with pain. Just how painful, might be judged from the ceaseless effort expended to dull its throbbings with the anesthesia of legend, myth, hypnotic ritual and narcotic modes of thinking. And not only have our popular culture, our newspapers, radio and cinema been devoted to justifying the Negro's condition and the conflict created thereby, but even our social sciences and serious literature have been conscripted—all in the effort to drown out the persistent voice of outraged conscience.

(13) This unwillingness to resolve the conflict in keeping with his democratic ideals has compelled the white American, figuratively, to force the Negro down into the deeper level of his consciousness, into the inner world, where reason and madness mingle with hope and memory and endlessly give birth to nightmare and to dream; down into the province of the psychiatrist and the artist, from whence spring the lunatic's fancy and the work of art. It is a dangerous region even for the artist and his tragedy lies in the fact that in order to tap the fluid fire of inspiration, he must perpetually descend and re-encounter not only the ghosts of his former selves, but all of the unconquered anguish of living.

(14) Obviously this position need not be absolutely disadvantageous for the Negro. It might, in a different culture, be highly strategic, enlisting in his cause the freedom-creating powers of art. For imprisoned in the deepest drives in human society, it is practically impossible for the white American to think of sex, of economics, his children or womenfolk, or of

sweeping socio-political changes, without summoning into consciousness fearflecked images of black men. Indeed, it seems that the Negro has become identified with those unpleasant aspects of conscience and consciousness which it is part of the American's character to avoid. Thus when the literary artist attempts to tap the charged springs issuing from his inner world, up float his misshapen and bloated images of the Negro, like the fetid bodies of the drowned, and he turns away, discarding an ambiguous substance which the artists of other cultures would confront boldly and humanize into the stuff of a tragic art. It is as though we were to discard the beneficial properties of the X-ray simply because when used without the protection of a leaden screen they might burn us or produce sterility.

(15) Indeed, the racial situation has exerted an influence upon the writer similar to that of an X-ray concealed in a radio. Moving about, perhaps ignoring, perhaps enjoying Jack Rochester or a hot jazz band, he is unaware of his exposure to a force that shrivels his vital sperm. Not that it has rendered him completely sterile, but that it has caused him to produce deformed progeny: literary offspring without hearts, without brains, viscera or vision, and some without genitalia.

(16) Thus it has not been its failure to depict racial matters that has determined the quality of American writing, but that the writer has formed the habit of living and thinking in a culture that is opposed to the deep thought and feeling necessary to profound art; hence its avoidance of emotion, its fear of ideas, its obsession with mere physical violence and pain, its overemphasis of understatement, its precise and complex verbal constructions for converting goatsong into carefully modulated squeaks.

(17) Nor are the stories and articles included in *Primer for White Folks* free of these faults. But if they bear the mark of the culture out of which they spring, they are also appeals for a superior society and a more vital literature. As arranged here, they offer a vivid statement of the strengths and weaknesses of the new mood born in the hearts of Americans during the war, a mood more precise in its fears (of racial bloodshed) than definite in its hopes (symbolized most concretely in the frantic efforts of interracial organizations and mayor's committees to discover a foolproof technique of riot control); but more significant than their obvious fears and vacillations, they are valuable for something practically missing from American writing since Huckleberry Finn: a search for images of black and white fraternity.

Questions for Discussion and Writing

1. What is the meaning of the title of the essay?

2. Can you explain the extended figure of speech in paragraph 2 of

the essay? How effective is it as a rhetorical device? Does it help to set the general tone of the essay?

3. The author states that the race problem has had a tremendous effect upon American literature in the twentieth century. What is this effect, and how is it exemplified in contemporary literature?

4. The author states that there is "an inescapable connection between the writer and the beliefs and attitudes current in his culture." Explain. Try to think of specific examples of literary works that will support this idea.

5. Can you determine what Mr. Ellison's basic opinion of *Primer for White Folks* is? What passage or passages in the essay would you use to justify your conclusion?

6. There are many figures of speech in this essay. Pick out and iden-tify those used in the following paragraphs: 2, 11, 13, 14, 15, 16. Does Ellison's use of figurative language enhance or detract from the effec-tiveness of the essay? In what ways?

LeRoi
Jones*

The Myth
of a "Negro Literature"

(1) The mediocrity
of what has been called "Negro Literature" is one of the most loosely held
secrets of American culture. From Phyllis Wheatley to Charles Chestnutt,
to the present generation of American Negro writers, the only recognizable accretion of tradition readily attributable to the black producer of a
formal literature in this country, with a few notable exceptions, had been
of an almost agonizing mediocrity. In most other fields of "high art" in
America, with the same few notable exceptions, the Negro contribution
has been, when one existed at all, one of impressive mediocrity. Only in
music, and most notably in blues, jazz, and spirituals, i.e., "Negro Music,"
has there been a significantly profound contribution by American Negroes.

*For a short biographical sketch of the author, see pp. 83–84.
Reprinted from LeRoi Jones, Home: Social Essays, by permission of William
Morrow and Company, Inc. Copyright © 1963 by LeRoi Jones.

(2) There are a great many reasons for the spectacular vapidity of the American Negro's accomplishment in other formal, serious art forms—social, economic, political, etc.—but one of the most persistent and aggravating reasons for the absence of achievement among serious Negro artists, except in Negro music, is that in most cases the Negroes who found themselves in a position to pursue some art, especially the art of literature, have been members of the Negro middle class, a group that has always gone out of its way to cultivate *any* mediocrity as long as that mediocrity was guaranteed to prove to America, and recently to the world at large, that they were not really who they were, i.e., Negroes. Negro music alone, because it drew its strengths and beauties out of the depth of the black man's soul, and because to a large extent its traditions could be carried on by the lowest classes of Negroes, has been able to survive the constant and willful dilutions of the black middle class. Blues and jazz have been the only consistent exhibitors of "Negritude" in formal American culture simply because the bearers of its tradition maintained their essential identities as Negroes; in no other art (and I will persist in calling Negro music, art) has this been possible. Phyllis Wheatley and her pleasant imitation of the 18th century English poetry are far and finally ludicrous departures from the huge black voices that splintered southern nights with their *hollers, chants, arwhoolies,* and *ballits*. The embarrassing and inverted paternalism of Charles Chestnutt and his "refined Afro-American" heroes are far cries from the richness and profundity of the blues. And it is impossible to mention the achievements of the Negro in any area of artistic endeavor with as much significance as in spirituals, blues and jazz. There has never been an equivalent to Duke Ellington or Louis Armstrong in Negro writing, and even the best of contemporary literature written by Negroes cannot yet be compared to the fantastic beauty of the music of Charlie Parker.

(3) American Negro music from its inception moved logically and powerfully out of a fusion between African musical tradition and the American experience. It was, and continues to be, a natural, yet highly stylized and personal version of the Negro's life in America. It is, indeed, a chronicle of the Negro's movement, from African slave to American slave, from Freedman to Citizen. And the literature of the blues is a much more profound contribution to Western culture than any other literary contribution made by American Negroes. Moreover, it is only recently that formal literature written by American Negroes has begun to approach the literary standards of its model, i.e., the literature of the white middle class. And only Jean Toomer, Richard Wright, Ralph Ellison, and James Baldwin have managed to bring off examples of writing, in this genre, that could succeed in passing themselves off as "serious" writing, in the sense that, say, the work of Somerset Maugham is "serious" writing. That is, serious, if one has never read Herman Melville or James Joyce. And it is part of the tragic naivete of the middle class (-brow) writer, that he has not.

(4) Literature, for the Negro writer, was always an example of "culture." Not in the sense of the more impressive philosophical characteristics of a particular social group, but in the narrow sense of "cultivation" or "sophistication" by an individual within that group. The Negro artist, because of his middle-class background, carried the artificial social burden as the "best and most intelligent" of Negroes, and usually entered into the "serious" arts to exhibit his familiarity with the social graces, i.e., as method or means of displaying his participation in the "serious" aspects of American culture. To be a writer was to be "cultivated," in the stunted bourgeois sense of the word. It was also to be a "quality" black man. It had nothing to do with the investigation of the human soul. It was, and is, a social preoccupation rather than an aesthetic one. A rather daring way of status seeking. The cultivated Negro leaving those ineffectual philanthropies, Negro colleges, looked at literature merely as another way of gaining prestige in the white world for the Negro middle class. And the literary and artistic models were always those that could be socially acceptable to the white middle class, which automatically limited them to the most spiritually debilitated imitations of literature available. Negro music, to the middle class, black and white, was never socially acceptable. It was shunned by blacks ambitious of "waking up white," as low and degrading. It was shunned by their white models simply because it was produced by blacks. As one of my professors at Howard University protested one day, "It's amazing how much bad taste the blues display." Suffice it to say, it is in part exactly this "bad taste" that has continued to keep Negro music as vital as it is. The abandonment of one's local (i.e., place or group) emotional attachments in favor of the abstract emotional response of what is called "the general public" (which is notoriously white and middle class) has always been the great diluter of any Negro culture. "You're acting a nigger," was the standard disparagement. I remember being chastised severely for daring to eat a piece of watermelon on the Howard campus. "Do you realize you're sitting near the highway?" is what the man said, "This is the capstone of Negro education." And it is too, in the sense that it teaches the Negro how to make out in the white society, using the agonizing overcompensation of pretending he's also white. James Baldwin's *The Amen Corner*, when it appeared at the Howard Players theatre, "set the speech department back ten years," an English professor groaned to me. The play depicted the lives of poor Negroes running a store-front church. Any reference to the Negro-ness of the American Negro has always been frowned upon by the black middle class in their frenzied dash toward the precipice of the American mainstream.

(5) High art, first of all, must reflect the experience of the human being, the emotional predicament of the man, as he exists, in the defined world of his being. It must be produced from the legitimate emotional resources of the soul in the world. It can *never* be produced by appropri-

ating the withered emotional responses of some strictly social idea of humanity. High art, and by this I mean any art that would attempt to describe or characterize some portion of the profound meaningfulness of human life with any finality or truth, cannot be based on the superficialities of human existence. It must issue from *real* categories of human activity, *truthful* accounts of human life, and not fancied accounts of the attainment of cultural privilege by some willingly preposterous apologists for one social "order" or another. Most of the formal literature produced by Negroes in America has never fulfilled these conditions. And aside from Negro music, it is only in the "popular traditions" of the so-called lower class Negro that these conditions are fulfilled as a basis for human life. And it is because of this "separation" between Negro life (as an emotional experience) and Negro art, that, say, Jack Johnson or Ray Robinson is a larger cultural hero than any Negro writer. It is because of this separation, even evasion, of the emotional experience of Negro life, that Jack Johnson is a more modern political symbol than most Negro writers. Johnson's life, as proposed, certainly, by his career, reflects much more accurately the symbolic yearnings for singular values among the great masses of Negroes than any black novelist has yet managed to convey. Where is the Negro-ness of a literature written in imitation of the meanest of social intelligences to be found in American culture, i.e., the white middle class? How can it even begin to express the emotional predicament of black Western man? Such a literature, even if its "characters" *are* black, takes on the emotional barrenness of its model, and the blackness of the characters is like the blackness of Al Jolson, an unconvincing device. It is like using black checkers instead of white. They are still checkers.

(6) The development of the Negro's music was, as I said, direct and instinctive. It was the one vector out of African culture impossible to eradicate completely. The appearance of blues as a native *American* music signified in many ways the appearance of American Negroes where once there were African Negroes. The emotional fabric of the music was colored by the emergence of an American Negro culture. It signified that culture's strength and vitality. In the evolution of the Negro as a cultural and social element of American culture, but also the evolution of that culture itself. The "Coon Shout" proposed one version of the American Negro—and of America; Ornette Coleman proposes another. But the point is that both these versions are accurate and informed with a legitimacy of emotional concern nowhere available in what is called "Negro Literature," and certainly not in the middle-brow literature of the white American.

(7) The artifacts of African art and sculpture were consciously eradicated by slavery. Any African art that based its validity on the production of an artifact, i.e., some *material* manifestation such as a wooden statue or a woven cloth, had little chance of survival. It was only the more "abstract"

aspects of African culture that could continue to exist in slave America. Africanisms still persist in the magic, religion, and popular cultural traditions of American Negroes. However, it is not an African art American Negroes are responsible for, but an American one. The traditions of Africa must be utilized within the culture of the American Negro where they *actually* exist, and not because of a defensive rationalization about the *worth* of one's ancestors or an attempt to capitalize on the recent eminence of the "new" African nations. Africanisms do exist in Negro culture, but they have been so translated and transmuted by the American experience that they have become integral parts of that experience.

(8) The American Negro has a definable and legitimate historical tradition, no matter how painful, in America, but it is the only place such a tradition exists, simply because America is the only place the American Negro exists. He is, as William Carlos Williams said, "A pure product of America." The paradox of the Negro experience in America is that it is a separate experience, but inseparable from the complete fabric of American life. The history of Western culture begins for the Negro with the importation of the slaves. It is almost as if all Western history before that must be strictly a learned concept. It is only the American experience that can be a persistent cultural catalyst for the Negro. In a sense, history for the Negro, before America, must remain an emotional abstraction. The cultural memory of Africa informs the Negro's life in America, but is impossible to separate it from its American transformation. Thus, the Negro writer if he wanted to tap his legitimate cultural tradition should have done it by utilizing the entire spectrum of the American experience from the point of view of the emotional history of the black man in this country: as its victim and its chronicler. The soul of such a man, as it exists outside the boundaries of commercial diversion or artificial social pretense. But without a deep commitment to cultural relevance and intellectual purity this was impossible. The Negro as a writer, was always a social object, whether glorifying the concept of white superiority, as a great many early Negro writers did, or in crying out against it, as exemplified by the stock "protest" literature of the thirties. He never moved into the position where he could propose his own symbols, erect his own personal myths, as any great literature must. Negro writing was always "after the fact," i.e., based on known social concepts within the structure of bourgeois idealistic projections of "their America," and an emotional climate that never really existed.

(9) The most successful fiction of most Negro writing is in its emotional content. The Negro protest novelist postures, and invents a protest quite amenable with the tradition of bourgeois American life. He never reaches the central core of the America which *can* cause such protest. The intellectual traditions of the white middle class prevent such exposure of reality, and the black imitators reflect this. The Negro writer on Negro life

in America postures, and invents a Negro life, and an America to contain it. And even most of those who tried to rebel against that *invented* America were trapped because they had lost all touch with the reality of their experience within the *real* America, either because of the hidden emotional allegiance to the white middle class, or because they did not realize where the reality of their experience lay. When the serious Negro writer disdained the "middle-brow" model, as is the case with a few contemporary black American writers, he usually rushed headlong into the groves of the Academy, perhaps the most insidious and clever dispenser of middle-brow standards of excellence under the guise of "recognizable tradition." That such recognizable tradition is necessary goes without saying, but even from the great philosophies of Europe a contemporary usage must be established. No poetry has come out of England of major importance for forty years, yet there are would-be Negro poets who reject the gaudy excellence of 20th century American poetry in favor of disembowelled academic models of second-rate English poetry, with the notion that somehow it is the only way poetry should be written. It would be better if such a poet listened to Bessie Smith sing *Gimme A Pigfoot*, or listened to the tragic verse of a Billie Holiday, than be content to imperfectly imitate the bad poetry of the ruined minds of Europe. And again, it is this striving for *respectability* that has it so. For an American, black or white, to say that some hideous imitation of Alexander Pope means more to him, emotionally, than the blues of Ray Charles or Lightnin' Hopkins, it would be required for him to have completely disappeared into the American Academy's version of a Europeanized and colonial American culture, or to be lying. In the end, the same emotional sterility results. It is somehow much more tragic for the black man.

(10) A Negro literature, to be a legitimate product of the Negro experience in America, must get at that experience in exactly the terms America has proposed for it, in its most ruthless identity. Negro reaction to America is as deep a part of America as the root causes of that reaction and it is impossible to accurately describe that reaction in terms of the American middle class; because for them, the Negro has never really existed, never been glimpsed in anything even approaching the complete reality of his humanity. The Negro writer has to go from where he actually is, completely outside of that conscious myopia. That the Negro does exist is the point, and as an element of American culture he is completely misunderstood by Americans. The middle-brow, commercial Negro writer assures the white American that, in fact, he doesn't exist, and that if he does, he does so within the perfectly predictable fingerpainting of white bourgeois sentiment and understanding. Nothing could be further from the truth. The Creoles of New Orleans resisted "Negro" music for a time as raw and raucous, because they thought they had found a place within

the white society which would preclude their being Negroes. But they were unsuccessful in their attempts to "disappear" because the whites themselves reminded them that they were still, for all their assimilation, "just coons." And this seems to me an extremely important idea, since it is precisely this bitter insistence that has kept what can be called "Negro Culture" a brilliant amalgam of diverse influences. There was always a border beyond which the Negro could not go, whether musically or socially. There was always a possible limitation to any dilution or excess of cultural or spiritual reference. The Negro could not ever become white and that was his strength; at some point, always, he could not participate in the dominant tenor of the white man's culture, yet he came to understand that culture as well as the white man. It was at this juncture that he had to make use of other resources, whether African, sub-cultural, or hermetic. And it was this boundary, this no-man's-land, that provided the logic and beauty of his music. And this is the only way for the Negro artist to provide his version of America—from that no-man's-land outside the mainstream. A no-man's-land, a black country, completely invisible to white America, but so essentially part of it as to stain its whole being an ominous gray. Were there really a Negro literature, now it could flower. At this point when the whole of Western society might go up in flames, the Negro remains an integral part of that society, but continually outside it, a figure like Melville's Bartleby. He is an American, capable of identifying emotionally with the fantastic cultural ingredients of this society, but he is also, forever, outside that culture, an invisible strength within it, an observer. If there is ever a Negro literature, it must disengage itself from the weak, heinous elements of the culture that spawned it, and use its very existence as evidence of a more profound America. But as long as the Negro writer contents himself with the imitation of the useless ugly inelegance of the stunted middle-class mind, academic or popular, and refuses to look around him and "tell it like it is"—preferring the false prestige of the black bourgeoisie or the deceitful "acceptance" of *buy and sell* America, something never included in the legitimate cultural tradition of "his people"—he will be a failure, and what is worse, not even a significant failure. Just another dead American.

Questions for Discussion and Writing

1. The author states that "Blues and jazz have been the only consistent exhibitors of 'Negritude' in formal American culture." What reasons does he give for this? In your opinion, are his reasons valid?

2. According to Jones, what is there in the character of the black bourgeoisie that renders him incapable of creating "serious" art? Com-

pare his appraisal of the black middle class with that of Nathan Hare in "The Exiles." Write a personal evaluation of the black middle class.

3. Are there examples in today's society that would tend to negate Mr. Hare's and Mr. Jones' evaluation of the black middle class? If so, can you cite examples from your own community or society?

4. In paragraph 8 of the essay, the author refers to the "paradox" of the Negro experience in America. Can you explain this paradox?

5. Mr. Jones suggests that we are living in a period in which a "true Negro literature" could genuinely flower. Do you agree with this idea? Why? Why not? What specific characteristics do you feel would distinguish a "true Negro literature"?

Marian E. Musgrave

Marian Musgrave, scholar of languages and literature, received the B.A. and M.A. degrees from Howard University (Washington, D.C.). She received the Ph.D. degree from Western Reserve University (now Case-Western Reserve) where her major field of concentration was seventeenth-century English literature. Professor Musgrave attended both Howard and Western Reserve Universities on full scholarships and fellowships. During her academic career, Professor Musgrave has served as Chairman of the English Department at Alcorn College (Lorman, Mississippi), as professor of English at Southern University in New Orleans, at Central State University (Wilberforce, Ohio) where she was director of the graduate English program, and at Miami University.

Through the years, Professor Musgrave has developed an interest in the area of language study and has written and spoken extensively on the problems of learning language. The following article was taken from the *College Language Association Journal* and presents a "new" approach to the teaching of English to students with sub-standard dialects. While the article is written from the teacher's point of view, it provides interesting and perhaps valuable information for both students and teachers.

Marian E.
Musgrave

Teaching English as a Foreign Language to Students with Sub-standard Dialects

(1) When I first began teaching at Alcorn A. and M. College in Lorman, Mississippi, I found the problems of teaching English there not difficult in type but in degree, as compared with the same task at other colleges for Negroes in the South. The student population at Alcorn is drawn mainly from rural areas and from very small towns, the better urban students tending to enroll at urban colleges or at least at colleges not far from urban centers. These factors, I feel, helped greatly to increase problems involving Freshman English. Students from land-locked areas, which are extremely common in Mississippi, are not exposed to contacts with our mobile American population. Except perhaps on the Gulf Coast, there is no steady flow in and out of persons speaking many varied dialects of American English; furthermore, the

Reprinted from Marian Musgrave, "Teaching English as a Foreign Language," CLA Journal (September 1963), by permission of the author and publisher.

blighting effects of total segregation prevent all but the most perfunctory contacts with speakers of standard Southern dialects and tend to prevent acquaintances with current movements and ideas in the mainstream of American civilization, so that my Alcorn students not only lacked the vocabulary to express many ideas but lacked also the intellectual stimulation which would encourage vocabulary growth.

(2) At Alcorn I encountered a number of dialectal peculiarities which I had not previously heard, though, since my experience with Southern colleges is limited to Arkansas, Louisiana, and Mississippi, it admittedly is not wide. Some of my students almost never used "we," "our," and "ours." One of these students, who lived on the road leading to the college said to me, "Us had rain at us house last night." I also found that inflected genitives were quite rare, as were, in fact, most inflections containing sibilants. This means, of course, that many students neither recognized nor used standard plural and possessive forms, nor did they use *s*'s on third person singular, present indicative verbs, surely the most wide-spread error among Negroes.

(3) Most of us are only too well acquainted with Freshman English programs. We know that constant floods of new texts appear each year, and it is always our wistful hope that somewhere, sometime, we will find a text that meets the need of the sub-standard freshman. It is obvious that most teachers are dissatisfied with the results obtained in our programs and that we are highly doubtful of the efficacy of the Sophomore or Junior Comprehensive. We also have our own opinion as to the justice of making the English Department responsible for the dismissal of those students who, unable to read and write acceptably, have nevertheless entered their junior year. I am sure, also, that none of us felt encouraged by the results of the Princeton experiment published two years ago and announced first at the convention of the National Reading Association at Texas Christian University in 1959. The experiment, which was done with freshmen students, involved testing in usage and mechanics before the semester began and after the semester was over. The students as a group not only showed no improvement in these areas, but actually showed marked regression. Knowing this, and believing that still simpler texts and exercises would not solve problems that date back to the student's formative years, I felt that the college, the students, and I would have nothing to lose by trying another method.

(4) The idea behind my experiment is certainly not new, and I do not pretend to take any credit for originating it. It is the method by which a child learns his native tongue. Used in teaching foreign languages, it has proved its superiority to the old grammatical approaches. It is the basis of the Berlitz system, but in my home town, Cleveland, Ohio, the method is called the de Sauze System, after the long-time director of the foreign

language program in the Cleveland Public Schools, Dr. Emile B. de Sauze. Dr. de Sauze believed in starting a second language early; in Cleveland, children in the Major Work Program begin their daily French lessons in the third grade. An important feature of these lessons is that no English at all is spoken either by teacher or pupil, except by permission, which must be asked in French. Using repetition, imitation, and acting-out, the child steadily builds up an active speaking vocabulary dealing with ordinary objects, ideas, and activities.

(5) I first began attempting to use this method at Alcorn with a class in Freshman English during the summer of 1959. My only excuse for attempting it is that I was one of those children taught by the de Sauze method, and I know that it works. I must apologize to any of you who are linguists or speech therapists, for I do not intend to invade your field, nor do I pretend to any specialized knowledge in those areas. But the situation was desperate, and desperate situations frequently call forth desperate remedies.

(6) I had an ideal class to start with, I feel, for they were students who saw clearly that their speech handicapped them and they wished to improve. I did not have to waste time trying to convince them of the advantages of speaking Standard English. They had, furthermore, a ready-made group spirit, a phenomenon which seems to have been the result of an accidental age differential. One-half of the class was composed of students in their late teens; the other half consisted of mature women who had taught or who were teaching. Along with their group loyalty, then, was a healthy spirit of rivalry.

(7) Since the first summer term was but five weeks long, we had no time to waste. During the first hour each day we had oral drill as a group; the second hour was spent on individual drills, while the rest of the class did written work. We started with introductions of ourselves in short sentences. I would say, "Who are you?" The student would reply, "I am ————."

(8) After going about the room, I would then say, pointing to a student, "Who is she?"

(9) This gambit forced students to listen to each other and to take an interest in each other. They felt a bit embarrassed if they articulated too poorly for the next persons to catch their names, so they began pronouncing carefully. One example is the woman who, in answer to the question, "Where do you live?" answered, "I live in Towtown," or so it seemed. But she was from Tylertown, and after this incident, she said *Tylertown*, not with the true *ai* sound, but with three syllables.

(10) Here I must pause and remark that at no time was it my goal to change Southern pronunciations or to tamper with what is called "Southern accent." In fact, I emphasized that speaking Standard English

does not mean imitating the speech of another region but means imitating the speech of standard speakers in one's own area. Normally, even educated Southerners and Westerners do not have true *er* and *ai* sounds in their dialects, and it was not my purpose to superimpose these sounds. By the same token I also did not waste time on forms that are rapidly passing out of American English, like *who* and *whom* used as relative pronouns.

(11) In that first week, really starting from scratch, we worked orally with the verb *to be* and with ordinary objects in the room. In this way we caught and dealt with common errors within their context. "What is this?" I would say, pointing to a desk. "This is a *dest*," was the common early answer. To catch that sort of error, I taught them to cup their hands behind their ears so that they could actually hear the sounds they were making, for we had no laboratory equipment. Then we said sequences of sounds to help distinguish between *est* and *esk*. Students suggested rhyming words, just as they would in a first grade class. I avoided writing these or any words on the board, for I did not want the issues confused by English orthography.

(12) I found that everyone said "I am" in this class though I have encountered other forms in Mississippi; but many students said "You is," and in a construction like "He is my neighbor," they would first contract the verb, I think, and then eliminate the sibilant altogether, so that they normally said, "He my neighbor."

(13) Part of the second week's work involved the verb *to have*. Here we unearthed many sub-standard forms, notably the use of *has* for every person *except* he, she, and it. I must make it clear that at no time did I talk to them about grammar, which presumably had been taught them for many years with no results. And, at any rate, sub-standard dialects have their grammar as well as standard ones, as many commentators have pointed out.

(14) During our second and third weeks we progressed from short statements dealing with the class, our home towns, and class relations, to two-person dialogues dealing with given situations. At first, I served as the second person, but as the class members grew more involved with each other, they were able to take both roles. A sample dialogue is this:

What time do you wake up in the morning?
I wake up at six o'clock in the morning.
What do you do when you wake up?
I make the coffee when I wake up.
Who drinks the coffee?
My husband drinks the coffee.
Does he like coffee?
Yes, he likes coffee.

Other dialogues dealt with a visit to the library, a vacation trip, going to the grocery store, and other homely, everyday situations calling for homely, everyday words. It will be noticed that most of the words in the question must be repeated in the answer. This fact gives an artificial sound to the speech, a sound which is not a defect. Answering the question completely involves thinking about word order, an important factor in speaking Standard English. When I was a fourth grade pupil in French, our teacher used to say to us, "Pensez, et alors parlez." Think, and then speak. My students had to think first, and that stopped a good deal of careless speech.

(15) During our fourth week, we had groups of students from the same town or who had classes together confer briefly and then tell the class what people in the town do in various seasons, or what they do in various classes. Two women who taught in a Louisiana school just over the Mississippi border told about their experiences, particularly about the nickel lunch program, which to me, at least, was fascinating.

(16) In the dialogues, students asked questions formally and were answered as formally:

> What do the men in your town do?
> Some of the men in my town farm. Other men work in the tung plant.
> What do they do in the tung plant?
> They press oil from tung nuts.
> What do they do with the oil?
> They put the oil in barrels.
> Do many men work in the tung plant?
> No, many men do not work in the tung plant. Part of the plant has been closed.
> Why has part of the plant been closed?
> Part of the plant has been closed because it was not needed.

One sure sign of improvement and new confidence in this class, besides the disappearance of certain written errors in the best students' papers, was that in the fourth week they began complaining about the simplicity of the hour-long drills. I brought Hemingway's "The Killers," which we read aloud, to show how effective simplicity can be; and, to show them the immense complexities of which the language is capable, while still keeping simple forms, I brought a recording of Edith Sitwell's *Facade*, a series of experimental poems which that distinguished British poet presented with especially composed music in 1920.

(17) Had Alcorn's library been better, I feel that I could have handled the inevitable reaction better. I would have assigned at least two short stories a week, particularly stories by Sherwood Anderson, Hemingway, Eudora Welty, Jesse Stuart, Erskine Caldwell, and other Southern regionalists. I believe that such readings could have reinforced my own reassur-

ances to the students that there is nothing wrong with a Southern accent, that it can, in fact, be a positive asset, and that saying what you mean, in the simplest way possible, is a positive virtue.

(18) At Southern University in New Orleans, I have, in a small way, worked with students once a week in the classroom and have had two students who came in regularly for a drill at my office. These experiences, I think, confirm the conclusions that I reached at Alcorn. One such conclusion is that the student must want to change before any changes can be effected. Another is that he must have the intellectual energy to practice on his own. I was fortunate enough to have one student who developed remarkably in one semester. He practiced regularly, both at home and with me, and in class recited without ever developing the self-consciousness that renders silent the sub-standard speaker. Another factor that caused great improvement in this young man is that he fell in love with the short story, which he seems never to have read before. I gave him a copy of *Twenty Grand*, a collection of adventure and mystery short stories, the type he liked best, and he devoured them.

(19) I should now mention some defects of the system. One is the tremendous consumption of time. One needs daily drill to learn any language including one's native tongue. Except in summer, classes meet three times a week at most colleges, for just an hour, so that the amount of attention that one can pay to each student is pitifully small. Individual practice sessions also consume much time, but of course many students will not come in for drill. In connection with this, I must say that they are frequently too embarrassed to come in; for they know as well as we that their speech is poor, and a sort of false pride keeps them from doing the only thing which will cure the ailment.

(20) I have found that my own speech defect greatly alleviates students' embarrassment. I have always had a slight lisp, a condition which was aggravated by my chipping a front tooth. I found that my students were really encouraged by my imperfection to try harder themselves. Before I chipped the tooth, I frequently heard students excuse themselves for mis-pronunciations on the grounds that they were tongue-tied, or, as they said, "tie-tongued." I almost never hear that excuse now, for it would take a deaf person to miss my lisp.

(21) I should close with one caution. All teachers are short on time and long on tasks that deans and principals and department heads want done immediately. The temptation, when trying the de Sauze method, is to whale away at the major errors which Southern Negroes make—such as omitting the sibilants on third person singular, present indicative verbs; not recognizing past tense verbs, particularly those whose -ed termination is pronounced; and eliding whole verbs or parts of verbs, as in "Who you?" "Where he gone?" "He crazy." "Why he act like that?"

(22) It is a mistake to attack these in isolation, for they are errors within a word-environment, or speech-context, so that attempting to eliminate one is self-defeating. The student's speech really becomes confused, so that in his writing and speaking one will find strange, bastard forms such as s's carefully appended to all tenses, or d's stuck on everywhere. I have found "he haves," "he haved," "he doos." Some of these odd forms, when spoken with the student's normal intonation, one might miss, supposing it to be the form customarily used, but on paper we can spot it for what it is, and I have found that when I compare early with late papers, these odd forms are the alien intruders.

(23) One last remark I must make, and that is that many students cannot admit to themselves that there is anything wrong with their speech, since their self-confidence is already upon precarious enough grounds. They will therefore resist any efforts the teacher makes and can easily contaminate the class's reaction, if the teacher is not on guard against this. There are others, just as resistant, who attempt to turn the practice session into a discussion of fine points of grammar. One of my students who habitually uses uninflected genitives—Bill car, John house—wanted to talk about the punctuation of the quote within a quote. For such students, not much can be done. The will to improve is all important.

Questions for Discussion and Writing

1. What, according to the author, prompted the project that she calls "teaching English as a foreign language" to American students?

2. Professor Musgrave indicates that her method was not original but was rather one by which she herself had once been taught and one which had proved to be successful. What name does she give to this method? Why? Describe the manner in which it operates. What is your opinion of it?

3. In paragraph 21, what are the three errors that the author found to be primary among Southern Negroes? If possible, listen to the speech of Southern Negroes (television, radio, tapes also may be used). Do you find the author's appraisal to be accurate? Nearly accurate? Inaccurate? Use the same test on speech of Southern whites. What are your findings? Write a brief paper on the results of your investigation of either project.

4. The author is careful to distinguish between sub-standard usage and regional accents. Why? Why did she not tamper with regional accents?

5. In paragraph 6, the author states the following: "I had an ideal class . . . for they were students who saw clearly that their speech handicapped them and they wished to improve." What does this suggest to you about the relationship which exists between desire for and acquisition of knowledge? Write a brief paper expressing your ideas on this subject.

ON THE ARTS

Alain
Locke

Alain Locke, educator, philosopher, and critic, received his Ph.D. degree from Harvard University in 1918. He also studied at Oxford University and at the University of Berlin. During his lifetime, Locke was especially interested in philosophy, literature, and art; and he served as professor of Philosophy at Howard University from 1912 until his retirement in 1954.

Locke became a major spokesman for the new Negro writers of the 1920's, a period known as the Harlem Renaissance. This period was characterized by the rebellion of young black writers against the stereotypes of the Negro in American literature. He urged all Americans to recognize the contributions of Negroes to American life and culture. Also he encouraged young Negro writers by publishing the works of the more promising ones in a magazine he edited, *Survey Graphic*.

The major publications of Alain Locke include *Race Contracts and Interpretation*, *The Negro in Art*, and *The Negro and His Music*, the work from which the following essay is taken. Before his death in 1954, he had planned *The Negro in American Culture*, a book which was to synthesize his basic ideas concerning the various aspects of Negro culture. Professor Locke did not live to complete the work, but it was completed by Margaret Just Butcher and published in 1956. An essay from that work "The Negro as Artist and in American Art," appears in this volume.

Alain
Locke

The Sorrow Songs:

The Spirituals

(1) The spirituals are
the most characteristic product of Negro genius to date. They are its great
folk-gift, and rank among the classic folk expressions in the whole world
because of their moving simplicity, their characteristic originality, and their
universal appeal. Although the products of the slave era and the religious
fervor of the plantation religion, they have outlived the generation and the
conditions which produced them. But they have not always been properly
appreciated or understood. One of the proofs of their classic immortality
lies in what abuses the spirituals have survived.

(2) They have lived through the contempt of the slave-owners. It was
only cultured observers with the Union armies like Wm. Allen and Colonel
Thos. Wentworth Higginson who called them to the attention of music-
lovers. Then, although they were never written down or formally composed
in definite versions, they have survived imperishably. Evolved from hymns,

they were again driven out of the church worship by the conventions of respectability and the repressions of Puritanism as the Negro church became more sophisticated. Finally, after enduring the neglect and disdain of second-generation respectability, spirituals have had to survive successive waves of false popularizations, first the corruptions of sentimental balladry, then a period of concert polishing and finally the contemporary stage of being "ragged" or "jazzed."

(3) They were first given to the musical world not as slave songs, but as "jubilees." It is a romantic story, told in Pike's "Story of the Jubilee Singers," and retold in Professor Work's "Folk Songs of the American Negro." It is the tale of that group of singers who started out from Fisk University in 1871 under the resolute leadership of George L. White, to make this music the appeal of that struggling college for funds. With all the cash in the Fisk treasury, except for a dollar held back by Principal Adam K. Spence, the troupe set out to Oberlin, where after an unsuccessful concert of current music, they instantly made an impression by a program of spirituals. Henry Ward Beecher's invitation to Brooklyn led to a national and international hearing, repeated tours all over America and Europe— fame for the singers, fortune for the college, but most important of all, recognition for Negro folk music. Other schools, Hampton, Atlanta, Calhoun, Tuskegee and a host of others joined the movement, and spread the knowledge of these songs far and wide in their concert campaigns. Later they were recorded and saved permanently as collection after collection was published. Thus they were saved during that critical period in which any folk product is likely to be snuffed out by the false pride of the second generation. Professor Work rightly estimates this a service worth much more to the race and the nation than the considerable sums of money brought to these struggling schools. Indeed it saved a folk art, preserved the most perfect registration of the Negro folk temperament and the most unique embodiment of its folk experience. Still during this period the spirituals were too often treated sentimentally, and their deepest tragic feeling and their purest folk artistry overlooked.

(4) Only since 1900 has the profundity and true folk character of the spirituals been gradually discovered and recognized. It was one of the great services of Dr. DuBois, in his unforgettable chapter on "The Sorrow Songs" to give them a serious and proper interpretation as the peasant's instinctive distillation of sorrow and his spiritual triumph over it in a religious ecstasy and hope. Men then began to realize that though naive and simple, they were really very profound. Underneath broken words, childish imagery, peasant simplicity, was an epic intensity and a tragic depth of religious emotion for which the only equal seems to have been the spiritual experience of the Jews, and for which the only analogue is the Psalms. The

spirituals stand out, therefore as one of the great classic expressions of all time of religious emotion and Christian moods and attitudes.

(5) Shortly after this, Henry Krehbiel, one of the great music critics of his generation, gave the spirituals their first serious and adequate musical analysis and interpretation in his "Afro-American Folk Songs." By this time, they had definitely come into their own and were recognized not only as unique folk music but as the main strand in American folk-song. Already they had been taken out of their original religious setting, and adapted to secular uses, some of them unworthy of their great dignity and spirituality. This was particularly true in their use as catch-penny sentimental appeals in the missionary campaigning of the Negro schools. Only with the original Fisk Singers was their real simplicity and dignity maintained. They were then carried still further from their proper sphere to the minstrel stage and the concert hall.

(6) But just about this time they received the highest possible recognition—that of being used as the thematic material for symphonic music through their incorporation in the epoch-making work of Anton Dvořák, the Bohemian composer, who chose them to represent American atmosphere in his symphony "From the New World" (1894).—Since then, the spirituals and even the secular Negro folk melodies and their harmonic style have been regarded by most musicians as the purest and most valuable musical ore in America; the raw materials of a native American music. So gradually ever since, their folk quality and purity of style have been emphasized by real musicians. Eventually on another level, they will come back to their original power and purity. We should always remember that they are not sentimental nor theatrical, but epic and full of simple dignity. They are also essentially choral in character, and not at their best in solo voice or solo instrumental form. They will find their truest development, then, in symphonic music or in the larger choral forms of the symphonic choir, like the development which the great modern Russian composers have brought to Russian folk music. At this stage, on a higher level, they will reachieve their folk atmosphere and epic spirituality.

(7) But let us go back to the originals,—the true spirituals. Many songs called spirituals are far from being so. The term is often very inaccurately used, especially to denote later artificial compositions which imitate the folk spirituals or dress them up in sentimental and concert versions. Yet age alone is not the hallmark of a true spiritual; for although the last generation of slavery from 1845–65 was their heyday, genuine spirituals are composed in primitive Negro communities even today. However, a genuine spiritual is always a folk composition or a group product, spontaneously composed as a choral expression of religious feeling, or as Miss Zora Hurston aptly puts it,—"by a group bent on the expression of feelings

and not on sound effects." She coins the useful term "neo-spirituals" to describe the artificial derivatives which we are all familiar with in the entertainment spirituals of the concert-hall and glee-club rendition. These "renovated spirituals," she says correctly, "are a valuable contribution to the musical literature, but they are not the genuine thing. Let no one imagine they are the true songs of the people as sung by them."

(8) Negro spirituals thus are not originally solo or quartette material. They are congregational outbursts under the pressure of great religious emotion,—choral improvisations on themes familiar to all the participants. Each singing of the piece is a new creation, and the changes, interpolations, variations defy the most expert musician's recording. Before they completely vanish in their original form, this congregational folk-singing, with its unique breaks and tricks, should be recorded by phonograph, the only way their values can be gotten.

(9) Needless to say, the early four-part hymn harmony versions are much more complex and irregular. Only recently have we recaptured in any art organization the true flavor and manner of these songs. But a record of the Eva Jessye Choir or the Hall Johnson Singers will give us our closest reproduction of the genuine Negro way of singing these songs. Both of them, it will be noticed, have the actual mechanics of improvised Negro choral singing, with its syllabic quavers, off-tones and tone glides, improvised interpolations, subtle rhythmic variation. In most conventional versions of the spirituals there is too much melody and formal harmony. Over-emphasize the melodic elements of a spiritual, and you get a sentimental ballad a la Stephen Foster. Stress the harmony and you get a cloying glee or "barber-shop" chorus. Over-emphasize, on the other hand, the rhythmic idiom and instantly you secularize the product and it becomes a syncopated shout, with the religious tone and mood completely evaporated. It is only in subtle fusion of these elements that the genuine folk spiritual exists or that it can be recaptured.

(10) At present, spirituals are at a very difficult point in their career; they are caught in the transitional stage between a folk-form and art-form. Their increasing popularity has brought a dangerous tendency to sophistication and over-elaboration. Even Negro composers have been too much influenced by formal European idioms and mannerisms in setting them. This is slightly true of the work of Mr. Henry T. Burleigh, who must be credited, however, as the musician who won for the spirituals the acclaim and acceptance of the concert stage. He is the father of the art spiritual, even though some of his settings have overlaid the folk spirit with concert furbelows and alien florid adornments.

(11) This does not mean that there is only one style of rendering spirituals. The folk itself has many styles. It only means that the folk quality

and atmosphere should be preserved as much as possible. To realize this, one has only to compare the robust and dramatic rendering of the Negro baritone Paul Robeson with the subdued, ecstatic and mystic renderings of Roland Hayes. Both are great interpretations; and each typical of a vein of Negro singing. As long as the peculiar quality of Negro song is maintained and the musical idiom kept pure, there can be no valid criticism. Complaint cannot legitimately be made against the concert use and the art development of the spirituals, but only against the glossed-over versions characteristic of those arrangers and singers who have not closely studied the primitive Negro folk-ways of singing.

(12) In spite of the effectiveness of the solo versions, especially when competently and reverently sung in the true Negro manner, it is being realized more and more that the proper idiom of these songs calls for choral arrangement. The vital sustained background of accompanying voices is important. The younger Negro musicians Nathaniel Dett, Carl Diton, Ballanta Taylor, Edward Boatner, Lawrence Brown, Hall Johnson and Eva Jessye, while they have written effective solo versions, are turning with increasing interest to the choral form. Herein lies the significance of the newer types of Negro choral choir that are beginning to appear or re-appear, among them the excellent choral organizations led by Eva Jessye and Hall Johnson. They have about restored the spirituals to their primitive choral basis and their original singing style. Developed along the lines of its own originality, we may expect a development of Negro folk song that may equal or even outstrip the phenomenal choral music of Russia.

(13) Negro music should be expected to flower most naturally in the field of vocal music, since its deepest folk roots are there. Commenting critically on a recent Carnegie Hall concert of a well-known and well-trained Negro University Chorus, Mr. Olin Downes, prominent music critic, soundly advised more singing in the true Negro idiom and less effort at imitation of other types of choral singing. Some interpreted this advice as a biased curtain-lecture to Negro singing groups to stick to their own limited province. But this was not the real issue. No one could ban from Negro groups the whole range of universal music. It was rather the advice to develop a great and unique musical style out of the powerful musical dialect which we have in our most characteristic folk-songs; as such organizations as the Ukranian Singers, the Russian Symphonic Choir, the Don Cossack Chorus have done from the Russian folk music and its unique styles of singing. Two Victor recordings of the Hall Johnson Chorus illustrate how this double uniqueness of singing style and folk melodies can be effectively used. Eventually choral works of an entirely new sort can and must come from Negro sources. While seculars like "St. James Infirmary Blues," "Water Boy" and "I'm an Eastman" are used in this particular

recording similar choral arrangement of the spirituals has been tried and found successful. Someday too a great composer might develop a great liturgical music out of the music materials of the spirituals.

(14) So these "sorrow songs" are more than a priceless heritage from the racial past, they are promising material for the Negro music of the future. And they are the common possession of all, part of the cultural currency of the land, as their popularity and universal appeal only too clearly proves. A "Society for the Preservation of the Spirituals" organized in Charleston, S.C. by a white singing organization is a striking symbol of this common duty to restore them to dignity and respect.

Identification

Briefly identify each of the following persons:

1. Eva Jessye

2. Edward Boatner

3. Hall Johnson

Questions for Discussion and Writing

1. The author states that the Negro spirituals "are the most characteristic product of Negro genius to date." What justification does he use for this statement? He further refers to the spirituals as classic. Is this statement defensible from the standpoint of any definition of the term "classic"?

2. What role did such universities as Fisk, Tuskegee, and Hampton play in the preservation of the Negro spirituals?

3. The author refers to an essay by W. E. B. DuBois, "The Sorrow Songs," which he sees as particularly relevant to a proper interpretation of the spirituals. Read the essay in *Souls of Black Folk*. Does it aid you to a fuller understanding of the Negro spiritual? From your reading of both essays, write a brief paper in which you express your opinions of the spirituals as a musical form.

4. What two events, occurring almost simultaneously, were largely responsible for elevating the spirituals to the highest peak of recognition as American folk music and as American classical music? Explain.

5. How does the author distinguish between the "true" and the "artificial" spiritual?

6. During the period in which this essay was written, the author felt that the spirituals were in a period of transition from folk to art forms. What distinguishes the folk spiritual from the art spiritual? Do you think that the transformation is now complete? Do you think that it will ever be? Why? Why not?

7. In the author's opinion, what is the proper idiom for the Negro spirituals? What reason does he give to support his idea? Can you agree or disagree with the author on this point? Discuss.

LeRoi
Jones*

Classic Blues

(1) What has been called "classic blues" was the result of more diverse sociological and musical influences than any other kind of American Negro music called blues. Musically, classic blues showed the Negro singer's appropriation of a great many elements of popular American music, notably the music associated with popular theater or vaudeville. The instrumental music that accompanied classic blues also reflected this development, as it did the Negro musician's maturing awareness of a more instrumental style, possibly as a foil to be used with his naturally vocal style. Classic blues appeared in America at about the same time as ragtime, the most instrumental or non-vocal music to issue from Negro inspiration. Ragtime is also a music that

*For a biographical sketch of LeRoi Jones, see pp. 83–84.
Reprinted from LeRoi Jones, Blues People (pp. 8–86), by permission of William Morrow and Company, Inc. Copyright © 1963 by LeRoi Jones.

is closely associated with the popular theater of the late nineteenth and early twentieth centuries. Although ragtime must be considered as a separate kind of music, borrowing more European elements than any other music commonly associated with Negroes, it contributed greatly to the development of Negro music from an almost purely vocal tradition to one that could begin to include the melodic and harmonic complexities of instrumental music.

(2) Socially, classic blues and the instrumental styles that went with it represented the Negro's entrance into the world of professional entertainment and the assumption of the psychological imperatives that must accompany such a phenomenon. Blues was a music that arose from the needs of a group, although it was assumed that each man had his *own* blues and that he would sing them. As such, the music was private and personal, although the wandering country blues singers of earlier times had from time to time casual audiences who would sometimes respond with gifts of food, clothes, or even money. But again it was assumed that *anybody* could sing the blues. If someone has lived in this world into manhood, it was taken for granted that he had been given the content of his verses, and as I pointed out earlier, musical training was not a part of African tradition—music like any art was the result of natural inclination. Given the deeply personal quality of blues-singing, there could be no particular method for learning blues. As a verse form, it was the lyrics which were most important, and they issued from life. But classic blues took on a certain degree of professionalism. It was no longer strictly the group singing to ease their labors or the casual expression of personal deliberations on the world. It became a music that could be used to entertain others *formally*. The artisan, the professional blues singer, appeared; blues-singing no longer had to be merely a passionately felt avocation, it could now become a way of making a living. An external and sophisticated idea of performance had come to the blues, moving it past the casualness of the "folk" to the conditioned emotional gesture of the "public."

(3) This professionalism came from the Negro theater: the black minstrel shows, traveling road shows, medicine shows, vaudeville shows, carnivals, and tiny circuses all included blues singers and small or large bands. The Negro theater, in form, was modeled on the earlier white minstrel shows and traveling shows which played around America, especially in rural areas where there was no other formal entertainment. The Negro theater did not, of course, come into being until after the Civil War, but the minstrel show is traceable back to the beginning of the nineteenth century. White performers using blackface to do "imitations of Negro life" appeared in America around 1800, usually in solo performances. By the 1840's, however, blackface was the rage of the country, and there were minstrel shows from America traveling all over the world. It was at least

thirty more years before there were groups of traveling entertainers who did not have to use burnt cork or greasepaint.

(4) It is essential to realize that minstrelsy was an extremely important sociological phenomenon in America. The idea of white men imitating, or caricaturing, what they consider certain generic characteristics of the black man's life in America to entertain other white men is important if only because of the Negro's reaction to it. (And it is the Negro's *reaction to* America, first white and then black and white America, that I consider to have made him a unique member of this society.)

(5) The reasons for the existence of minstrelsy are important also because in considering them we find out even more about the way in which the white man's concept of the Negro changed and why it changed. This gradual change, no matter how it was manifested, makes a graph of the movement of the Negro through American society, and provides an historical context for the rest of my speculations.

(6) I suppose the "childlike" qualities of the African must have always been amusing to the American. I mentioned before how the black man's penchant for the supernatural was held up for ridicule by his white captors, as were other characteristics of African culture. Also, I am certain that most white Americans never thought of the plight of the black man as tragic. Even the Christian Church justified slavery until well into the nineteenth century. The "darky" at his most human excursion into the mainstream of American society was a comic figure. The idea that somehow the slavery of the black man in America was a tragic situation did not occur to white Americans until the growth of the Abolition movement. But it is interesting that minstrelsy grew as the Abolition movement grew. I would say that as the "wild savage" took on more and more of what New England Humanists and church workers considered a human aspect, there was also more in his way of life that Americans found amusing. (As who has not laughed at the cork-faced "Negro" lawmakers in D. W. Griffiths' *Birth of a Nation*? It is a ridiculous situation, ignorant savages pretending they know as much as Southern senators.) As the image of the Negro in America was given more basic human qualities, e.g., the ability to feel pain, perhaps the only consistent way of justifying what had been done to him—now that he had reached what can be called a post-bestial stage—was to demonstrate the ridiculousness of his inability to act as a "normal" human being. American Negroes were much funnier than Africans. (And I hope that Negro "low" comedy persists even long after all the gangsters on television are named Smith and Brown.)

(7) The white minstrel shows were, at their best, merely parodies of Negro life, though I do not think that the idea of "the parody" was always present. It was sufficiently amusing for a white man with a painted face to attempt to reproduce some easily identifiable characteristic of "the darky." There was room for artistic imprecision in a minstrel show because it

wasn't so much the performance that was side-splitting as the very idea of the show itself: "Watch these Niggers. . . ."

(8) The black minstrel shows were also what might be called parodies, or exaggerations, of certain aspects of Negro life in America. But in one sense the colored minstrel was poking fun at himself, and in another and probably more profound sense he was poking fun at the white man. The minstrel shows introduced new dance steps to what could then be considered a mass audience. The cakewalk was one of the most famous dance steps to come out of minstrelsy; it has been described as "a takeoff on the high manners of the white folks in the 'big house'." (If the cakewalk is a Negro dance caricaturing certain white customs, what is that dance when, say, a white theater company attempts to satirize it as a Negro dance? I find the idea of white minstrels in blackface satirizing a dance satirizing themselves a remarkable kind of irony–which, I suppose, is the whole point of minstrel shows.

(9) Early Negro minstrel companies like the Georgia Minstrels, Pringle Minstrels, McCabe and Young Minstrels, provided the first real employment for Negro entertainers. Blues singers, musicians, dancers, comedians, all found fairly steady work with these large touring shows. For the first time Negro music was heard on a wider scale throughout the country, and began to exert a tremendous influence on the mainstream of the American entertainment world; a great many of the shows even made extensive tours of England and the Continent, introducing the older forms of blues as well as classic blues and early jazz to the entire world.

(10) Classic blues is called "classic" because it was the music that seemed to contain all the diverse and conflicting elements of Negro Music, plus the smoother emotional appeal of the "performance." It was the first Negro music that appeared in a formal context as entertainment, though it still contained the harsh, uncompromising reality of the earlier blues forms. It was, in effect, the perfect balance between the two worlds and as such, it represented a clearly definable step by the Negro back into the mainstream of American Society. Primitive blues had been almost a conscious expression of the Negro's *individuality* and equally important, his separateness. The first years of the Civil War saw the Negro as far away from the whole of American society as it was ever possible for him to be. Such a separation was never possible again. To the idea of metasociety is opposed the concept of integration, two concepts that must always be present in any discussion of Negro life in America.

Questions for Discussion and Writing

1. Distinguish between the early blues and classic blues. At what two points in the essay does the author make clear the distinction between these forms?

2. According to the author, why was there no particular method for *learning* the blues?

3. What development during the nineteenth century contributed to the emergence of blues as a "classic" form? Explain.

4. The author suggests that the minstrel shows may serve as an indicator of the changing concept of the Negro in the minds of white Americans. Does he clearly support this idea in the essay? How?

5. What is the "remarkable kind of irony" to which the author refers in paragraph 8 of the essay? Out of what does it arise?

6. In what way did the emergence of the blues as a classic form effect the status of the Negro in American society?

Alain
Locke*

Jazz and
the Jazz Age:
1918-1926

(1) Although 1918
is the official birthday of jazz, jazz had an embryonic start much before
that. In fact, jazz was carried in the bosom of ragtime and as, has been
said, is only ragtime more fully evolved. The Negro folk idiom in melody
and syncopated rhythm gives us "ragtime"; carried over to harmony and
orchestration, it gives us "jazz." It is one and the same musical spirit and
tradition in two different musical dimensions. In fact, if Isaac Goldberg's
analysis of ragtime and its connection with the spirituals is correct, we may
actually have on our hands, in seemingly quite different things, one essential Negro style of music with three different dimensions—the spirituals,
ragtime, jazz. Strange, it may seem! But before coming to that, any close
observance of the intermediate period between ragtime and jazz will
convince us that at least ragtime is the mother of jazz, not just merely its

*For a biographical sketch of the author, see pp. 129–30.

predecessor. When we realize this, we can then quite clearly see that the Carnegie concert of 1912 was truly the birthday party of jazz, while the Whiteman concert of 1924 from which we have seemed to take credit, actually deserves credit in another connection, for it was the "coming of age" party for jazz.

(2) Goldberg suggests, following no less an authority than W. C. Handy, that the spirituals, ragtime and jazz form one continuous sequence of Negro music, being just different facets of the same jewel. Says he:

> Handy, the recognized pioneer of the "blues" insists that ragtime, essentially is nothing more than a pepped-up secular version of the Negro spirituals. He recalls how in the old minstrel days they rendered such haunting exhortations as "Git on Board, Little Chillun." To sing it in the traditional fashion of the earnest if ecstatic spiritual was too tame. So, sung faster to the accompaniment of eccentric hand-clapping gestures, it becomes the "spiritual" disintegrating, breaking up into its ragtime successor. . .

(In fact, in the camp-meeting style of jubilation, the dividing line between the spiritual, and ragtime almost completely breaks down.) "Today," he continues, "hearing Handy jazz up the invitation to a ride on the heavenly railroad, one would exclaim, "Why, he's simply jazzing it." In Handy's minstrel days, they called it "jubing," from the word "jubilee." Ragtime, then, is already found lurking beneath the ecstasy and the rhythms of the more jubilant songs to the Lord, just as in the slower-paced spirituals, one hears the mood, though not the peculiar pattern of the "blues." And when we recall how jazz budded out of the improvised break interval of the blues, this theory grows even more plausible, for then we have approximately the same contrast between the stately spiritual chorale and the jubilant spiritual camp-meeting shout in the religious music that in the secular music we have between the slow swaying melancholy blues and the skipping rag and fast-rocking jazz. The extreme contrast but common root of the slow and the fast elements of the Hungarian Czardas is another case in point and, clearly, a close analogy. As Goldberg later says:

> Ragtime is then, in part, the pagan release of the Negro from his own addiction to holiness, and his rhythms brought to us something of that profane deliverance. It is in brief a balancing of the psychological accounts. . . . The spirituals translate the Bible; ragtime translates the other six days of the week.

(3) Time and again, in spite of the obvious development of ragtime and jazz from Negro sources and the pioneer artistry and tricks of Negro dancers and musicians, the question comes up in sceptical quarters: How

Negro is it after all? No one will deny that the elements of ragtime and jazz can be found elsewhere in the world, not only in other folk music, but as a device of syncopation, in some of the most classical music—Beethoven, for instance. But in spite of this, jazz and ragtime are distinctively Negro, in fact, the further back one goes the more racial it is found to be. Today's jazz is a cosmopolitan affair, an amalgam of modern tempo and mood. But original jazz is more than syncopation and close eccentric harmony. With it goes, like Gypsy music, a distinctive racial intensity of mood and a peculiar style of technical performance, that can be imitated, it is true, but of which the original pattern was Negro. Moreover it is inborn in the typical or folky type of Negro. It can be detected even in a stevedore's swing, a preacher's sway, or a bootblack's flick, and heard equally in an amen corner-quaver, a blue cadence or a chromatic cascade of Negro laughter. An authority insists rightly that it is what he calls "a rubato of pitch as well as of accent," that is a subtle irregularity of interval of tone quality and pace of rhythm that once was a Negro secret and still is a Negro characteristic. "It began," this critic says, "in the restless feet of the black; it rippled through his limbs and communicated itself to every instrument upon which he could lay his hands. . . . It still remains a racial accent which the white, for all the uncanny skill with which he has translated it from its original black, has not fully mastered. And yet, by paradox, it is the white, the Northern white (and we should add, the Jew) in association with the Negro, who has developed ragtime and jazz to their fullest (not yet their fullest) possibilities." So jazz is basically Negro, then, although fortunately, also human enough to be universal in appeal and expressiveness.

(4) But as jazz has spread out from its Mississippi headwaters and become the international ocean it now is, it has become more diluted, more cosmopolitan and less racial. It was the early jazz that was the most typically racial—and musically the most powerful. To sense the difference instantly, one has only to contrast, for example, one of the early blues, like Bessie Smith's old version of the "Gulf Coast Blues" with any up-to-the-minute cabaret blues or to compare a real folky rendition of the "Memphis Blues" with some modern fancy-dress version. Jazz is more at home in Harlem than in Paris, unless Paris imports Harlem to play, sing and dance it as she used to do; but beyond that, jazz is more at home in its humble folk haunts even than in Harlem. "The earliest jazz-makers were the itinerant piano players who wandered up and down the Mississippi towns from saloon to saloon, from dive to dive. Often wholly illiterate, these humble troubadours knew nothing about written music or composition, but with minds like cameras they would listen to the rude improvisations of the dock laborers and the railroad gangs and reproduce them, reflecting per-

fectly the sentiments and moods of these humble folk. Seated at the piano with a carefree air that a king might envy, their box-back coats flowing over the stool, their Stetsons pulled well over their eyes and cigars at a forty-five degree angle, they would 'whip the ivories' to marvelous chords and hidden racy meanings, evoking the intense delight of their hearers who would smother them at the close with huzzas and whiskey."

(5) The same commentator, J. A. Rogers, writes about the exact origin of jazz: "More cities claim its birthplace than claimed Homer dead. New Orleans, St. Louis, Memphis, Chicago, all assert the honor is theirs. But jazz, as it is today, seems to have come into being this way. W. C. Handy, after having digested the airs of the itinerant musicians referred to, experimented with the blues form from 1909 until 1912, and by 1912 had evolved the first jazz classic, 'The Memphis Blues.' Then came, as a fairly authentic legend has it, Jasbo Brown, a reckless musician of a Negro cabaret in Chicago, who played this and other blues, blowing his own extravagant moods and risque interpretations into them, while hilarious with gin. To give further emphasis to his veiled allusions he would make his trombone 'talk,' by putting a derby hat and later a tin can at its mouth. The delighted patrons would shout, 'More, Jasbo! More Jas, more!' And so the name originated."

(6) Another cradle element of jazz was in Handy's "Blues." It was the *habanera* or tango rhythm, an eight and two-quarter note's sequence, first used by him in the original "Memphis Blues." The justification for the use of the tango rhythm as characteristically Negro, and its popularity among Negroes becomes very plausible when it is realized that this is originally an African rhythm—(the native word for it is "Tangana"—Niles, p. 16), and that it probably became Spanish through the Moors. This is corroborated by the fact that this same tango rhythm is basic in the purest and oldest strains of the Afro-Cuban music, in the folk music of Mexico and Brazil where the Negro influence has been dominant, and in Negro dances of even the Bahamas and the Barbadoes. Further, an authority, Friedenthal, traces the Charleston to a compounding of this rhythm to the regular two-four beat. Says he: "Clap your hands on the dotted quarter and the eighth note which follows it, pat your feet regularly, four times to the bar, and you have the Charleston rhythm."

(7) But in addition to jazz rhythm and harmony, jazz improvisation came rocketing out of the blues. It grew out of the improvised musical "filling-in" of the gap between the short measure of the blues and the longer eight bar line, the break interval in the original folk-form of the three-line blues. Such filling in and compounding of the basic rhythm are characteristic of Negro music everywhere, from deepest Africa to the streets of Charleston, from the unaccompanied hand-clapping of the street corner "hoe-down" to the interpolations of shouts, amens and exclama-

tions in Negro church revivals. Handy's own theory of jazz is that it is, in essence, "spontaneous deviation from the musical score," in other words an impromptu musical embroidery woven around and into the musical tune and the regular harmony. In short, daring and inspired musical play. When this style was incorporated into orchestral music, instrumental jazz was born out of the folk jazz which was its origin. Thus jazz is but a towering and elaborate superstructure built upon the basic foundation of the blues.

(8) This fact disposes of the controversy as to whether jazz is a new type of music or simply another method of playing music, because it shows the difference between mere surface jazz and the real solid variety. The one is a mere set of musical tricks by which any tune whatsoever can be "ragged" or "jazzed"; the other is an organic trinity of jazz rhythm, harmony and creative improvisation. Surface jazz is the cheap alloy of Tin Pan Alley; many are the classical compositions that have suffered this trick adulteration. Beethoven, Verdi, Mozart, Tchaikovsky have all paid their unprofitable toll as the "high-brow" music of the elect has been stepped down for popular consumption as "the music of the millions." Nevertheless it is only half true to say as Gilbert Seldes does: "There is no such thing as jazz music; jazz is a method of playing music." Eccentric tone distortion and rhythm antics are only one side of jazz, and the more superficial side at that. What is deeper is the mood out of which it is generated and the instinctive gift of doing it spontaneously. No really Negro musical group worries about what the other musicians are going to do; they are just as apt to vary and embroider at will and whimsy, with nobody put out on musical base, so to speak, as to follow score. No one approaching it from the side of experience rather than academic debate could be in doubt about the racial color and feeling of jazz; it is just as unique and characteristic as Gypsy is Gypsy. As a matter of fact, in the world of musical idiom, it has no other serious rival.

(9) Niles puts it neatly. He says: "Up to this time, every other type of orchestra had played as best it could what was set before it in black and white. Successive and competitive improvisation was unknown and a heresy. After this, it was different." Louis Armstrong, in his clever recent book, Swing That Music (p. 121), says "to become a front rank 'swing player,' a musician must learn to read expertly and be just as able to play to score as any 'regular' musician. Then he must never forget for one minute of his life that the true spirit of swing music lies in free playing and that he must always keep his own musical feeling free. He must try to originate and not just imitate. And if he is a well-trained musician in the first place, he will be able to express his own musical ideas as they come to him with more versatility, more richness and more body. . . . To be a real swing artist, he must be a composer as well as a player." Most of the

members of today's Negro jazz orchestras are highly trained musicians, but more of their pieces are worked out by ear in improvised experiment than are played from set arrangements. The arranger, more often, just copies down the good "break" or the happy inspiration so that it won't get forgotten.

(10) For the process of composing by group improvisation, the jazz musician must have a whole chain of musical expertness, a sure musical ear, an instinctive feeling for harmony, the courage and gift to improvise and interpolate, and a canny sense for the total effect. This free style that Negro musicians introduced into playing really has generations of experience back of it; it is derived from the voice tricks and vocal habits characteristic of Negro choral singing. Out of the voice slur and quaver between the flat and the natural came the whole jazz cadenza and all the myriad jazz tone tricks, and out of the use of a single sustained voice tone as a suspension note for chorus changes of harmony came the now elaborate system of jazz harmonic style. It is most interesting to note that the African has this same fluid shifting musical scale, even more subtle than the scale shifts of American Negro folk music. In fact, it seems that the American Negro musical traits are the original African ones toned down and held in leash somewhat by the more regular patterns of European music. These basic racial idioms are more apparent in the simpler earlier forms of jazz, and still more in the vocal rather than the instrumental pieces. Some day, when Negro folk music is being scientifically studied, the old cheap discarded Okeh and Columbian records of "The Memphis Students," "The McKinney Cotton Pickers," "The Chicago Rhythm Kings," "The Dixieland Orchestra" and of the early "Blues-singers"—Bessie, Clara and Mamie Smith and Ma Rainey—will be priceless material in showing how jazz was created.

(11) For better or worse, jazz is, however, the spiritual child of this age. Phases of it will disappear with the particular phase of civilization which gave birth to it; but some permanent contributions to music and art will have been made. More than that, jazz will always be an important factor in interpreting the subtle spirit of our time, more so after it has passed into history. One naturally wonders why it is that jazz has become so characteristic an expression of the modern spirit.

(12) There are many interpretations; each perhaps with its share of the truth. George Antheil, himself an important modernistic composer, stresses jazz as a gift of "primitive joy and vigor." "Negro music," he says, "appeared suddenly (in Europe) after the greatest war of all time . . . it came upon a bankrupt spirituality. To have continued with Slavic mysticism (Russian music was the great vogue when the World War broke out), would in 1918 have induced us all to commit suicide. We needed the roar of the lion to remind us that life had been going on for a long while and would probably go on a while longer. Weak, miserable and anaemic, we

needed the stalwart shoulders of a younger race to hold the cart awhile till we had gotten the wheel back on. . . . The Negro taught us to put our noses to the ground, to follow the scent, to come back to the elementary principles of self-preservation."

(13) Then, there is the theory of emotional escape, seemingly contradicting this first theory of emotional rejuvenation. Jazz, according to these theorists, was a marvelous antidote to Twentieth-Century boredom and nervous exhaustion, a subtle combination of narcotic and stimulant; opium for the mind, a tonic for the feelings and instincts echoing the quick nervous tempo and pace of the hectic civilization of ours, which had originally caused that neurasthenia and disillusionment. It would be a curious fact if jazz really was such a cultural anti-toxin, working against the most morbid symptoms of the very disease of which it itself was a by-product. Many competent observers think it is.

(14) In some important way, jazz has become diluted and tinctured with modernism. Otherwise, as purely a Negro dialect of emotion, it could not have become the dominant recreational vogue of our time, even to date, the most prolonged fad on record. More importantly, jazz in its more serious form, has also become the characteristic musical speech of the modern age. Beginning as the primitive rhythms of the Congo, taking on the American Negro's emotional revolt against the hardships and shackles of his life, jazz became more than the Negro's desperate antidote and cure for sorrow. It incorporated the typical American restlessness and unconventionality, embodied its revolt against the drabness of commonplace life, put pagan force behind the revolt against Puritan restraint, and finally became the Western World's life-saving flight from boredom and over-sophistication to the refuge of elemental emotion and primitive vigor. This is the credit side of the jazz ledger, against which the debit side we have already mentioned must be balanced, according to one's judgment and temperament and taste. Both detractors and enthusiasts must admit the power and widespread influence of jazz. It is now part Negro, part American, part modern; a whole period of modern civilization may ultimately be best known and understood as "The Jazz Age."

Questions for Discussion and Writing

1. Explain the relationship between the spirituals, ragtime, and jazz.

2. In what ways is jazz reflective of the Negro temperament, according to Locke? How does he support the idea that jazz is strictly a contribution of the Negro?

3. According to J. A. Rogers, what is the legend that underlies the origin of the term, "jazz"?

4. Why is W. C. Handy referred to as "the father of the blues"? How did jazz evolve from the blues? How did Handy create the first jazz classic?

5. Who were some of the most important men among the early jazz musicians and composers? Are you acquainted with any contemporary jazz musicians? Discuss.

6. Throughout the essay, the author refers to the freedom of style that constitutes jazz compositions. Does he indicate the nature of this freedom of style? Explain.

7. Do you agree that jazz reflects the American tempo and the modern mood in general as well as the emotions of the Negro in particular? Write a defense for or a negation of this idea.

8. Try to find recordings by the early jazz musicians and recordings by contemporary jazz musicians. Write a brief discussion of the styles and effects of each group. Which do you prefer, if either? Why?

Ralph
Ellison*

Living

with Music

(1) In those days it was either live with music or die with noise, and we chose rather desperately to live. In the process our apartment—what with its booby-trappings of audio equipment, wires, discs and tapes—came to resemble the Collier mansion, but that was later. First there was the neighborhood, assorted drunks and a singer.

(2) We were living at the time in a tiny ground-floor-rear apartment in which I was also trying to write. I say "trying" advisedly. To our right, separated by a thin wall, was a small restaurant with a juke box the size of the Roxy. To our left, a night-employed swing enthusiast who took his

*For a biographical note about the author, see pp. 101–2.

lullaby music so loud that every morning promptly at nine Basie's brasses started blasting my typewriter off its stand. Our living room looked out across a small back yard to a rough stone wall to an apartment building which, towering above, caught every passing thoroughfare sound and rifled it straight down to me. There were also howling cats and barking dogs, none capable of music worth living with, so we'll pass them by.

(3) But the court behind the wall, which on the far side came knee-high to a short Iroquois, was a forum for various singing and/or preaching drunks who wandered back from the corner bar. From these you sometimes heard a fair barbershop style "Bill Bailey," free-wheeling versions of "The Bastard King of England," the sage of Uncle Bud, or a deeply felt rendition of Leroy Carr's "How Long Blues." The preaching drunks took on any topic that came to mind: current events, the fate of the long-sunk *Titanic* or the relative merits of the Giants and the Dodgers. Naturally there was great argument and occasional fighting—none of it fatal but all of it loud.

(4) I shouldn't complain, however, for these were rather entertaining drunks, who like the birds appeared in the spring and left with the first fall cold. A more dedicated fellow was there all the time, day and night, come rain, come shine. Up on the corner lived a drunk of legend, a true phenomenon, who could surely have qualified as the king of all the world's winos—not excluding the French. He was neither poetic like the others nor ambitious like the singer (to whom we'll presently come) but his drinking bouts were truly awe-inspiring and he was not without his sensitivity. In the throes of his passion he would shout to the whole wide world one concise command, "Shut up!" which was disconcerting enough to all who heard (except, perhaps, the singer), but such were the labyrinthine acoustics of courtyards and areaways that he seemed to direct his command at me. The writer's block which this produced is indescribable. On one heroic occasion he yelled his obsessive command without one interruption longer than necessary to take another drink (and with no appreciable loss of volume, penetration or authority) for three long summer days and nights, and shortly afterwards he died. Just how many lines of agitated prose he cost me I'll never know, but in all that chaos of sound I sympathized with his obsession, for I too, hungered and thirsted for quiet. Nor did he inspire me to a painful identification, and for that I was thankful. Identification after all, involves feelings of guilt and responsibility, and since I could hardly hear my own typewriter keys I felt in no way accountable for his condition. We were simply fellow victims of the madding crowd. May he rest in peace.

(5) No, these more involved feelings were aroused by a more intimate source of noise, one that got beneath the skin and worked into the very structure of one's consciousness—like the "fate" motif in Beethoven's

Fifth or the knocking-at-the-gates scene in *Macbeth*. For at the top of our pyramid of noise there was a singer who lived directly above us; you might say we had a singer on our ceiling.

(6) Now, I had learned from the jazz musicians I had known as a boy in Oklahoma City something of the discipline and devotion to his art required of the artist. Hence I knew something of what the singer faced. These jazzmen, many of them now world-famous, lived for and with music intensely. Their driving motivation was neither money nor fame, but the will to achieve the most eloquent expression of idea-emotions through the technical mastery of their instruments (which, incidentally, some of them wore as a priest wears the cross) and the give and take, the subtle rhythmical shaping and blending of idea, tone and imagination demanded of group improvisation. The delicate balance struck between strong individual personality and the group during those early jam sessions was a marvel of social organization. I had learned too that the end of all this discipline and technical mastery was the desire to express an affirmative way of life through its musical tradition and that this tradition insisted that each artist achieve his creativity within its frame. He must learn the best of the past, and add to it his personal vision. Life could be harsh, loud and wrong if it wished, but they lived it fully, and when they expressed their attitude toward the world it was with a fluid style that reduced the chaos of living to form.

(7) The objectives of these jazzmen were not at all those of the singer on our ceiling, but though a purist committed to the mastery of the *bel canto*, style, German lieder, modern French art songs and a few American slave songs sung as if *bel canto*, she was intensely devoted to her art. From morning to night she vocalized, regardless of the condition of her voice, the weather or my screaming nerves. There were times when her notes sifting through her floor and my ceiling, bouncing down the walls and ricocheting off the building in the rear, whistled like tenpenny nails, buzzed like a saw, wheezed like the asthma of a Hercules, trumpeted like an enraged African elephant—and the squeaky pedal of her piano rested plumb center above my typing chair. After a year of noncooperation from the neighbor on my left I became desperate enough to cool down the hot blast of his phonograph by calling the cops, but the singer presented a serious ethical problem: Could I, an aspiring artist, complain against the hard work and devotion to craft of another aspiring artist?

(8) Then there was my sense of guilt. Each time I prepared to shatter the ceiling in protest, I was restrained by the knowledge that I, too, during my boyhood, had tried to master a musical instrument and to the great distress of my neighbors—perhaps even greater than that which I now suffered. For while our singer was concerned basically with a single tradition and style, I had been caught actively between two: that of the Negro

folk music, both sacred and profane, slave song and jazz, and that of western classical music. It was most confusing; the folk tradition demanded that I play what I heard and felt around me, while those who were seeking to teach the classical tradition in the schools demanded that I play strictly according to the book and express that which I was *supposed* to feel. This sometimes led to heated clashes of wills. Once during a third grade music appreciation class a friend of mine insisted that it was a large green snake he saw swimming down a quiet brook instead of the snowy bird the teacher felt that Saint-Saëns' *Carnival of the Animals* should evoke. The rest of us sat there and lied like little black, brown, and yellow trojans about that swan, but our stalwart classmate held firm to his snake. In the end he got himself spanked and reduced the teacher to tears, but truth, reality and our environment were redeemed. For we were all familiar with snakes, while a swan was simply something the Ugly Duckling of the story grew up to be. Fortunately some of us grew up with a genuine appreciation of classical music *despite* such teaching methods. But as an aspiring trumpeter I was to wallow in sin for years before being awakened to guilt by our singer.

(9) Caught mid-range between my two traditions, where one attitude often clashed with the other and one technique of playing was by the other opposed. I caused whole blocks of people to suffer.

(10) Indeed, I terrorized a good part of an entire city section. During summer vacation I blew sustained tones out of the window for hours, usually starting—especially on Sunday morning—before breakfast. I sputtered whole days through M. Arban's (he's the great authority on the instrument) double- and triple-tonguing exercises—with an effect like that of a jackass hiccupping off a big meal of briars. During school term mornings I practiced a truly exhibitionist "Reveille" before leaving for school, and in the evening I generously gave the ever-listening world a long, slow version of "Taps," ineptly played but throbbing with what I in my adolescent vagueness felt was a romantic sadness. For it was farewell to day and a love song to life and a peace-be-with-you to all the dead and dying.

(11) On hot summer afternoons I tormented the ears of all not blessedly deaf with imitations of the latest hot solos of Hot Lips Paige (then a local hero), the leaping right hand of Earl "Fatha" Hines, or the rowdy poetic flights of Louis Armstrong. Naturally I rehearsed also such school-band standbys as the *Light Cavalry* Overture, Sousa's "Stars and Stripes Forever," the *William Tell* Overture, and "Tiger Rag." (Not even an after-school job as office boy to a dentist could stop my efforts. Frequently, by way of encouraging my development in the proper cultural direction, the dentist asked me proudly to render Schubert's *Serenade* for some poor devil with his jaw propped open in the dental chair. When the drill got going, or the forceps bit deep, I blew real strong.)

(12) Sometimes, inspired by the even then considerable virtuosity of the late Charlie Christian (who during our school days played marvelous

riffs on a cigar box banjo), I'd give whole summer afternoons and the evening hours after heavy suppers of black-eyed peas and turnip greens, cracklin' bread and buttermilk, lemonade and sweet potato cobbler, to practicing hard-driving blues. Such food oversupplied me with bursting energy, and from listening to Ma Rainey, Ida Cox and Clara Smith, who made regular appearances in our town, I knew exactly how I wanted my horn to sound. But in the effort to make it so (I was no embryo Joe Smith or Tricky Sam Nanton) I sustained the curses of both Christian and infidel —along with the encouragement of those more sympathetic citizens who understood the profound satisfaction to be found in expressing oneself in the blues.

(13) Despite those who complained and cried to heaven for Gabriel to blow a chorus so heavenly sweet and so hellishly hot that I'd forever put down my horn, there were more tolerant ones who were willing to pay in present pain for future pride.

(14) For who knew what skinny kid with his chops wrapped around a trumpet mouthpiece and a faraway look in his eyes might become the next Armstrong? Yes, and send you, at some big dance a few years hence, into an ecstasy of rhythm and memory and brassy affirmation of the goodness of being alive and part of the community? Someone had to: for it was part of the group tradition—though that was not how they said it.

(15) "Let that boy blow," they'd say to the protesting ones. "He's got to talk baby talk on that thing before he can preach on it. Next thing you know he's liable to be up there with Duke Ellington. Sure, plenty Oklahoma boys are up there with big bands. Son, let's hear you try those 'Trouble in Mind Blues.' Now try and make it sound like ole Ida Cox sings it."

(16) And I'd draw in my breath and do Miss Cox great violence.

(17) Thus the crimes and aspirations of my youth. It had been years since I had played the trumpet or irritated a single ear with other than the spoken or written word, but as far as my singing neighbor was concerned I had to hold my peace. I was forced to listen, and in listening I soon became involved to the point of identification. If she sang badly I'd hear my own futility in the windy sound; if well, I'd stare at my typewriter in despair that I should ever make my prose so sing. She left me neither night nor day, this singer on our ceiling, and as my writing languished I became more and more upset. Thus one desperate morning I decided that since I seemed doomed to live within a shrieking chaos I might as well contribute my share; perhaps if I fought noise with noise I'd attain some small peace. Then a miracle: I turned on my radio (an old Philco AM set connected to a small Pilot AM tuner) and I heard the words

Art thou troubled?
Music will calm thee . . .

I stopped as though struck by the voice of an angel. It was Kathleen Ferrier, that loveliest of singers, giving voice to the aria from Handel's *Rodelinda*. The voice was so completely expressive of words and music that I accepted it without question—what lover of the vocal art could resist her?

(18) Yet it was ironic, for after giving up my trumpet for the type-writer I had avoided too close a contact with the very art which she recommended as balm. For I had started music early and lived with it daily, and when I broke I tried to break clean. Now in this magical moment all the old love, the old fascination with music superbly rendered, flooded back. When she finished I realized that with such music in my own apartment, the chaotic sounds from without and above had sunk, if not into silence, then well below the level where they mattered. Here was a way out. If I was to live and write in that apartment, it would be only through the grace of music. I had tuned in a Ferrier recital, and when it ended I rushed out for several of her records, certain that now deliverance was mine.

(19) But not yet. Between the hi-fi record and the ear, I learned, there was a new electronic world. In that realization our apartment was well on its way toward becoming an audio booby trap. It was 1949 and I rushed to the Audio Fair. I have, I confess, as much gadget-resistance as the next American of my age, weight and slight income; but little did I dream of the test to which it would be put. I had hardly entered the fair before I heard David Sarser's and Mel Sprinkle's Musician's Amplifier, took a look at its schematic and, recalling a boyhood acquaintance with such matters, decided that I could build one. I did, several times before it measured within specifications. And still our system was lacking. Fortunately my wife shared my passion for music, so we went on to buy, piece by piece, a fine speaker system, a first-rate AM-FM tuner, a transcription turntable and a speaker cabinet. I built half a dozen or more preamplifiers and record compensators before finding a commercial one that satisfied my ear, and, finally we acquired an arm, a magnetic cartridge and—glory of the house— a tape recorder. All this plunge into electronics, mind you, had as its simple end the enjoyment of recorded music as it was intended to be heard. I was obsessed with the idea of reproducing sound with such fidelity that even when using music as a defense behind which I could write, it would reach the unconscious levels of the mind with the least distortion. And it didn't come easily. There were wires and pieces of equipment all over the tiny apartment (I became a compulsive experimenter) and it was worth your life to move about without first taking careful bearings. Once we were almost crushed in our sleep by the tape machine, for which there was space only on a shelf at the head of our bed. But it was worth it.

(20) For now when we played a recording on our system even the drunks on the wall could recognize its quality. I'm ashamed to admit, how-

ever, that I did not always restrict its use to the demands of pleasure or defense. Indeed, with such marvels of science at my control I lost my humility. My ethical consideration for the singer up above shriveled like a plant in too much sunlight. For instead of soothing, music seemed to release the beast in me. Now when jarred from my writer's reveries by some especially enthusiastic flourish of our singer, I'd rush to my music system with blood in my eyes and burst a few decibels in her direction. If she defied me with a few more pounds of pressure against her diaphragm, then a war of decibels was declared.

(21) If, let us say, she were singing "Depuis le Jour" from *Louise*, I'd put on a tape of Bidu Sayao performing the same aria, and let the rafters ring. If it was some song by Mahler, I'd match her spitefully with Marian Anderson or Kathleen Ferrier; if she offended with something from *Der Rosenkavalier*, I'd attack her flank with Lotte Lehmann. If she brought me up from my desk with art songs by Ravel or Rachmaninoff, I'd defend myself with Maggie Teyte or Jennie Tourel. If she polished a spiritual to a meaningless artiness I'd play Bessie Smith to remind her of the earth out of which we came. Once in a while I'd forget completely that I was supposed to be a gentleman and blast her with Strauss' *Zarathustra*, Bartok's *Concerto for Orchestra*, Ellington's "Flaming Sword," the famous cresendo from *The Pines of Rome*, or Satchmo scatting, "I'll be Glad When You're Dead" (you rascal you!). Oh, I was living with music with a sweet vengeance.

(22) One might think that all this would have made me her most hated enemy, but not at all. When I met her on the stoop a few weeks after my rebellion, expecting her fully to slap my face, she astonished me by complimenting our music system. She even questioned me concerning the artists I had used against her. After that, on days when the acoustics were right, she'd stop singing until the piece was finished and then applaud—not always, I guessed, without a justifiable touch of sarcasm. And although I was now getting on with my writing, the unfairness of this business bore in upon me. Aware that I could not have withstood a similar comparison with literary artists of like caliber, I grew remorseful. I also came to admire the singer's courage and control, for she was neither intimidated into silence nor goaded into undisciplined screaming; she persevered, she marked the phrasing of the great singers I sent her way, she improved her style.

(23) Better still, she vocalized more softly, and I, in turn, used music less and less as a weapon and more for its magic with mood and memory. After a while a simple twirl of the volume control up a few decibels and down again would bring a live-and-let-live reduction of her volume. We have long since moved from that apartment and that most interesting neighborhood and now the floors and walls of our present apartment are

adequately thick and there is even a closet large enough to house the audio system; the only wire visible is that leading from the closet to the corner speaker system. Still we are indebted to the singer and the old environment for forcing us to discover one of the most deeply satisfying aspects of our living. Perhaps the enjoyment of music is always suffused with past experience, for me, at least, this is true.

(24) It seems a long way and a long time from the glorious days of Oklahoma jazz dances, the jam sessions at Halley Richardson's place on Deep Second, from the phonographs shouting the blues in the back alleys I knew as a delivery boy, and from the days when watermelon men with voices like mellow bugles shouted their wares in time with the rhythm of their horses' hoofs and farther still from the washerwomen singing slave songs as they stirred sooty tubs in sunny yards; and a long time, too, from those intense, conflicting days when the school music program of Oklahoma City was tuning our earthy young ears to classical accents—with music appreciation classes and free musical instruments and basic instructions for any child who cared to learn and uniforms for all who made the band. There was a mistaken notion on the part of some of the teachers that classical music had nothing to do with the rhythms, relaxed or hectic, of daily living, and that one should crook the little finger when listening to such refined strains. And the blues and the spirituals—jazz—? They would have destroyed them and scattered the pieces. Nevertheless, we learned some of it all, for in the United States when traditions are juxtaposed they tend, regardless of what we do to prevent it, irresistibly to merge. Thus musically at least each child in our town was an heir of all the ages. One learns by moving from the familiar to the unfamiliar, and while it might sound incongruous at first, the step from the spirituality of the spirituals to that of the Beethoven of the symphonies or the Bach of the chorales is not as vast as it seems. Nor is the romanticism of a Brahms or Chopin completely unrelated to that of Louis Armstrong. Those who know their native culture and love it unchauvinistically are never lost when encountering the unfamiliar.

(25) Living with music today we find Mozart and Ellington, Kirsten Flagstad and Chippie Hill, William L. Dawson and Carl Orff all forming part of our regular fare. For all exalt life in rhythm and melody; all add to its significance. Perhaps in the swift change of American society in which the meanings of one's origin are so quickly lost, one of the chief values of living with music lies in its power to give us an orientation in time. In doing so, it gives significance to all those indefinable aspects of experience which nevertheless help to make us what we are. In the swift whirl of time music is a constant, reminding us of what we were and of that toward which we aspire. Art thou troubled? Music will not only calm, it will ennoble thee.

Identification

Briefly identify each of the following persons:

1. Charlie Christian

2. Earl "Fatha" Hines

3. Louis Armstrong

4. Duke Ellington

5. Ma Rainey

6. Bessie Smith

7. Ida Cox

Questions for Discussion and Writing

1. What is the tone of this essay? Can you point to specific passages in the essay that help to establish the tone?

2. In the first paragraph of the essay, Ellison says that in those days "it was either live with music or die with noise." How does he develop this idea? Is the development systematic and clear? Does he employ adequate and appropriate transitional devices as he moves from one idea to the next? Point out these devices.

3. Ellison describes the singer on the ceiling as an "intimate source of noise." Why? What comparison and contrast does he draw between the singer and the jazz musicians that he had known as a boy?

4. In the explanation of his hesitancy to complain about the singer on the ceiling, Ellison provides the reader with a brief but amusing account of his own musical assays. Discuss briefly.

5. In what way does the author finally decide to combat the noise created by the singer? In paragraph 21, he gives a very graphic account of the "battle" between himself and the singer. What is the effect of the pseudo-serious description of the battle? What is the ultimate outcome of the battle?

6. Ellison is quite fond of figurative language—a fact that is everywhere evident in this essay. Point out those figures of speech used in the following paragraphs: 2, 4, 7, 10. Can you find other examples in the work? What purpose, if any, do they serve?

7. Perhaps you have had some experience with music and/or musicians that you found amusing, frustrating, fascinating, etc. Write a brief account of your experience.

Margaret
Just
Butcher

Margaret Just Butch-
er, professor of English, received the B.A. degree from Howard University
and the Ph.D. degree from Boston University. She has taught at Miner's
Teacher's College, at Virginia Union and at Howard University. She has
also been a Fulbright visiting professor at Grenoble, Lyon, and Dijon. For
a time, she served as associate consultant for the National Association for
the Advancement of Colored People.

The following essay is taken from *The Negro in American Culture*, a
work begun by Alain Locke (see Locke biographical sketch). In the introduction, Mrs. Butcher states: "The purpose of the book as Alain conceived
it, and as I have tried to develop it is this: to trace in historical sequence
. . . both the folk and the formal contributions of the American Negro to
American Culture. . . . Its main thesis is that by setting up an inveterate
tradition of racial differences in the absence of any fixed or basic differences of culture and tradition on the Negro's part, American slavery intro-

duced into the very heart of American society a crucial dilemma whose resultant problems, with their progressive resolution, account for many fateful events in American history and for some of the most characteristic qualities of American culture." This essay is concerned with the artistic heritage of the Negro, its loss and rediscovery, and its impact upon Negro art in the twentieth century.

Margaret
Just
Butcher

The Negro

as Artist and

in American Art

(1) When, near the
close of the last century, a few American Negroes began to paint and to
model, it was thought strange and unusually ambitious. By most people,
including the Negroes themselves, it was also thought to be the Negroes'
first attempt at art. Actually, late nineteenth-century cultural provincialism
was such that art was regarded as the ultimate expression of a civilized
people. That Negroes should identify themselves with the creative arts was
regarded as a pretension. The Western world had yet to learn that primitive
civilizations had had not only artists, but also great art. The Western world
had yet to learn, too, that of the many types of primitive art that of the
Negro in Africa was one of the greatest and most sophisticated. Artistic
tradition and skill in all the major craft arts run back for generations, even
centuries, among the principal African tribes, particularly those of the

West Coast and Equatorial Africa, from which Afro-Americans are descended. These arts are wood and metal sculpture, metal-forging, wood-carving, ivory and bone-carving, weaving, pottery-making, and skillful surface decoration in line and color. In fact, everything in the category of the European fine arts except easel painting, marble sculpture, engraving, and etching (and even the techniques of engraving and etching are represented in the surface carving of much African art) was known to Africans. Actually, therefore, the pioneer Negro artists were unknown to their American descendants; starting the Negroes' second career in art, they were unconsciously recapturing a lost artistic heritage. Actually this was a "third career," for in Brazil there had been early Negro artists.

(2) But how was this heritage lost? The answer explains much about Negro slavery. Slavery not only transplanted the Negro physically, but also cut him off decisively from his cultural roots. By taking away his languages, abruptly changing his habits, and putting him in a strangely different civilization, slavery reduced the Negro to what might be termed "cultural zero." No matter how divided one may be as to the relative values of human civilizations, no one can really believe that the African stood, after centuries of living and a long intertribal history, at a point of "cultural zero." One of the high developments in African civilization, as in all primitive cultures, was dexterity of hand and foot and co-ordination of eye and muscle. These abilities were useful in the development of elaborate native crafts, the traditions of which had been built upon generations of trial and error. These skills were lost in the horror of the slave ship, where families, castes, and tribes were ruthlessly disrupted. When slavery later substituted the crudest body labor, providing for it only the crudest tools, it finally stultified any impulse the Negro might have had for exerting technical skill or manual dexterity. Alexander Jacovleff, a Russian artist whose drawings of African types are classic, once commented that Africa is "a continent of beautiful bodies, but above all, of beautiful hands." There is a symbolic connotation in the observation: life in Africa required skill of hands and foot, almost perfect co-ordination of nerve and muscle, so that weapons could be thrown accurately and materials woven or tied accurately. Naturally, a people endowed with these capacities and skills was able to carve, trace, or scrape; the primitive artisan was also a primitive artist.

(3) We will never know, and cannot estimate, how much technical African skill was blotted out in America. The hardships of cotton- and rice-field labor, the crudities of the hoe, the ax, and the plow, certainly reduced the typical Negro hand to a gnarled stump incapable of fine craftsmanship even if artistic incentives, materials, and patterns had been available. But we may believe that there was some memory of beauty; by way of compensation some obviously artistic urges flowed with the peasant Negro toward the only channels of expression left open—song, graceful

movement, and poetic speech. Stripped of all else, the Negro's own body became his prime and only artistic instrument; dance, pantomine, and song were the compensation for his pent-up emotions. It was environment that forced American Negroes away from the craft arts and their old ancestral skills to the emotional arts of song and dance for which they are known and noted in America. When a few Negroes did achieve contact with the skilled crafts, their work showed the latent instinct of the artisan. In the early colonial days, for example, before plantation slavery had become dominant, Negro craftsmen were well known as cabinetmakers, marquetry-setters, woodcarvers, and ironsmiths, as the workmanship of many old mansions in Charleston, New Orleans, Savannah, and other centers of colonial wealth and luxury attest.

(4) Even in surviving, the Negro's artistry was reversed; in Africa the dominant arts were sculpture, metal-working, and weaving. In America the Negro's chief arts have been song, dance, music, and, considerably later, poetry. African art skills were technical, rigid, controlled, and disciplined; characteristic African art expression is, therefore, sober, heavily conventionalized, and restrained. The American African arts are freely emotional, exuberant, and sentimental. The American Negro, for example, is credited with a "barbaric love of color" which, indeed, he frequently possesses. African arts, on the other hand, are in most instances very sober and subtle in the use of color. The notion of tropical extravagance about color is a myth that facts do not sustain: in typical African art formal decoration and design are much more important than color. What we have thought "primitive" in the American Negro (his naïve exuberance, spontaneity, sentimentalism) are not characteristically African, and cannot be explained as ancestral heritage. They seem to be the result of the American Negro's peculiar experience with emotional hardships. True, they are now characteristic traits, but they represent the Negro's acquired rather than his original artistic temperament.

(5) The Negro artist in America had to make a new beginning; he has not yet recaptured his ancestral gifts or recovered his ancient skills. He must achieve this, of course, in the medium and manner of his adopted and acquired civilization and the modern techniques of painting, sculpture, and the craft arts. But when this development finally matures, it may be expected to reflect something of the original endowment, if not as a carry-over of instinct (which many insist is unlikely), at least as a result of the proud inspirations of the reconstructed past.

(6) In the dislocating process of being transplanted from Africa to America, Negro art and the Negro artist were somehow separated; it was generations before they came together again. In the interval, African art was forgotten, "Negro themes and subject matter" were neglected by artists generally, and many Negro artists regarded "Negro Art" as ghetto restric-

tion and fled from it in protest and indignation. Now African art is both recognized and prized. Gradually American artists have come to treat Negro subjects as something more than a passing subject of secondary interest. Negro types presented with dignity and understanding are now a major theme in the program for developing a "native American art." More important, a younger generation of Negro artists has taken as one of its main objectives and opportunities the interpretation of the Negro and the development of what is now called "Negro Art." For though the Negro as a part of the American scene is the common property of American artists, Negro and white, he is certainly the special and particular artistic asset of his own people.

(7) If history texts were either lost or destroyed in their entirety, we could, in large measure, rewrite history from art. A keen and perceptive eye could tell from the way in which the Negro was artistically depicted what the eighteenth, nineteenth, and twentieth centuries thought of him—or, indeed, what it thought of any other class, race, or type. Any significant change or special attitude has always been reflected in the art of the period; actually art has sometimes registered the change before it has become generally apparent in the conventional attitudes of society. For example, we may reliably judge that for the seventeenth century, the Negro was an unfamiliar figure exciting curiosity and romantic interest. This is revealed first in the blackamoor figures of the Negro king among the three magi who went to Bethlehem with gold, myrrh, and frankincense; this romantic concept of the Negro continued into the eighteenth century, when most Negroes were shown as the attendants of noblemen, in fancy and elaborate dress, symbolic of their position as petted and prized possessions. Few portraits of the Empire and Pompadour periods were complete without the traditional figure of the black page or personal attendant elegantly dressed and obviously displayed as a pet. Nor can we forget the occasional black notable or scholar whose idealized portrait reflected the admiration and sentimental interest of the eighteenth century in the Negro. *Oronooko*, a novel cited earlier in a different context, is an example; Johnson's *Rasselas* is again a case in point. Men like Juan Latino, the Spanish Negro scholar; Capitein, the Dutch Negro theologian; and others down to Samuel Brown, the learned servant of Samuel Johnson, sat for the best painters and engravers of their day. From this tradition we have the occasional, but important, Negro figure portraits by Velazquez, Rembrandt, Rubens, Goya, Reynolds, and Hograth.

(8) The tradition carried over into early colonial America wherever the aristocratic tradition was strong. We see it unmistakably in the portrait of George Washington's family, where the dark-brown, elegantly groomed family "retainer," Lee, is a prominent figure in the group. In fact, there is scarcely a grotesque or carelessly painted Negro figure before the begin-

ning of the nineteenth century, the moment of the Negro's lapse into chattel slavery and plantation bondage. Then, for a time, the Negro disappeared from painting. When he made his reappearance, it was in the background as a clownish, grotesque object setting off the glory of his master or portraying the comic subject of the master's condescending amusement. The "old faithful uncle"—later literature's "Uncle Tom," "Uncle Ned," and "Uncle Remus"—and the broad, expansive Mammy, the inevitable literary Mammy, from "Aunt Chloe" to "Aunt Jemima," were initial stereotypes. No less conventional were the jigging plantation hands (invariably in tattered jeans) and the sprawling, grinning pickaninnies. Scarcely any nineteenth century art show was without its genre portrait study of one or more of these types or its realistically painted or sketched portrayal of "The Plantation Quarters," "Ole Virginia Life," or some equally glorified version of the slave system. The tradition was so strong that it lasted at least forty years after the nominal fall of slavery; it has been (and to some extent still is) one of the mainstays of the literary and artistic defenses of the "lost cause" of the Confederacy. One of the cleverest arguments, if not the cleverest, was this misrepresentation of the patriarchal regime of the southern plantation. It was against this falsification that American art had to react in the latter decades of the nineteenth century, and it was this falsification that made the Negro artist, during all that period, dread and avoid Negro subjects.

(9) Few were able to remember that Negro subjects had been treated with dignity and even with a romantic touch in the previous century; no one dared to resume the dignified or romantic interpretation in opposition to such strong and flourishing Nordic pride and prejudice. A Negro figure, decently dressed, not obviously a peasant or servant, and without reflection of inferior status, was a rarity; a book rather than a tray in a Negro hand would have been an intolerable heresy. (To many, it might be added, it still is.) Oddly enough, no Negro painters and sculptors realized that it was their duty and opportunity to challenge this hardening tradition and stereotype. For the most part they ignored Negro subjects entirely. Yet, in spite of the Negro artist's failure to attack the stereotype, it was undermined by white artists who, for artistic rather than social reasons were pioneers in the cause of realism. So-called "Americanists" were developing a realistic art of native types, including a new and revolutionizing portrayal of the Negro subject. Some of them, like Winslow Homer, began with sketches of the exotic Negro in the West Indies. Others started with some bias toward the plantation school, but a bias tempered by the new concept of realism which demanded *true* type portraiture. Wayman Adams can be identified with this trend. Finally, with the great realists like Robert Henri and George Luks of early-twentieth-century fame, Negro types commanded the technical thoroughness of a major artistic problem. Eventually, por-

trayal of Negroes was to reflect the dignity and honesty of an entirely changed artistic approach and social attitude. George Bellows, John Curry, Julius Bloch, Thomas Benton, and other artists of the twentieth century have made the Negro a subject of major interest and have interpreted him in dignified, sympathetic, even spiritual terms.

(10) The task of the early Negro artist was to prove to a skeptical world that the Negro *could* be an artist. That world did not know that the African had been a capable artist in his native culture and that, independent of European culture, he had built up his own techniques and traditions. It had the notion that for a Negro to aspire to the fine arts was ridiculous. Before 1885, any Negro man or woman with artistic talent and ambition confronted an almost impassable barrier. Yet, in a long period of trying apprenticeship, several Negro artists surmounted both the natural and the artificial obstacles with sufficient success to disprove, but not dispel, the prevailing prejudice.

(11) The first Negro artists in America can never be known by name, but only by their craft work. They were the woodcarvers and cabinet-makers whose skillful work went into many colonial mansions of the handcraft period. The most authentic tracing of any considerable school of master Negro craftsmen has been in connection with the famous Negro blacksmiths of New Orleans, who furnished the handwrought iron grilles that ornamented the balconies and step-balustrades of the more pretentious homes. Interestingly enough, they were working with an original African skill without knowing it, for metal-forging is one of Africa's oldest and greatest arts. However, this was retaught the Negro in his new home, and the probable reason for his almost complete monopoly of the trade was his ability to endure the extreme heat.

(12) There are two important reasons for mentioning these nameless craft artisans. Their early craftsmanship proves the artistic capacity of the group to be broader than just an occasional flowering talent of formal art at the top level, and a sound art should have a handicraft basis. Also, the development of isolated "fine art" is not a profitable way of starting the artistic education of a group. When curves were beaten out freehand, when ornament was improvised in a quick turn of mechanical skill, when the designs were wrought from memory instead of with blueprints and calipers, there was that original creative skill out of which the best art naturally and inevitably comes.

Questions for Discussion and Writing

1. What erroneous assumptions about Negro art and artists existed at the close of the nineteenth century? Out of what set of circumstances did these assumptions arise? Were these assumptions held by white Americans only?

2. What are the nature and sources of the artistic heritage to which the American Negro artist is heir? What has accounted for the loss of this heritage? Explain.

3. According to the author, how did African life contribute to the development of manual dexterity and subsequently to the development of artistic talent in the Negro?

4. The author suggests that the thwarting of the "craft arts" in the Negro resulted in the development of the "emotional arts." How does she explain this? In your opinion, is this explanation plausible?

5. Are there any recognizable differences between African and Afro-American art, according to Butcher? If so, what are some of the basic ones?

6. In what ways have American attitudes, both of blacks and whites, changed toward African and Afro-American art?

7. In paragraph 7, the author makes the following statement: "If history texts were either lost or destroyed in their entirety, we could, in large measure, rewrite history from art." How does she support this idea?

Adam
David
Miller

Adam David Miller,
actor and director, received the M.A. degree in English from the University
of California at Berkeley. He has taught at the University of California at
Berkeley, at San Francisco State College, and is presently teaching at Laney
College. Aside from his career as a teacher, Mr. Miller has contributed
much to the development of the new Black Theater Movement. Together
with being actor and director for Aldridge Players/West, an Afro-American
drama group in San Francisco, he is a member of the board of directors
for that group. He also serves on the board of directors for a book co-
operative, Books Unlimited, and on the board of advisors of Ecology
Action, a group which Mr. Miller says is "interested in restoring some
sense to our handling of our environment."

Mr. Miller is intensely concerned with the revelation of Afro-American culture and hopes that his work will "stay what might be cultural
genocide" for black people. In the following essay, published in *The
Drama Review*, he concerns himself with the extent to which the black
dramatist is influenced by the audience for which he writes.

Adam
David
Miller

It's a Long Way
to St. Louis

(1) As we examine
a play, we can experience the playwright grappling with such questions
as: Who am I? Who are these characters I people my world with? What
is my world? *Who am I creating it for?* The play, that most public, most
social of the arts, is created for an audience, and it is this question of
audience, more than any other single question, that has bedeviled this
country's Negro playwrights.

(2) James Weldon Johnson thought the question not one of a single
audience but rather one of audiences. In "The Dilemma of the Negro
Author" (*The American Mercury*, December, 1928, p. 477), he wrote:

> . . . the Aframerican author faces a special problem which the plain Ameri-
> can author knows nothing about—the problem of the double audience. It is

First published in The Drama Review, *Vol. 12, no. 4, T40 (Black Theatre issue),*
Summer 1968. Copyright 1968 The Drama Review. *Reprinted by permission; all rights*
reserved.

more than a double audience; it is a divided audience, an audience made up of two elements with differing and often opposite points of view. His audience is always both white America and black America. The moment a Negro writer takes up his pen or sits down to his typewriter, he is immediately called upon to solve, consciously or *unconsciously*, this problem of the double audience. To whom shall he address himself, to his own black group or to white America? *Many a Negro writer has fallen down, as it were, between these two stools.* (emphasis added)

(3) Johnson's white audience, though ignorant of Negro experience, had nonetheless hard-to-change preconceptions about what Negro experience was and how it wanted to see it presented; it demanded that the Negro playwright lie about his experience. Since most white playwrights up to Johnson's time had defined Negro life in a way that enabled their white audiences to feel superior to Negroes, thus contributing to the view of Negroes as objects rather than subjects, most whites were willing to see Negroes presented only in images that permitted white comfort. While Johnson's black audience would permit a "real" Negro to be shown in a "Harlem," with all his foibles and faults—all his humanness—they would object to this same Negro on Broadway. For Broadway and the eyes of whites certain subjects and manners dear to the hearts of Negroes were taboo. To Broadway the Negro audience wanted only a *nice* Negro to be shown. So, to please either audience, the Aframerican playwright had to cut a stencil and fill it in with whichever viciousness or banality he imagined one or the other of his audiences conceived. This was a real dilemma.

(4) Johnson considered for a moment the idea of the Negro author saying: "Damn the white audience! . . . What I have written, I have written. I hope you'll be interested and like it. If not, I can't help it." But only for a moment. These words were hardly written when he acknowledged: "But it is impossible for a sane American Negro to write with total disregard for nine-tenths of the people of the United States. Situated as his own race is amidst and amongst them, their influence is irresistible" (*The American Mercury*, pp. 480–81). Thus 40 years ago, in the infancy of black playwriting, Johnson was able to predict with accuracy that our best playwrights would, often unconsciously, vitiate their creative energies by diverting their attention to a white audience that was often hostile, ignorant, deaf, and blind.

(5) What Johnson might have said but didn't was that the white audience could act as cultural tyrant partly because white society apparently offered great rewards to those authors whose creations fitted within socially acceptable limits, rewards the non-white society could not match. All of the cultural apparatus, publishing, radio, film, was under the control of whites, and if the Aframerican writer wanted to continue the recognition he had begun to receive, he had better toe the line.

(6) As long as the black playwright himself sought the rewards held out by the white society, he had his characters seek them, with the result that most of the work done was less a frontal attack on the society as evil than on certain evils of the society. Such a playwright felt and showed in his work that if only certain evils, such as racial discrimination and segregation, were removed, then he and other blacks could take their "rightful places" alongside whites.

(7) Even such a playwright as Langston Hughes—who knew his proper subject matter, who proclaimed at the beginning of his career his rejection of the self-denying "urge to whiteness" and was proud to use his "racial individuality" ("The Negro Artist and the Racial Mountain," *The Nation*, June 23, 1926)—was an integrationist at his core, and felt that the society could be changed so that whites and Negroes could live side by side in harmony. The Hughes statement went something like this: "You are mistaken about me. I am a better man than you think, give me the chance to prove it. Once you understand this, we can work together to create a better world for both of us." Hughes was essentially an optimist about the society and about its potential for change.

(8) Because of what he was saying, Hughes needed a white audience to say it to, despite the fact that the lives of his characters were little understood by that audience; indeed, they were little understood by those "literate" Aframericans who felt they had nothing in common with the *poor* blacks making up Hughes' fictive world.

(9) The racial values that make up Lorraine Hansberry's fictive world also could make sense only if projected to a white-seeking audience. The virtues of the Younger women in *A Raisin in the Sun*—thrift, caution, hard work, good sense—contrast with the lack of these virtues in the men. Walter Younger attempted to make a quick killing, and in the process lost the family's savings to a black con-man. The women want to leave the black ghetto. To do this they attempt to buy a house in an all-white district. When the whites try to buy them out, Walter is willing, but the women convince him that it is in the interest of his manhood to insist on a fulfillment of the deal. The Youngers have the viability of their black lives destroyed but are denied the white life they seek. They are being forced to measure their lives by the standards set by their oppressors. This, of course, is senseless for Negroes. In short, Miss Hansberry is saying to a white audience: here are the Youngers, a good American family operating in the tradition of thrift and hard work, the trademark of successful mobility in the society. They only want a chance to prove to you what good neighbors they can be. Why don't you let them?

(10) James Baldwin bases his *Blues for Mister Charlie* on the murder of Emmet Till, a young Negro boy, by at least two Mississippi white men. In the play the murderers become one man, and it is the psyche of this

man Baldwin presents for his audience's understanding. In these "Notes" Baldwin addressed himself to what appears to be an *American* audience, that is, the entire body politic of the country. But his words trip him up. When we look closely, we see that they could not possibly have been meant for Negroes. How could he ask Negroes to be responsible for white crimes? By what twisted logic could he expect Negroes to see themselves *causing* white violence and oppression?

(11) And the play itself, about the murderer's trial and the events preceding, poses questions for whites, not for Negroes, to answer. Nor is the asking of them likely to help a Negro audience "understand this wretched man." Besides, it is not the duty of the Negro to understand this man. It is the duty of a white audience to understand him and his duty to understand himself. Too often Negroes have been offered the job of civilizing whites; it is high time whites began civilizing themselves. It is the duty of the black audience to understand itself, and the duty of the black playwright to help in this understanding.

(12) Even the comic playwrights fall into the trap of either catering to the good will of a white audience, or of making statements irrelevant to Negroes. Young white Cotchipee of Ossie Davis' *Purlie Victorious* becomes the first member of Big Bethel, the church the Negroes wrestle away from his father. He is happy to join, they are happy to have him. In Douglas Turner Ward's *Day of Absence*, we see a black audience laughing at the whites in their helplessness at the loss of their Negroes for a day. "Look," they say, "the white folks need us. Ha, ha." One must ask if this is something Negroes need to be told. The image of the black woman who raises Miss Ann's children at the sacrifice of her own is one all too familiar to Negroes. What Negroes need to know is not that they are needed by whites but that they are needed by one another. They need to be shown by their playwrights how to reach out to each other across this need.

(13) There are, fortunately, playwrights who do address their work to Negro audiences. Ed Bullins' *How Do You Do* speaks to the middle-class white-seeking Negro, who was the despair of Langston Hughes. Bullins' *Clara's Ole Man* gives the ghetto Negro a picture of life that is "just around the corner" or perhaps the block. Marvin X's *Take Care of Business* shows a young black's determination to try to understand his father. Dorothy Ahmad's play shows a young girl helping her father see that she is his daughter, not his wife. (LeRoi Jones should belong here but despite his brilliance, he is still trying to do something with whites, either flagellating them verbally, or parading them as beasts. The results are often vivid but shallow abstractions.) These are plays about Negroes addressed to Negroes. They provide characters blacks can identify with. They speak to the black experience in ways blacks can understand.

(14) To return to James Weldon Johnson. Johnson felt the Negro author could solve the dilemma of the divided audience by "standing on his racial foundation . . . fashion something that rises above race, and reaches into the universal in truth and beauty" (*op. cit.*, p. 481). Johnson here is buying a particularly limited idea of "universal." The Negro playwright must reach the "universal" *through* race. He should write in such a way that he makes sense to his Negro audience. If this playwright addresses himself to the needs of his Aframerican audience, their need for an understanding of both their African and American history, their need for heroes who look like themselves, for women who are not abstractions of neuter, their need to see themselves in their complexity, then the question of "universality" will be answered, and the question of audience will be academic.

(15) It is a long way to St. Louis, but with some of the younger playwrights at work, the distance gets shorter all the time.

Identification

Briefly identify each of the following persons:

1. Lorraine Hansberry

2. Ossie Davis

3. Ed Bullins

Questions for Discussion and Writing

1. State the central theme of the essay.

2. What problem has been created for the Negro playwright as a result of the "double audience" for whom he writes? How did the earlier playwrights react to this problem?

3. Generally, what were the basic themes of the early playwrights? Toward what audience were the plays directed? For what reasons? In your opinion, were these reasons valid? Discuss.

4. Did the themes of the Negro dramatists change significantly with the emergence of such modern writers as James Baldwin and Lorraine Hansberry?

5. Miller suggests that a new Black Theatre is emerging—a theatre

consisting of playwrights whose views contrast sharply with those of the traditional black playwrights? What themes are handled by these playwrights? Toward what audience are the plays directed? What is the philosophy that engendered this type of theatre?

6. How does the author's interpretation of universality differ from that of James Weldon Johnson? With which interpretation do you agree? Why? Do you have an interpretation of your own which differs from both of these?

7. Try to locate information on the new Black Theatre groups. Following is a list of a few such groups: The New Lafayette Theatre, New York; The Spirit House, Newark, New Jersey; Black Arts/West, San Francisco; Free Southern Theatre, New Orleans; Afro-Arts Theatre, Chicago; Theatre Black, Cleveland; Black House, Philadelphia. Write a brief paper in which you discuss some aspect of the new theatre movement or of one of the black theatre groups.

ON RELIGION

Louis E.

Lomax

Louis Lomax, author and free-lance writer, received his undergraduate training at Paine College in Augusta, Georgia and his graduate training at American University. For several years, Mr. Lomax worked as the feature editor for the *Chicago American* as well as a member of Mike Wallace's news staff. He also served for two years as a television newscaster in New York City. In addition to his work as a journalist and newscaster, Mr. Lomax was at one time assistant professor of philosophy at Georgia State College.

Since 1958, Mr. Lomax has been a free-lance writer, his articles having appeared in some of the leading magazines of this country. His books include *The Negro Mood, When the Word is Given*, and *The Reluctant African*, for which he won the *Saturday Review* Anisfield-Wolf Award in 1961.

The following essay is taken from *When the Word is Given*, an in-depth investigation of the Muslim Movement in America, its character, its philosophy, its leaders, and its adherents.

Louis E.
Lomax

The Nation of Islam—

Is This

a True Religion?

(1) Although Elijah has made his holy pilgrimage to Mecca, the debate over the religious validity of the Black Muslims still rages, with the movement's critics holding to their charge that Elijah Muhammad teaches hate whereas true religion teaches love. A case can be made that these critics are doubly in error, first in their assumption that their own faith teaches universal love, and secondly in their conclusion—aided by news accounts—that the Black Muslims actually preach hatred of others.

(2) Every religion is a closed network of believers; it has its dogma, its ritual, its gods. The followers of that faith are taught to love one another and are urged to proselytize sinners (outsiders) wherever they can be found. Most religions draw creedal, not racial, lines. Persons of any race

Reprinted from Louis Lomax, When the Word is Given *(pp. 64–73) by permission of the author and of the World Book Publishing Co., Inc.*

may embrace the tenets of the faith and become members. However, this is not always the case and racial overtones have crept into major world faiths.

(3) The late, and loved, Pope John flirted with immortality by coming to grips with the issue of racism in religion. Not only did he infuse the church with the fresh air of universalism, but he halted a service because a priest violated—forgot, actually—His Holiness' order that a reference to the Jews as a "perfidious people" be stricken from the Catholic prayer service. The pending second session of the ecumenical council may see the introduction of a proposal that would call on the Church to speak out against anti-Semitism. The proposal was not brought up in the first session because the Church fathers feared what the Arabs might say.

The Jews and the Protestants face essentially the same problems as the Roman Catholics. St. Paul rose to glory because he translated being a Jew from a biological to a spiritual proposition. Many Jews have not accepted that translation and they snicker when Sammy Davis, Jr., walks into their temple. Racism is such a fact of American Protestant church life that most major denominations are divided along racial lines. Then there is the question of religion and geography. The world's major faiths were spawned in ethnic stock. Thus the followers of Buddha are apt to be Orientals; but for slavery and colonization all of the followers of Christ would be European. But for the same kind of cultural intermingling, Allah's followers would be the peoples of Asia Minor and North Africa, and the black peoples below the Sahara would still be practicing the varied tribal and family faiths mentioned earlier in this essay.

(5) But time and trouble make saints of everybody . . . and universalism occurs only when feuding faiths clash on the plains of practical reality. Thus American Protestants now have a commission that is given over entirely to eliminating all anti-Semitism from the gospel of Christ. The Episcopal Bishop of California, James Pike, has gone so far as to suggest that we take down the cross as a symbol of our faith lest this encourage the teaching that the Jews killed Our Lord. This teaching—that the Jews killed Christ—is no longer fashionable as it was when I was baptized. Now one is told that the Romans killed Christ. And since the once-heathen Romans are now Christians—even though they are Catholic—I suppose this makes things better.

(6) Now let's turn to the other side of the coin.

(7) During a recent lecture before the Jewish Graduate Club at Columbia University I talked about the need for all orthodox religions to relax their dogmas and accept other peoples as equals. One fiercely intent man leaped to his feet and shouted to me, "You want to rob us of our culture because you people don't have one of your own!" This was sheer nonsense and the host rabbi rose to say so. But I pressed the issue: Could

I join their temple? The younger Jews shouted "Yes—we would love to have you." The older fellows were not quite so sure.

(8) "Are you as Jews chosen of God, thus the only ones who are really blessed?" I asked one of the fundamentalists.

(9) "Yes," he shot back.

(10) "Are you chosen in a way that I can never be?" I continued.

(11) "Yes." He faltered. "You are not a Jew; you cannot be among the elect."

(12) By this time the younger Jews were on their feet screaming denunciations of him. But the issue of ethnic exclusiveness that splits today's Jewish community had been laid bare.

(13) Dogma and ritual are further evidences of the tribalism endemic to religion. I was born and raised a Baptist; long before I could read and write I knew that any person who had not been immersed in water was doomed to Hell. There was nothing to argue about, no need for polemics and reasoning; there would be no Methodists in Heaven.

(14) The point of truth is this: Ethnic and dogmatic bigotry are imbedded in every religious faith plying its wares in the world market; we religious liberals are students of apologetics, sophisticated believers who prefer to forget our crude and tribalistic roots in favor of an enlightened social ethic. Alas, along came Elijah and made us see ourselves as we once were; along came Malcolm X and made us understand what we are now, and why.

(15) The argument that the Black Muslims are not a valid religion because of the exclusivity of their fellowship, then, is clearly spurious. Every religion is a sort of sanctified country club, a coming together of peers in the name of their god. The second argument against the religiosity of the Black Muslims is equally spurious: like all faiths, the Black Muslims never hate the other fellow; they say love your own kind. Religious bigotry is Western civilization's major blind spot, and Malcolm X has taken up squatters' rights just there.

(16) Thus it is that secularism must save the church—the layman must lead the clergyman to the mourner's bench and make him confess brotherhood in the name of a democratic and pluralistic society. The nature of our social moment demands that we free God from racialism and dogmatics. Racialism, the malignant one of the two cancers, must be dealt with first since it is the prime moral issue of our time. And it must be dealt with by all peoples of all faiths working in concert. Should our social order change, should we somehow come to grips with the evils that have spawned the Black Muslims, the movement would be forced to refine itself or perish.

(17) Malcolm X is the best authority for this. I have often pressed him on his categorical denunciation of the white man as a devil, and his

reply is always the same: "The Honorable Elijah Muhammad teaches us that the white man is a devil. We hold to that teaching because history proves the white man is a devil. If he is not a devil," Malcolm X concludes, "then let him prove it. Let him give justice, freedom, and equality to our people."

(18) I have deliberately kept my analysis of the Black Muslims in personal terms of reference because this is precisely how most Negroes feel about the matter—after all, the attraction of the movement for Negroes is one of the major points of this essay. "Of course I disagree with Malcolm," the wife of a Negro newsman told me. "But I disagree with a lot of other religions, too. If he teaches hate, so do they; what's the difference? I wonder why the white people are after him." She smiled. "Could it be because he is colored?"

(19) The Black Muslims have their God, their gospel, their ritual trappings, their approval from official heads of the Islamic faith. As a religion, then, there is little left to do but disagree with them and then leave them alone.

(20) This, of course, pains liberals, Negro and white, who want to hear a ringing denunciation of the Black Muslims. Negro leaders are always quick to denounce Elijah, but the Negro masses are strangely silent. There is a reason for this silence, something both the Negro leadership and the white power structure would do well to examine: Deep down in their hearts, as James Baldwin so accurately states, the black masses don't believe in white people any more. They don't believe in Malcolm either, except when he articulates their disbelief in white people. In the end—and this is the thing white people will be a long time in grasping—the Negro masses neither join nor denounce the Black Muslims. They just sit at home in the ghetto amid the heat, the roaches, the rats, the vice, the disgrace, and rue the fact that come daylight they must meet the man—the white man—and work at a job that leads only to a dead end.

(21) This brings me to the core of the matter, to the final measure of every religion: it is a thing called *compassion*, a concern and caring about the other fellow. It is rooted in the glaring awareness that we all have fallen short of the high mark set for us, and thus we need the honest sympathy and understanding of all men everywhere.

(22) For though you may have your God, your holy book, your ritual, and your symbols; though you may give of your wages to build the temple; and though you may have been to Mecca, or Jerusalem, if you have not compassion you are but meanness couched in Scripture, you are but an ancient stink, a reason for men to hold their noses as they crawl on toward a land of human understanding and brotherhood.

(23) Once the convert becomes a Black Muslim he is baptized as a citizen in the Nation of Islam. They have a flag, a symbol, and a cause.

From this day forward his life centers around activity at the Muslim restaurant and temple.

(24) Who are these Black Muslims? Where do they live, and what do they do for a living?

(25) These questions baffle all observers because any Negro you encounter could be a Black Muslim. Usually the men wear identifying pins, and the Muslim women can generally be spotted by their dress, particularly the long, flowing headpiece. But these identifying signs are not always present. I have encountered Black Muslims working in printing plants, in barbershops, as messenger boys, as night-club entertainers, and as cab drivers. I will never forget taking a stroll in Central Park where I came across a Muslim sister working as a nursemaid to three white children. Since most nurses and maids are Negroes the rise of the Black Muslims has sent a quiet but very real chill through the employment agencies in several major cities. After all, there is no telling what these Muslim women will do when the "word" comes, when the Battle of Armageddon is declared. And there is no way for employment agencies to determine if Negro applicants are Black Muslims before sending them out as servants in white homes. Nor is there any way for heads of households to know just who their butlers and cooks are. To borrow from James Baldwin, nobody knows their name. It could be "X."

(26) The Black Muslims flatly refuse to discuss their organizational finances with anyone. However, observers of the movement are convinced that the tithes collected at temples and the income from temple restaurants form the basis of the Muslim economy. The local restaurant—and most of them are called "Shabazz" restaurants after Malcolm X whose "restored" Arab name is Shabazz—is under the supervision of the local minister. He seems to have fairly complete control, but all matters are subject to review by Malcolm X as Elijah's roving ambassador. The local ministers are allowed a certain portion of what they raise, but only top insiders know just how Mr. Muhammad makes this determination. The major leaders of the movement all seem to have taken a vow of poverty and live on expenses furnished by the movement itself. I know this is true of Malcolm X and I suspect it to be true of others.

(27) But it must be remembered that the Black Muslims are both thrifty and industrious; they are encouraged to open their own businesses and many of the top leaders are themselves businessmen. Elijah Muhammad, Jr. runs one of the largest bakeries in Chicago; Raymond Sharrieff is said to have ownership in a clothing store there. All evidence indicates that local Muslim leaders finance themselves through various enterprises and that the bulk of the funds raised in the temple itself flow on to the movement headquarters in Chicago.

(28) Whoever and wherever these Black Muslims are they lead an

exacting, regimented life. In their homes they practice strict dietary laws—precisely those of the kosher Jews—and avoid contact with white people as much as possible. The private role of both the man and the woman in the family is clearly defined, and the children are indoctrinated with the faith while they are still young. Muslim men are watched by The Fruit and must engage in some kind of gainful employment. They are encouraged to go into small businesses whenever possible; they are assured of patronage from their fellow Muslims. A number of Negro businessmen have been attracted to the Nation of Islam because it provides them with a ready source of customers. Other Muslim brothers can be seen on the streets every day selling Muslim newspapers. They are allowed to keep a goodly portion of what they earn and are thus independent. The temple restaurants employ scores of Muslim men and women, thus decreasing the ranks of their unemployed. Other Muslims are door-to-door salesmen and find easy entry in the Negro community, where the white door-to-door salesmen have become anathema.

(29) But the average Black Muslim works for some white man somewhere in some capacity. He is urged to learn a trade and thus ready himself for the day when he will be called upon to be one of the heads of industry and commerce in the Muslims' own, separate state.

(30) The Black Muslim men are lectured constantly about family responsibility and are subject to trial before their peers if they violate the rules of the order. Punishment can vary from a small fine to temporary or permanent banishment from the temple. No Muslim will associate with an offender for the duration of his exile. It is said that Malcolm X's brother was once banished and that Malcolm refused even to write the man until the period of punishment had been served.

(31) Black Muslim women are schooled in the art and need for homemaking, and are taught to take a back seat in the presence of their husbands. Muslim women almost never talk to strangers—non Muslims, that is—and maintain a general silence that is unnerving. They also eschew makeup and fancy dress. When I first encountered the Muslims some five years ago, this ban on feminine adornment was rigidly enforced. But there seems to have been a strong revolt among temple women and the ban has been relaxed to the point where employing makeup is now optional. Yet I have seen few Muslim women exercise this option. The wife of a major Muslim official, say Joseph X of New York, certainly wouldn't exercise it.

(32) The Black Muslims are a male-oriented organization. A man reaches real stature in the movement when he becomes a member of The Fruit of Islam, the functional and disciplinary arm of the movement. The Fruit hold separate temple services, where they are taught, among other things, every possible method of self-defense. Every local temple has a Captain of The Fruit—in New York it is Joseph X—and the entire network

is headed by the son-in-law of Elijah Muhammad, Raymond Sharrieff. The Fruit enforce brotherhood among the men of the temple and form the honor guard whenever Malcolm X or Elijah Muhammad makes a public appearance. The Fruit work under the local minister, but there is a line of authority that runs down to the local captains directly from Sharrieff's Chicago headquarters. The Muslim Girls Training Class (MGT), for young women, is headed by Sister Lottie X, also of Chicago.

(33) The division of authority seems to be along these lines: The local Fruit and MGT work under the local minister on local matters. But unless the matter in question is one of clearly defined doctrine the local minister gets clearance from Chicago before issuing his orders. On national matters, those affecting the movement as a whole, The Fruit and the MGT take orders directly from headquarters. These orders are issued to members of the temple who obey without question.

(34) One of the functions of The Fruit and the MGT is fund-raising. None of the rumors about Muslims receiving help from outside—Communist or segregationist—sources has proved true. The fact of the matter is that the Black Muslims are hard-working, frugal people; they never buy on installment, and give a tenth—at least—of their earnings to the temple. This income is augmented by bazaars, plays, rallies, and the sale of their own newspapers and magazines. Then there is the matter of the various lawsuits the Muslims have carried on with astonishing success. The Black Muslims have collected upward of a quarter of a million dollars I know about in the past four years or so, mostly as a result of police brutality against their members. These suits are filed in the name of the individual Muslim but they are carried on by the temple, and I suspect the temple shares in the results.

(35) Further regimentation of life within the Nation is achieved by demanding that members send their children to Black Muslim schools wherever possible. In two cities, Chicago and Detroit, the Muslims have "universities" where they train the children from kindergarten through high school. It will be recalled that Elijah Muhammad first got into trouble with the law when he decided to send his children to the Muslim school rather than the public schools. Now authorities in both cities have approved the Muslim schools as accredited centers of learning.

(36) These schools are well disciplined and skillfully run. Early in 1962 there was considerable concern in Chicago over just what the Black Muslims were teaching in their schools. A biracial committee visited the University of Islam there and came away stunned. Said committee member Judge Edyth Sampson, a former U.S. delegate to the United Nations, "These people are doing a magnificent job with their young students. I am deeply impressed by what I saw."

(37) What Mrs. Sampson and her fellow committee members saw

was essentially this: Black Muslim boys and girls stand muster for cleanliness and decorum each morning. The classes are separated, boys in one section, girls in the other, and the students' day is divided between religious and secular education. They are taught both English and Arabic; they are drilled in the history of the black man in Africa and America. They are taught the history of the Black Muslim movement from Fard down to Minister Malcolm X.

(38) In 1963 Sister Christine X, one of the directors of the school, authored a new first reader which is now being employed. The exercises in the book are something American educators would do well to study:

> My name is Nora X. My father's name is James X, and my mother is Frances X. We are Muslims. We have our own flag. Our flag is over there on the wall. The symbols on our flag are a star and a crescent.

(39) Then the students are told to use the following words in sentences: Allah, black, Muhammad, God, Temple, nation, flag, Armageddon, Elijah.

(40) Other exercises in the book call for the student to write short essays on Mr. Muhammad and other notables within the movement. Then as the students progress through school they are taught to link subject matter to the history of the black man. For example, when the students are being taught mathematics they are repeatedly reminded that much of modern math is based on work done by the Egyptians; they are not allowed to forget that English is not their native tongue, that their language is Arabic, that the white man robbed them of their tongue when he kidnaped their fore-parents from Africa.

(41) The thing that arrests me most about these schools is that they are now turning out the first generation of youth completely schooled in the Black Muslim doctrine. Unlike Malcolm X, John Ali, and other prominent Muslims of today who had to be "de-brainwashed" before they saw the light, the movement now has several score teen-agers who have been grounded in their faith just as a devout Catholic child is reared in his. As of now the movement suffers greatly from a lack of trained leaders. Only a handful of capable men and women are available to the organization and the nature of their doctrine is such that trained Negroes are hardly apt to join. But a few more years will see the emergence of well-trained Black Muslims who, I am certain, will give the organization more administrative order than it now has.

(42) Meanwhile the Black Muslims are bombarding Negroes all over the nation with their message to the "lost-found, so-called Negro in the wilderness of North America." For a number of years Mr. Muhammad had a weekly column in some of the nation's best Negro newspapers. Now the

Muslims publish their own weekly, *Mr. Muhammad Speaks*, a thirty-six page tabloid that has the largest circulation of any Negro newspaper being published. The Muslims also conduct a weekly radio program on stations in some forty cities throughout the nation. All this is augmented by the appearances of Malcolm X on radio and TV programs each week. All in all, the Black Muslims have covered the nation; their basic teachings are known and debated by Negroes everywhere.

(43) On the whole, then, the state of the Nation of Islam is good; its population is growing, its economy is well into the black, and its foreign relations—though strained—are better than they have ever been before.

Questions for Discussion and Writing

1. In paragraph 2, Mr. Lomax states that "racial overtones have crept into major world faiths." Can you cite examples from your own experiences that would support this statement? Read Thurman's "The Luminous Darkness" (last essay in this section). What ideas in that essay support Lomax's statement?

2. According to the author, what two arguments are used to discredit the Black Muslims as a true religious sect? Is his refutation of these arguments logical? Is his evidence adequate?

3. Explain the following statement: "Should our social order change, should we somehow come to grips with the evils that have spawned the Black Muslims, the movement would be forced to refine itself or perish." In a brief paper, write your reaction to this idea.

4. Locate additional material on the Muslim movement, its nature and character and write a brief paper on some aspect of it. You might begin with the following works: Louis Lomax, *When the Word is Given*; Malcolm X, *Autobiography*; Archie Epps, *The Speeches of Malcolm X*; and Eric Lincoln, *The Black Muslims in America*.

5. Despite the controversial nature of the Black Muslim movement, it is generally felt that this movement has done more toward promoting a sense of identity and pride among black people than any other single movement or organization. Might this be a result of the structure of the Muslim community as outlined in the last section of this essay? Discuss.

Malcolm X

Malcolm X, founder of the Organization for Afro-American Unity, was at one time before his death, the most powerful minister and spokesman for the Muslim movement. He was born Malcolm Little, son of a baptist minister in Omaha, Nebraska. As a boy of six, he witnessed his home burned by the Ku Klux Klan. Shortly thereafter, Malcolm's father moved the family to Lansing, Michigan and became an adherent of the teachings of the Black Nationalist leader, Marcus Garvey.

After the death of his father, Malcolm's mother attempted to keep her family together, the family then consisting of eleven children. She was unsuccessful, however, and eventually Malcolm had to be sent to an institution for boys. While there, he was encouraged to attend school. He was alert and intelligent, but his quick mind gained for him the censure of his white classmates. Becoming disillusioned with school, he went to New York where, while still a teen-ager, he became deeply involved in under-

189

ground activities. Eventually, he was arrested and sent to prison for burglary; and it was in prison in Concord, Massachusetts that he was converted to the Muslim religion. After his release from prison, he ultimately became the chief minister and spokesman for the Honorable Elijah Muhammad, founder of the Muslim Movement. Through his impassioned speeches, many of which were made on the American college campuses, Malcolm X gained the admiration of young Americans all over the country.

After serving for some time as Muhammad's spokesman, Malcolm finally broke with Muhammad and established the Organization for Afro-American Unity. In order to acquire a deeper insight into the nature and character of Orthodox Islam, Malcolm traveled to Africa and the Near East, ending his tour with a pilgrimage to Mecca. When he returned to the United States, many of his racist views had been abandoned, and he began in earnest to build the Organization for Afro-American Unity. Unfortunately, however, he was assassinated not long after, on Feb. 21, 1965.

Malcolm X

The Harvard Law School Forum Speech of March 24, 1961

(1) We thank you for inviting us here to the Harvard Law School Forum this evening to present our views on this timely topic: *The American Negro: Problems and Solutions*. However, to understand our views, the views of the Muslims, you must first realize that we are a religious group, and you must also know something about our religion, the religion of Islam. The creator of the universe, whom many of you call God or Jehovah, is known to the Muslims by the name Allah. The Muslims believe there is but one God, and that all the prophets came from this one God. We believe also that all prophets taught the same religion, and that they themselves called that religion Islam, an Arabic word that means complete submission and obedi-

ence to the will of Allah. One who practices divine obedience is called a Muslim (commonly known, spelled and referred to here in the West as Moslem). There are over seven hundred twenty-five million Muslims on this earth, predominantly in Africa and Asia, the non-white world. We here in America are under the divine leadership of the Honorable Elijah Muhammad, and we are an integral part of the vast world of Islam that stretches from the China seas to the sunny shores of West Africa. A unique situation faces the twenty million ex-slaves here in America because of our unique condition. Our acceptance of Islam and conversion to the religion affects us also in a unique way, different from the way in which it affects all other Muslim converts elsewhere on this earth.

(2) Mr. Elijah Muhammad is our divine leader and teacher here in America. Mr. Muhammad believes in and obeys God one hundred percent, and he is even now teaching and working among our people to fulfill God's divine purpose. I am here at this forum tonight to represent Mr. Elijah Muhammad, the spiritual head of the fastest-growing group of Muslims in the Western Hemisphere. We who follow Mr. Muhammad know that he has been divinely taught and sent to us by God himself. We believe that the miserable plight of the twenty million black people in America is the fulfillment of divine prophecy. We believe that the serious race problem that [the Negro's] presence here poses for America is also the fulfillment of divine prophecy. We also believe that the presence today in America of the Honorable Elijah Muhammad, his teachings among the twenty million so-called Negroes, and his naked warning to America concerning her treatment of these twenty million ex-slaves is also the fulfillment of divine prophecy. Therefore, when Mr. Muhammad declares that the only solution to America's serious race problem is complete separation of the two races, he is reiterating what was already predicted for this time by all the Biblical prophets. Because Mr. Muhammad takes this uncompromising stand, those of you who don't understand Biblical prophecy wrongly label him a racist and hate-teacher and accuse him of being anti-white and teaching black supremacy. But this evening since we are all here at the Harvard Law School Forum, together, both races face to face, we can question and examine for ourselves the wisdom or folly of what Mr. Muhammad is teaching.

(3) Many of you who classify yourselves as white express surprise and shock at the truth that Mr. Muhammad is teaching your twenty million ex-slaves here in America, but you should be neither surprised nor shocked. As students, teachers, professors and scientists, you should be well aware that we are living in a world where great changes are taking place. New ideas are replacing the old ones. Old governments are collapsing and new nations are being born. The entire old system which held the old world

together has lost its effectiveness, and now that old world is going out. A new system or a new world must replace the old world. Just as the old ideas must be removed to make way for the new, God has declared to Mr. Muhammad that the evil features of this wicked old world must be exposed, faced up to, and removed in order to make way for the new world which God Himself is preparing to establish. The divine mission of Mr. Muhammad here in America today is to prepare us for the new world of righteousness by teaching us a better understanding of the old world's defects. Thus we may come to agree that God must remove this wicked old world.

(4) We see by reports in the daily press that even many of you who are scholars and scientists think that the message of Islam that is being preached here in America among your twenty million ex-slaves is new, or that it is something Mr. Muhammad himself has made up. Mr. Muhammad's religious message is not new. All of the scientists and prophets of old predicted that a man such as he with such a doctrine or message, would make his appearance among us at a time as that in which we are living today. It is written too in your own scriptures that this prophetic figure would not be raised up from the midst of the educated class, but that God would make His choice from among the lowest element of America's twenty million ex-slaves. It would be as in the days when God raised up Moses from among the lowly Hebrew slaves and [com]missioned him to separate his oppressed people from a slave master named Pharaoh. Moses found himself opposed by the scholars and scientists of that day, who are symbolically described in the Bible as "Pharaoh's magicians." Jesus himself, a lowly carpenter, was also [com]missioned by God to find his people, the "lost sheep," and to separate them from their Gentile enemies and restore them to their own nation. Jesus also found himself opposed by the scholars and scientists of his day, who are symbolically described in the Bible as "scribes, priests, and Pharisees." Just as the learned class of those days disagreed with and opposed both Moses and Jesus primarily because of their humble origin, Mr. Elijah Muhammad is today likewise being opposed by the learned, educated intellectuals of his own kind, because of [his] humble origin. These modern-day "magicians, scribes, and Pharisees" try to ridicule Mr. Muhammad by emphasizing the humble origin of him and his many followers."

(5) Moses was raised up among his enslaved people at a time when God was planning to restore them to a land of their own where they could give birth to a new civilization, completely independent of their former slave masters. Pharaoh opposed God's plan and God's servant, so Pharaoh and his people were destroyed. Jesus was sent among his people at a time when God was planning to bring about another great change. The dispen-

sation preached by Jesus two thousand years ago ushered in a new type of civilization, the Christian civilization, better known as the Christian world. The Holy Prophet Muhammad (may the peace and blessing of Allah be upon him) came six hundred years after Jesus with another dispensation that did not destroy or remove the Christian civilization, but which put a dent in it, a wound that has lasted even until today. Now, today, God has sent Mr. Elijah Muhammad among the downtrodden and oppressed so-called American Negroes to warn that God is again preparing to bring about another great change, only this time it will be a final change. This is the day and the time for a complete change. Mr. Muhammad teaches that the religion of Islam is the only solution to the problems confronting our people here in America. He warns us that it is even more important, however, to know the base or foundation upon which we must build tomorrow. Therefore, although the way in which Mr. Muhammad teaches the religion of Islam and the particular kind of Islam he teaches may appear to be different from the teaching of Islam in the Old World, the basic principles and practices are the same.

(6) You must remember: The condition of America's twenty million ex-slaves is uniquely pitiful. But just as the old religious leaders in the days of Moses and Jesus refused to accept Moses and Jesus as religious reformers, many of the religious leaders in the old Muslim world today may also refute the teachings of Mr. Elijah Muhammad, neither realizing the unique condition of these twenty million ex-slaves nor understanding that Mr. Elijah Muhammad's teachings are divinely prescribed to rectify the miserable condition of our oppressed people here. But as God made Pharaoh's magicians bow before Moses, He plans today to make all opposition, both at home and abroad, bow before the truth that is now being taught by the Honorable Elijah Muhammad.

(7) We are two thousand years from the time of the great change which took place in Jesus' day. If you will but look around you on this earth today, it will be as clear as the five fingers on your hand that we are again living at a time of great change. God has come to close out the entire old world, the old world where for the past six thousand years most of the earth's population has been deceived, conquered, colonized, ruled, enslaved, oppressed, and exploited by the Caucasian race. At the time when Pharaoh's civilization reached its peak and his period of rule of the slaves was up, God appeared unto Moses and revealed to him that He had something different for his people. Likewise, God told Mr. Muhammad that He has something different for his people, the so-called Negroes here in America today—something that until now has never before been revealed. Mr. Muhammad teaches us that this old world has seen nothing yet, that the real thing is yet to come.

Questions for Discussion and Writing

1. What parallels does the author draw between the Muslim religion and the Christian religion? Can you find other parallels?

2. In paragraph 1, the author states "a unique situation faces the twenty million ex-slaves here in America because of our unique condition, thus our acceptance of Islam, and into Islam, affects us uniquely." Does he clearly indicate wherein this uniqueness lies?

3. In paragraph 2, the author states three "beliefs" of the Muslims. Each he says is a "fulfillment of divine prophecy." Does he give evidence to support this?

4. At the end of paragraph 2, the author invites his audience to question and examine with him the "wisdom or folly" of Muhammad's teachings. Trace his development through the following paragraphs. How thorough is his examination. Discuss.

5. Try to state the basic philosophy of the Muslim religion. What makes the teachings of Muhammad, according to Malcolm X "a peculiar kind of Islam"?

Martin
Luther
King, Jr.

Martin Luther King, Jr., a Baptist minister and the leader of the Negro Civil Rights Movement, was chief spokesman for the philosophy of nonviolence. Dr. King received the B.A. degree from Morehouse College and the Ph.D. degree from Boston University. He was President of the Southern Christian Leadership Council and co-pastor of Ebenezer Baptist Church in Atlanta, Georgia. His life and teachings reflected the philosophy of Jesus, Thoreau, and Ghandi, to whom he has often been compared.

Dr. King was the recipient of the Nobel Peace Prize for 1964. His major published works include *Stride Toward Freedom, Why We Can't Wait* and *Strength to Love*, the work from which the following essay is taken. Dr. King's great appeal and the source of his magnetism were his public addresses, through which he fired the imagination of millions of Negroes and touched the conscience of millions of white Americans.

He was assassinated in Memphis, Tennessee in the spring of 1968.

Martin
Luther
King, Jr.

The Answer to
a Perplexing Question

(1) Human life
through the centuries has been characterized by man's persistent efforts to
remove evil from the earth. Seldom has man thoroughly adjusted himself
to evil, for in spite of his rationalizations, compromises, and alibis, he
knows the "is" is not the "ought" and the actual is not the possible.
Though the evils of sensuality, selfishness, and cruelty often rise aggres-
sively in his soul, something within tells him that they are intruders and
reminds him of his higher destiny and more noble allegiance. Man's hankering after the demonic is always disturbed by his longing for the divine.
As he seeks to adjust to the demands of time, he knows that eternity is his
ultimate habitat. When man comes to himself, he knows that evil is a

foreign invader that must be driven from the native soils of his soul before he can achieve moral and spiritual dignity. . . .

(2) How can evil be cast out? Men have usually pursued two paths to eliminate evil and thereby save the world. The first calls upon man to remove evil through his own power and ingenuity in the strange conviction that by thinking, inventing, he will at last conquer the nagging forces of evil. Give people a fair chance and a decent education, and they will save themselves. This idea, sweeping across the modern world like a plague, has ushered God out and escorted man in and has substituted human ingenuity for divine guidance. Some people suggest that this concept was introduced during the Renaissance when reason dethroned religion, or later when Darwin's *Origin of Species* replaced belief in creation by the theory of evolution, or when the industrial revolution turned the hearts of men to material comforts and physical conveniences. At any rate, the idea of adequacy of man to solve the evils of history captured the minds of people, giving rise to the easy optimism of the nineteenth century, the doctrine of inevitable progress, Rousseau's maxim of "the original goodness of human nature," and Condorcet's conviction that by reason alone the whole world would soon be cleansed of crime, poverty, and war.

(3) Armed with this growing faith in the capability of reason and science modern man set out to change the world. He turned his attention from God and the human soul to the outer world and its possibilities. He observed, analyzed, and explored. The laboratory became man's sanctuary and scientists his priests and prophets. A modern humanist confidently affirmed:

> The future is not with the churches but with the laboratories, not with prophets but with scientists, not with piety but with efficiency. Man is at last becoming aware that he alone is responsible for the realization of the world of his dreams, that he has within himself the power for its achievement.

Man has subpoenaed nature to appear before the judgment seat of scientific investigation. None doubt that man's work in the scientific laboratories has brought unbelievable advances in power and comfort, producing machines that think and gadgets that soar majestically through the skies, stand impressively on the land, and move with stately dignity on the seas.

(4) But in spite of these astounding new scientific developments, the old evils continue and the age of reason has been transformed into an age of terror. Selfishness and hatred have not vanished with an enlargement of our educational system and an extension of our legislative policies. A once optimistic generation now asks in utter bewilderment, "Why could not we cast it out?"

(5) The answer is rather simple: Man by his own power can never

cast evil from the world. The humanist's hope is an illusion, based on too great an optimism concerning the inherent goodness of human nature.

(6) I would be the last to condemn the thousands of sincere and dedicated people outside the churches who have labored unselfishly through various humanitarian movements to cure the world of social evils, for I would rather a man be a committed humanist than an uncommitted Christian. But so many of these dedicated persons, seeking salvation within the human context, have become understandably pessimistic and disillusioned, because their efforts are based on a kind of self-delusion which ignores fundamental facts about our mortal nature.

(7) Nor would I minimize the importance of science and the great contributions which have come in the wake of the Renaissance. These have lifted us from the stagnating valleys of superstition and half-truths to the sunlit mountains of creative analysis and objective appraisal. The unquestioned authority of the church in scientific matters needed to be freed from paralyzing obscurantism, antiquated notions, and shameful inquisitions. But the exalted Renaissance optimism, while attempting to free the mind of man, forgot about man's capacity for sin.

(8) The second idea for removing evil from the world stipulates that if man waits submissively upon the Lord, in his own good time God alone will redeem the world. Rooted in a pessimistic doctrine of human nature, the idea, which eliminates completely the capability of sinful man to do anything, was prominent in the Reformation, that great spiritual movement which gave birth to the Protestant concern for moral and spiritual freedom and served as a necessary corrective for a corrupt and stagnant medieval church. The doctrines of justification by faith and the priesthood of all believers are towering principles which we as Protestants must forever affirm, but the Reformation doctrine of human nature overstressed the corruption of man. The Renaissance was too optimistic, and the Reformation too pessimistic. The former so concentrated on the goodness of man that it overlooked his capacity for goodness. While rightly affirming the sinfulness of human nature and man's incapacity to save himself, the Reformation wrongly affirmed that the image of God had been completely erased from man.

(9) This led to the Calvinistic concept of the total depravity of man and to a resurrection of the terrible idea of infant damnation. So depraved is human nature, said the doctrinaire Calvinist, that if a baby dies without baptism he will burn forever in hell. Certainly this carries the idea of man's sinfulness too far.

(10) This lopsided Reformation theology has often emphasized a purely other-worldly religion, which stresses the utter hopelessness of this world and calls upon the individual to concentrate on preparing his soul for the world to come. By ignoring the need for social reform, religion is

divorced from the mainstream of human life. A pulpit committee listed as the first essential qualification for a new minister: "He must preach the true gospel and not talk about social issues." This is a blueprint for a dangerously irrelevant church where people assemble to hear only pious platitudes.

(11) By disregarding the fact that the gospel deals with man's body as well as with his soul, such a one-sided emphasis creates a tragic dichotomy between the sacred and the secular. To be worthy of its New Testament origin, the church must seek to transform both individual lives and the social situation that brings to many people anguish of spirit and cruel bondage.

(12) The idea that man expects God to do everything leads inevitably to a callous misuse of prayer. For if God does everything, man then asks for anything, and God becomes little more than a "cosmic bellhop" who is summoned for every trivial need. Or God is considered so omnipotent and man so powerless that prayer is a substitute for work and intelligence. A man said to me, "I believe in integration, but I know it will not come until God wants it to come. You Negroes should stop protesting and start praying." I am certain we need to pray for God's help and guidance in this integration struggle, but we are gravely misled if we think the struggle will be won only by prayer. God, who gave us minds for thinking and bodies for working, would defeat his own purpose if he permitted us to obtain through prayer what may come through work and intelligence. Prayer is a marvelous and necessary supplement of our feeble efforts, but it is a dangerous substitute. When Moses strove to lead the Israelites to the Promised Land God made it clear that he would not do for them what they could do for themselves. "And the Lord said unto Moses, Wherefore criest thou unto me? speak unto the children of Israel, that they go forward."

(13) We must pray earnestly for peace, but we must also work vigorously for disarmament and the suspension of weapon testing. We must use our minds as rigorously to plan for peace as we have used them to plan for war. We must pray with unceasing passion for racial justice, but we must also use our minds to develop a program, organize ourselves into mass nonviolent action, and employ every resource of our bodies and souls to bring into being those social changes that make for a better distribution of wealth within our nation and in the underdeveloped countries of the world.

(14) Does not all of this reveal the fallacy of thinking that God will cast evil from the earth, even if man does nothing except to sit complacently by the wayside? No prodigious thunderbolt from heaven will blast away evil. No mighty army of angels will descend to force men to do what their wills resist. The Bible portrays God, not as an omnipotent czar who makes all decisions for his subjects nor as a cosmic tyrant who with gestapolike methods invades the inner lives of men, but rather as a loving

Father who gives to his children such abundant blessings as they may be willing to receive. Always man must do something. "Stand upon thy feet," says God to Ezekiel, "and I will speak unto you." Man is no helpless invalid left in a valley of total depravity until God pulls him out. Man is rather an upstanding human being whose vision has been impaired by the cataracts of sin and whose soul has been weakened by the virus of pride, but there is sufficient vision left for him to lift his eyes unto the hills, and there remains enough of God's image for him to turn his weak and sin-battered life toward the Great Physician, the curer of the ravages of sin.

(15) The real weakness of the idea that God will do everything is its false conception of both God and man. It makes God so absolutely sovereign that man is absolutely helpless. It makes man so absolutely depraved that he can do nothing but wait on God. It sees the world as so contaminated with sin that God totally transcends it and touches it only here and there through a mighty invasion. This view ends up with a God who is a despot and not a Father. It ends up with such a pessimism concerning human nature that it leaves man little more than a helpless worm crawling through the morass of an evil world. But man is neither totally depraved, nor is God an almighty dictator. We must surely affirm the majesty and sovereignty of God, but this should not lead us to believe that God is an Almighty Monarch who will impose his will upon us and deprive us of the freedom to choose what is good or what is not good. He will not thrust himself upon us nor force us to stay home when our minds are bent on journeying to some far country. But he follows us in love, and when we come to ourselves and turn our tired feet back to the Father's house, he stands waiting with outstretched arms of forgiveness.

(16) Therefore we must never feel that God will, through some breathtaking miracle or a wave of the hand, cast evil out of the world. As long as we believe this we will pray unanswerable prayers and ask God to do things that he will never do. The belief that God will do everything for man is as untenable as the belief that man can do everything for himself. It, too, is based on a lack of faith. We must learn that to expect God to do everything while we do nothing is not faith, but superstition.

(17) What, then is the answer to life's perplexing question: "How can evil be cast out of our individual and collective lives?" If the world is not to be purified by God alone nor by man alone, who will do it?

(18) The answer is found in an idea which is distinctly different from the two we have discussed, for neither God nor man will individually bring the world's salvation. Rather, *both* man and God, made one in a marvelous unity of purpose through an overflowing love as the free gift of himself on the part of God and by perfect obedience and receptivity on the part of man, can transform the old into the new and drive out the deadly cancer of sin.

(19) The principle which opens the door for God to work through

man is faith. This is what the disciples lacked when they desperately tried to remove the nagging evil from the body of the sick child. Jesus reminded them that they had been attempting to do themselves what could be done only when their lives were open receptacles, as it were, into which God's strength could be freely poured.

(20) Two types of faith in God are clearly set forth in the Scriptures. One may be called the mind's faith, wherein the intellect assents to a belief that God exists. The other may be referred to as the heart's faith, whereby the whole man is involved in a trusting act of self-surrender. To know God, a man must possess this latter type of faith, for the mind's faith is directed toward a theory, but the heart's faith is centered in a Person. Gabriel Marcel claims that faith is *believing in, not believing that.* It is "opening a credit; which puts me at the disposal of the one in whom I believe." When I believe, he says "I rally to with that sort of interior gathering of oneself which the act of rallying implies." Faith is the opening of all sides and at every level of one's life to the divine inflow.

(21) This is what the Apostle Paul emphasized in his doctrine of salvation by faith. For him, faith is man's capacity to accept God's willingness through Christ to rescue us from the bondage of sin. In his magnanimous love, God freely offers to do for us what we cannot do for ourselves. Our humble and openhearted acceptance is faith. So by faith we are saved. Man filled with God and God operating through man bring unbelievable changes in our individual and social lives.

(22) Social evils have trapped multitudes of men in a dark and murky corridor where there is no exit sign and plunged others into a dark abyss of psychological fatalism. These deadly, paralyzing evils can be removed by a humanity perfectly united through obedience with God. Moral victory will come as God fills man and man opens his life by faith to God, even as the gulf opens to the overflowing waters of the river. Racial justice, a genuine possibility in our nation and in the world, will come neither by our frail and often misguided efforts nor by God imposing his will on wayward men, but when enough people open their lives to God and allow him to pour his triumphant, divine energy into their souls. Our age-old and noble dream of a world of peace may yet become a reality, but it will come neither by man working alone nor by God destroying the wicked schemes of men, but when men so open their lives to God that he may fill them with love, mutual respect, understanding, and goodwill. Social salvation will come only through man's willing acceptance of God's mighty gift.

(23) Let me apply what I have been saying to our personal lives. Many of you know what it means to struggle with sin. Year by year you were aware that a terrible sin—slavery to drink, perhaps, or untruthfulness, impurity, selfishness—was taking possession of your life. As the years unfolded and the vice widened its landmarks on your soul, you knew that it

was an unnatural intruder. You may have thought, "One day I shall drive this evil out. I know it is destroying my character and embarrassing my family." At last you determined to purge yourself of the evil by making a New Year's resolution. Do you remember your surprise and disappointment when you discovered, three hundred and sixty-five days later, that your most sincere efforts had not banished the old habit from your life? In complete amazement you asked, "Why could not I cast it out?"

(24) In despair you decided to take your problem to God, but instead of asking him to work through you, you said, "God, you must solve this problem for me. I can't do anything about it." But days and months later the evil was still with you. God would not cast it out, for he never removes sin without the cordial co-operation of the sinner. No problem is solved when we idly wait for God to undertake full responsibility.

(25) One cannot remove an evil habit by mere resolution nor by simply calling on God to do the job, but only as he surrenders himself and becomes an instrument of God. We shall be delivered from the accumulated weight of evil only when we permit the energy of God to come into our souls.

Questions for Discussion and Writing

1. The author uses figurative language extensively throughout the essay: "He [man] knows that evil is a foreign invader that must be driven from the native soils of his soul" (paragraph 1). Science "lifted us from the stagnating valleys of superstition and half truth to the sunlit mountains of creative analysis" (paragraph 7). Point out other such examples in the essay. What is the effect of such figures? Do they enhance your enjoyment of the essay? Why? Why not?

2. State as clearly and as concisely as possible the central idea of the essay. Is it comparable to the central idea of the following essay by Howard Thurman? In what ways? Explain.

3. Examine the structure of this essay. Are the divisions, introduction, body, and conclusion clearly delineated? How many paragraphs are devoted to each? Point out the transitional devices and comment upon their effectiveness or ineffectiveness.

4. The author suggests that the church should be integrally involved in the problems of society and should not be "divorced from the mainstream of human life." Do you agree or disagree with this concept? Give reasons to support your position. Do you feel that the present-day church is involved or is becoming involved more with the problems of humanity?

5. At the beginning of the essay, the author poses the question "How can evil be cast out?" In paragraph 18, he begins to answer this question. What is his answer? In your opinion, is his support of his answer adequate and logical? What is your reaction to the essential context of his answer?

Howard
Thurman

Howard   Thurman, selected by *Life* magazine as one of America's greatest preachers, received his academic and religious training at Florida Baptist Academy, Morehouse College, Oberlin, and Dartmouth-Rochester Divinity School. During his career, he toured many colleges in the United States and Canada lecturing to students, primarily on intellectual apathy. Nevertheless, he had a unique approach to students and their problems which earned him their respect. His ability to gain confidence of people in general and students in particular contributed much to his success as a clergyman-philosopher.

Dr. Thurman has held several positions, among these being Professor of Systematic Theology and Dean of the Chapel at Harvard University. He was also the founder and Minister of the Church for the Fellowship of All Peoples in San Francisco, and Dean of the Chapel at Boston University (a position from which he recently retired).

His works include *Disciplines of the Spirit, The Inward Journey, The*

Greatest of These, Deep River, and *The Luminous Darkness.* The following selection is taken from the latter work. It examines the role of the Christian and the Christian Church in today's society and emphasizes strongly the Christian's responsibility for promoting brotherhood among all peoples.

Howard
Thurman

From

The Luminous Darkness

(1) There has
emerged in the tradition of the Christian movement a secondary consideration, which is that the Christian must love especially those who are Christians. Here is a tie that binds all Christians as members of the Body of
Christ. If this is the case, then to be a part of the Body of Christ is to share
the love of all those who are a part of the body of Christ. To spell it out:
not only would a Baptist be under the demand to love all other Baptists
and a Methodist to love all other Methodists, etc., but it would be binding
upon each one who claimed to be a Christian, and therefore a part of the
Body of Christ, to love all others who make such a claim. It would follow
then that the Christian would be unique among other men in that the
Christian is secure in the love of other Christians. Indeed at one time in

Reprinted from Howard Thurman, The Luminous Darkness *(pp. 102–9) by per-*
mission of Harper & Row, Publishers. Copyright © *1965 by Howard Thurman.*

the history of Christianity it was this that separated the Christian from the world. "Behold how the Christians love each other." The formula can be stated categorically: The Christian has a special sense of being loved by God because he accepts the idea that God loved him by giving His son for his redemption. His response to the redemptive giving of God is to love God. "I love him because he first loved me." All Christians are involved in this relationship with God, therefore all Christians must give love to one another as a part of the giving of love to God.

(2) The tragedy is that even among those whose profession of faith subscribes completely to the above, the total relationship gives evidence of another kind. In fact, it is precisely accurate to say that the church, which is the institutional expression of the doctrine, has given little indication that being a member of the body of Christ has any bearing on how one member relates to the other members. Granted it may be less evident among those who are part of the same sectarian tradition. There is much to indicate that the further a particular group may be from the so-called mainstream of the convention of the doctrine, the more apt we may be to find the practice of love of all who belong to the household of faith. One of my earliest memories is that of greeting people at our door who asked for my parents because they wanted to talk to them about religion. Two things I remember: they called themselves Russellites, and despite the fact that they were white they made themselves at home in the living room. Nothing entered into what they did or what they said that drew the color line.

(3) Until most recently, no one expected the white Christian to love the black Christian or the black Christian to love the white Christian. Historically in this country, the church has given the sweep of its moral force to the practice of segregation within its own community of believers. To the extent to which this has been done, the church has violated one of the central elements in its own commitment. It has dared to demonstrate that the commitment is not central, that it does not believe that Christians are bound to love one another.

(4) The effect of its position with references to Christians of other races is far-reaching. It is to be noted that the doctrine has to be accommodated and dealt with in a manner that will hold the doctrine secure and at the same time tolerate its profound violation. How is this accomplished? With reference to the Negro, the church has promulgated a doctrine that makes the Negro the object of its salvation while at the same time it denies him the status of a human being, thereby enhancing the difficulties he must face in his effort to experience himself as a human being. Time after weary time, the church has dishonored its Lord. When I asked Mr. Gandhi, "What is the greatest handicap that Jesus has in India?" instantly he replied, "Christianity." And this is what he meant.

(5) The purpose here is not to indict but rather it is to lament the fact that such is the situation. The point must be clear that the commitment to love as it stands at the center of the Christian doctrine of God has not prevented the Christian from excluding Negroes from his Christian fellowship, nor has it prevented the Christian who is Negro from excluding white people from his Christian fellowship. To the extent that this is true, being Christian may not involve a person either in experiencing himself as a human being or in relating to others so as to experience them as human beings. The sad fact is that being Jewish, Catholic, or Protestant seems to make little difference in this regard.

(6) If being Christian does not demand that all Christians love each other and thereby become deeply engaged in experiencing themselves as human beings, it would seem futile to expect that Christians as Christians would be concerned about the secular community in its gross practices of prejudice and discrimination. If a black Christian and a white Christian, in encounter, cannot reach out to each other in mutual realization because of that which they are experiencing in common, then there should be no surprise that the Christian institution has been powerless in the presence of the color bar in society. Rather it has reflected the presence of the color bar within its own institutional life.

(7) On the other hand, if Christians practiced brotherhood among Christians this would be one limited step in the direction of a new order among men. Think of what this would mean. Wherever one Christian met or dealt with another Christian, there would be a socially redemptive encounter. They would be like the Gulf Stream or the Japanese Current tempering and softening the climate in all directions. Indeed the Christian would be a leaven at all levels of the community and in public and private living. Of course, such a situation may lend itself to all kinds of exploitation and betrayals—but the Christian would be one of the bulwarks of integrity in human relations in an immoral society.

(8) If the Christian limited his practice to other Christians, thereby guaranteeing that the church, wherever it existed, at whatever cost, would not tolerate segregation within its body, then there would be a kind of fierce logic in its position. It would be consistent within itself because it would practice brotherhood without regard to race, color and all the other barriers. It would make for a kind of arrogance and bigotry toward those who were not fortunate or wise enough to put themselves in the way of being Christian. This would narrow the basis of the faith deliberately, while at the same time providing enough room for the outsider to come in and belong. But the church has historically tended to reject this alternative.

(9) It is true and freely acknowledged that there are many changes afoot. Here and there through the years the Gospel has been at work despite the prohibition placed upon it by many denials. There is a power in

the teaching which when released, goes on to work its perfect work. Slowly there have emerged certain ingredients in the social climate that have had a softening effect. Much of this is due to the introduction of the teachings of Jesus and the Christian religious experience into society.

(10) In recent time it has become increasingly a part of the public policy and private practice of the church to put itself squarely on the side of cleaning its own house of the evils that separate the brethren. It has become more and more aggressive in attacking the presence of those same evils wherever they are in our society. It is a prestige factor in the church to take a challenging position in the matter of the treatment of Negroes. Very often when I am visiting in a city, clergymen and laymen proudly announce that their particular church is "integrated," or they may complain that they are wide open in the welcome of Negroes but that Negroes do not come. One is glad to witness the changes that are taking place and may regard the changes as delayed reactions to the impact of the Gospel in the church itself. But the thought persists that this is the response of the church to the pressure of the secular community upon it, rather than the response of the church to the genius of the Gospel which it proclaims. Perhaps it is both. Even the church cannot be in the position of establishing the ground rules by which God works in the development of the good life for His children.

(11) But why has the church been such a tragic witness to its own Gospel? It does seem to me at times that it is because the church is not sufficiently religious. By this I mean that it is not wide open to the Spirit of the living God. Its genius as an institution has to be sectarian in character. Perhaps there can be no such thing among men as the Church of God; it is the nature of institutionalism to be adjectival; some qualifying word must always precede the word "church." It has to be some *kind* of church, and this gives it its unique character and position.

(12) This fact creates a terrible dilemma. How important is the limiting and defining character? It may be that the church as such is an abstraction which only becomes concrete when a peculiar pattern or style of worship, etiquette, or doctrine emerges to define the character and give context to the abstraction. Nothing is ultimately admissible that may threaten the institutional structure that gives to the Christian religion its form and substance. But suppose as a part of the form and substance of the church all believers must commit themselves to loving all men, believers and nonbelievers, as children of God and therefore members one of another? Then the tremendous resources of such a church would be at the disposal of the performing ethic. Under such a circumstance, the whole missionary-conversion process would be reversed—men would knock at the door of the church to find out what they need to do to become what, in evidence, the Christian is. The life that the church lives in the world

would "bring the world to Christ." This surely means first of all to go ye into one's very own world, one's very own life, to go into every part of one's very own being and proclaim the good news that one can be free to experience oneself as a child of God and to experience all other men as children of God. Of such is a part of the miracle of Jesus. Men came to him with the searching question, What must I do? How may I? He made the life of God contagious!

(13) The problem may not be so simple. It is too easy to say or to believe that the church has not been true to its own Gospel. The question that deserves probing is Why? Is it because of human frailty? Is it because man has not evolved to the point that he is sufficiently human to deal justly and to promote the common good? Is there some inherent limitation in the nature of man that works against his doing for himself and with and on behalf of others that which makes for harmony, wholeness, love? Is it because of what the church recognizes as original sin? If not, precisely from what is the believer saved by the death and resurrection of Christ? Are the roots of conflict deep into a long forgotten past?

(14) Why is it that in many aspects of life that are regarded as secular one is apt to see more sharing, more of a tendency for human beings to experience themselves as human beings, than in those areas that are recognized as being religious? There seems to be more of a striving toward equality of treatment in many so-called secular institutions in our society than has characterized those institutions whose whole formal religious commitment demands that they practice the art of brotherhood. When I was in college, I heard two Negro men arguing on this very issue. We were on an all-day train ride in the third of the day coach designated to Negroes. Finally, one of the men, to clinch his point, said, "If I had committed a crime and was being tried in court, I would much rather have a jury made up of gamblers, race track men, pimps, than one of people who profess Christianity. I know I'd get much fairer treatment."

(15) There is something out of line somewhere. Can it be that matters which have to do with human relations are not the legitimate concern of religion? Hardly. The fact cannot be ignored that generally our society does not expect the church to be any kind of guide in these matters. It seems to me that one of the really tremendous things that is happening before our very eyes is that the religious community is now being judged by the same standards of human relations as the secular institutions in our society. This means that the church is slowly winning the right to regard as an institution that has a stake in the earthly fate of mankind. It has always concerned itself with charity, with good works, with the meeting of the creature needs of man; it has always concerned itself with the preaching of a doctrine of salvation which addressed itself to the spiritual condition as far as the soul was concerned; but for some reason that has

puzzled me all of my life, the religious community tended not to concern itself with the total needs of a man as a human being. And that, after all, is what matters most. Always it is a human being who hungers, who is sick, who is ignorant, who suffers. And he cannot be touched in any way that counts unless the word gets through to him that he is being experienced as a human being by the persons for whom he is the object of good works.

Questions for Discussion and Writing

1. State the major idea of the essay. By what method or methods is the essay developed?

2. It has been suggested that the Church has lost much of its appeal in the twentieth century because it is essentially isolated from the society in which it operates. Do you agree with this statement? Do you disagree? Why? Is the idea either implicit or explicit in the essay? Discuss.

3. The author states "There seems to be more striving toward equality of treatment in many so-called secular institutions in our society than has characterized those institutions whose whole religious commitment demands that they practice the art of brotherhood." Are there examples in today's society that would support that idea? Point out some of these and explain them.

4. Do you feel that the Church should lead the way in promoting brotherhood among peoples? Is there any evidence that the Church is beginning to feel this responsibility? If so, do you think that this results from secular pressures? From religious pressures? Support your answer.

5. In paragraph 7, the author uses a figure of speech to describe the effect of Christians practicing brotherhood among Christians: "They would be like the Gulf Stream or the Japanese Current tempering and softening the climate in all directions." Explain the figure. Does the idea seem logical to you?

6. Paragraph 13 consists of a series of questions. Are these questions answered in the essay, or are the answers implicit in the questions? Does the author create any special effect by the use of this device?

ON POLITICS

Gladys J.
Curry

Black Politics:
a Brief Survey

The evolution of the politics of the black man in America is many-faceted and complex—its beginning rooted in the early history of this country. Since the political strategy of black people in America is an integral part of American culture, certainly some aspect of it should be treated here.

For the past hundred years or more, political theory and practice of black people in America have been essentially integrationist or assimilationist. From time to time during this period, however, there have been upsurges of the politics of isolationism and nationalism. We may, then, survey briefly the trends of black politics from the earlier periods to the present as they reflect integrationism and isolationism.

During the late nineteenth and early twentieth centuries, the assimilationist theory was in ascendency, espoused by such men as Frederick Douglass, Booker T. Washington, and W. E. B. DuBois in varying degrees and methods. Douglass' method was an appeal to the conscience of white

Americans through his passionate oratory and through his writings; Washington's method was accommodation, reflected in what has become known as the "Atlanta Compromise" speech; DuBois' method was open protest and demands for justice, reflected in the Niagara movement. This assimilationist or integrationist theory continued to obtain as such organizations as the National Association for the Advancement of Colored People (NAACP) and the Urban League were formed in the early part of this century. Both these organizations were concerned with civil rights for the Negro, using litigation through the United States' courts as a chief means of attaining these rights.

During the 1920's, however, the temper of black political theory began to change from one of assimilation to one of isolationism and nationalism. This temper was epitomized in two movements: the "Back to Africa" movement instituted by Marcus Garvey, founder of the Universal Negro Improvement Association, and the Black Muslim movement instituted by Elijah Muhammad in the 1930's. While the "Back to Africa" movement died with the deportation of Marcus Garvey, the Black Muslim movement gained considerable force in the 1940's and 1950's.

It is important to note here that paralleling these nationalistic groups were such integrationist groups as the NAACP and the Urban League which were still operating and still quite powerful. In the 1940's and 1950's, integrationist theory and practice in black politics was further reinforced by the organization of the Congress of Racial Equality (CORE) under James Farmer and the Southern Christian Leadership Conference (SCLC) under Martin Luther King. The 1960's, however, saw the rise of two other groups that were essentially nationalistic: the Student Nonviolent Coordinating Committee (SNCC) led by Stokely Carmichael and Rap Brown and the Organization of Afro-American Unity founded by Malcolm X. These groups instituted what has come to be known as the politics of black power.

It is evident here, then, that the politics of the black man in America have been like a pendulum, swinging back and forth between two poles: isolationism and integrationism. While integration has been and is now, I believe, the dominant political theory, isolationism has gained tremendous force in the 1960's. The two essays included in this section, both concerned with the black power concept, may give the reader some understanding of the nature and scope of the isolationist movement. The excerpt from the United States Committee on Civil Rights which precedes these essays may serve as a general introduction to the new Negro revolution which began in the 1950's and may provide some background for the essays that follow.

Beginning

the New Revolution

in the 1950's[*]

In 1955, a group of Montgomery, Alabama, Negroes under the leadership of the Reverend Martin Luther King protested segregated seating on city bus lines. When Mrs. Rosa Parks was arrested for refusing to move to the rear of the bus, the group instituted a boycott. For 12 months makeshift car pools substituted for public transportation. Many persons walked several miles to and from their jobs. The bus company at first scoffed at the Negro protest. But as the economic effects of the boycott began to be felt, the company sought a settlement. When negotiations broke down, legal action was brought to end bus segregation. On June 5, 1956, a federal district court ruled that segregation on local public transportation violated the due proc-

*From *Freedom to the Free: A Report to the President by the United States Commission on Civil Rights* (Washington, D.C.: U. S. Government Printing Office, 1963), pp. 175–81.

ess and equal protection clauses of the Fourteenth Amendment. Later that year, the Supreme Court, citing the *School Segregation Cases*, affirmed the judgment. The boycott was ended.

The success in Montgomery gave new stimulus to organizations committed to nonviolent action. The Congress of Racial Equality and the Southern Christian Leadership Conference intensified their efforts. Created in 1943, the Congress of Racial Equality (CORE), from its early beginnings, utilized the nonviolent protest to achieve its goals. The Southern Christian Leadership Conference (SCLC), a direct outgrowth of the Montgomery bus boycott, was formed to serve as a coordinating agency for those employing the technique and philosophy of nonviolent protest. At its organizational meeting in Atlanta in 1957, the Reverend Martin Luther King was elected as its president. The NAACP, itself a participant in direct action, the Southern Regional Council, religious groups, and various labor and civic organizations gave support and aid to those involved in direct action.

Then on February 1, 1960, four students from the Negro Agricultural and Technical College of Greensboro, North Carolina, entered a variety store, made several purchases, sat down at the lunch counter, ordered coffee, and were refused service because they were Negroes. They remained in their seats until the store closed.

In the spring and summer of 1960, young people, both white and Negro, participated in similar protests against segregation and discrimination wherever it was to be found. They sat in white libraries, waded at white beaches, and slept in the lobbies of white hotels. Many were arrested for trespassing, disturbing the peace, and disobeying police officers who ordered them off the premises. As a result of the sit-ins, literally hundreds of lunch counters began to serve Negroes for the first time and other facilities were open to them.

Thus began a sweeping protest movement against entrenched practices of segregation. In summing up the movement, Reverend King said that legislation and court orders tend to declare rights but can never thoroughly deliver them. "Only when people themselves begin to act are rights on paper given life blood. . . . Nonviolent resistance also makes it possible for the individual to struggle to secure moral ends through moral means." By 1962, the sit-in movement had achieved considerable success. As a result of the sit-ins and negotiations undertaken because of them, department store lunch counters and other facilities had been desegregated in more than 100 cities in 14 states in various parts of the nation.

The sit-in movement did not escape executive attention. On March 16, 1960, President Eisenhower commented that he was "deeply sympathetic with efforts of any group to enjoy the rights . . . of equality that they are guaranteed by the Constitution" and that "if a person is expressing such an aspiration as this in a perfectly legal way," the President did not see any reason why he should not do so. On June 1, Attorney General William P. Rogers met with representatives of several national variety stores and secured their promises to have their local managers confer with public officials and citizens' committees to work out means of desegregating their lunch counters. On August 10, the attorney general announced that the national chains had made good on their promises by desegregating lunch counters in 69 southern communities.

The judiciary was soon to become involved in the sit-ins. For while some of the sit-in demonstrators voluntarily went to jail, many appealed their convictions on the ground that the ejections, arrests, and convictions by local government officials constituted enforcement of the private proprietor's discrimination and therefore constituted state action in violation of the Fourteenth Amendment. Three cases involving 16 students reached the Supreme Court from Louisiana in the fall of 1961. On December 11, 1961, without reaching the broader constitutional questions, the Court reversed the convictions because of lack of evidence that the sit-ins disturbed the peace either by outwardly boisterous conduct or by passive conduct likely to cause a public disturbance.

In November 1962, the Supreme Court heard arguments in six cases in which the arrest of sit-in demonstrators was attacked as unconstitutional. The Solicitor General of the United States, appearing as a friend of the Court, maintained that four of the criminal convictions were based on unconstitutional State laws, and the fifth on a pervasive state policy of segregation, and that the sixth should be reversed because the agent who evicted the defendants also served as the arresting officer. The Court's decision is awaited at this writing.

One of the most dramatic attacks on segregation and discrimination was undertaken in May 1961 by the Congress of Racial Equality. A group of CORE-sponsored "freedom riders" toured the South to test segregation laws and practices in interstate transportation and terminal facilities. The "freedom riders" encountered no difficulties until they arrived in Alabama and Mississippi. In Montgomery, Alabama, 20 persons were injured on May 20, 1961, by mob action. When local police failed to restore order, 400 federal marshals were brought in to maintain order. President Kennedy said the situation was "the source of the deepest concern to me as it must be to the vast majority of the citizens of Alabama and all Americans." On May 21, after initially resisting federal authority, Governor Patterson called out the National Guard and order was quickly restored. The Department of Justice secured a temporary restraining order from the federal district court prohibiting any further attempt by force to stop "freedom riders" from continuing their test of bus segregation. On June 2, Montgomery city officials, together with several private individuals and organizations, were enjoined by the court from interfering with travel of passengers in interstate commerce. The city officials were also enjoined from refusing to provide protection for such travelers.

When the "freedom riders" rode into Mississippi, the Governor called out the National Guard to escort them into Jackson. On May 24, 1961, the first contingent was arrested for refusing to obey a police officer's command to move from segregated terminal waiting room facilities. In the following months, more than 300 "freedom riders" were arrested and convicted. On July 10, the Department of Justice intervened before a three-judge federal court to halt the arrest of the riders in Mississippi. The attorney general charged that local authorities had gone "beyond the scope of their lawful power" in making the arrests. On November 17, the court ruled that the arrests must be challenged in state courts. An application to the Supreme Court for an injunction to stay state criminal prosecutions was denied. President Kennedy, in reply to a question at his July 19 news conference, upheld the right of American citizens to move in interstate commerce "for whatever reasons they travel."

By the summer of 1962, the leaders of the direct action movements could see results in the form of government response to their demands and favorable changes in business attitudes and policies.

Stokely
Carmichael

Stokely   Carmichael
is the former chairman of the Student Nonviolent Coordinating Committee
(SNCC). Having been active in that organization almost from its inception
(1960), he was elected chairman in May 1967. He also played a major role
in the Mississippi Summer Project in 1964 and was the first to use the term
Black Power publicly in relation to the civil rights movement. The term has
since been subjected to many interpretations and has evoked many and
varied reactions.

Mr. Carmichael received the Bachelor of Arts Degree from Howard
University (Washington, D.C.). His major work is *Black Power: The Politics
of Liberation in America*, a book written in collaboration with Charles V.
Hamilton, Chairman of the Department of Political Science at Roosevelt
University in Chicago.

The following essay is essentially a definition of the concept of Black

Power. In it, Carmichael places special emphasis on the positive values of the concept. He expresses the idea that black people must attain "psychological equality" and that this can best be attained through black solidarity. He intimates that this does not exclude the friendship of other peoples.

Stokely Carmichael

Power

and Racism

(1) To most whites, black power seems to mean that the Mau Mau are coming to the suburbs at night. The Mau Mau are coming and whites must stop them. Articles appear about plots to "get Whitey," creating an atmosphere in which "law and order must be maintained." Once again, responsibility is shifted from the oppressor to the oppressed. Other whites chide, "don't forget—you're only 10 percent of the population; if you get too smart, we'll wipe you out." If they are liberals, they complain, "What about me?—don't you want my help any more?" These are people supposedly concerned about black Americans, but today they think first of themselves, of their feelings of rejection. Or they admonish, "You can't get anywhere without coalitions," without considering the problems of coalition with whom; on what terms

Stokely Carmichael, "Power and Racism." Reprinted by special permission of the Student Nonviolent Coordinating Committee.

(coalescing from weakness can mean absorption, betrayal); when? Or they accuse us of "polarizing the races" by our calls for black unity, when the true responsibility for polarization lies with the whites who will not accept their responsibility as the majority power for making the democratic process work.

(2) White America will not face the problem of color, the reality of it. The well-intended say: "We're all human, everybody is really decent, we must forget color." But color cannot be "forgotten" until its weight is recognized and dealt with. White America will not acknowledge that the ways in which this country sees itself are contradicted by being black—and always have been. Whereas most of the people who settled this country came here for freedom or for economic opportunity, blacks were brought here to be slaves. When the Lowndes County Freedom Organization chose the black panther as its symbol, it was christened by the press "the Black Panther Party"—but the Alabama Democratic Party, whose symbol is a rooster, has never been called the White Cock Party. No one ever talked about "white power" because power in this country *is* white. All this adds up to more than merely identifying a group phenomenon by some catch name or adjective. The furor over "black power" reveals how deep racism runs and the great fear which is attached to it.

(3) Whites will not see that I, for example, as a person oppressed because of my blackness, have common cause with other blacks who are oppressed because of blackness. This is not to say that there are no white people who see things as I do, but that it is black people I must speak to first. It must be the oppressed to whom SNCC addresses itself primarily, not to friends from the oppressing group.

(4) From birth, black people are told a set of lies about themselves. We are told that we are lazy—yet I drive through the Delta area of Mississippi and watch black people picking cotton in the hot sun for fourteen hours. We are told, "If you work hard, you'll succeed"—but if that were true, black people would own this country. We are oppressed because we are black—not because we are ignorant, nor because we are lazy, not because we're stupid (and got good rhythm), but because we're black.

(5) I remember that when I was a boy, I used to go to see Tarzan movies on Saturday. White Tarzan used to beat up the black natives. I would sit there yelling, "Kill the beasts, kill the savages, kill 'em!" I was saying: Kill *me*. It was as if a Jewish boy watched Nazis taking Jews off to concentration camps and cheered them on. Today, I want the chief to beat hell out of Tarzan and send him back to Europe. But it takes time to become free of the lies and their shaming effect on black minds. It takes time to reject the most important lies: that black people inherently can't do the same things white people do, unless white people help them.

(6) The need for psychological equality is the reason why SNCC

today believes that blacks must organize in the black community. Only black people can convey the revolutionary idea that black people are able to do things themselves. Only they can help create in the community an aroused and continuing black consciousness that will provide the basis for political strength. In the past, white allies have furthered white supremacy without the whites involved realizing it—or wanting it, I think. Black people must do things for themselves; they must get poverty money they will control and spend themselves, they must conduct tutorial programs themselves so that black children can identify with black people. This is one reason Africa has such importance: The reality of black men ruling their own nations gives blacks elsewhere a sense of possibility, or power which they do not now have.

(7) This does not mean we don't welcome help, or friends. But we want the right to decide whether anyone is, in fact, our friend. In the past, black Americans have been almost the only people whom everybody and his momma could jump up and call their friends. We have been tokens, symbols, objects—as I was in high school to many young whites, who liked having "a Negro friend." We want to decide who is our friend, and we will not accept someone who comes to us and says: "If you do X, Y, and Z, then I'll help you." We will not be told whom we should choose as allies. We will not be isolated from any group or nation except by our own choice. We cannot have the oppressors telling the oppressed how to rid themselves of the oppressor.

(8) I have said that most liberal whites react to "black power" with the question, What about me? rather than saying: Tell me what you want me to do and I'll see if I can do it. There are answers to the right question. One of the most disturbing things about almost all white supporters of the movement has been that they are afraid to go into their own communities —which is where the racism exists—and work to get rid of it. They want to run from Berkeley to tell us what to do in Mississippi; let them look instead at Berkeley. They admonish blacks to be nonviolent; let them preach non-violence in the white community. They come to teach me Negro history; let them go to the suburbs and open up freedom schools for whites. Let them work to stop America's racist foreign policy; let them press this government to cease supporting the economy of South Africa.

(9) There is a vital job to be done among poor whites. We hope to see, eventually, a coalition between poor blacks and poor whites. That is the only coalition which seems acceptable to us, and we see such a coalition as the major internal instrument of change in American society. SNCC has tried several times to organize poor whites; we are trying again now, with an initial training program in Tennessee. It is purely academic today to talk about bringing poor blacks and whites together, but the job of creating a poor-white power bloc must be attempted. The main responsi-

bility for it falls upon whites. Black and white can work together in the white community where possible; it is not possible, however, to go into a poor Southern town and talk about integration. Poor whites everywhere are becoming more hostile—not less—partly because they see the nation's attention focused on black poverty and nobody coming to them. Too many young middle-class Americans, like some sort of Pepsi generation, have wanted to come alive through the black community; they've wanted to be where the action is—and the action has been in the black community.

(10) Black people do not want to "take over" this country. They don't want to "get Whitey," they just want to get him off their backs, as the saying goes. It was, for example, the exploitation by Jewish landlords and merchants which first created black resentment toward Jews—not Judaism. The white man is irrelevant to blacks, except as an oppressive force. Blacks want to be in his place, yes, but not in order to terrorize and lynch and starve him. They want to be in his place because that is where a decent life can be had.

(11) But our vision is not merely of a society in which all black men have enough to buy the good things of life. When we urge that black money go into black pockets, we mean the communal pocket. We want to see money go back into the community and used to benefit it. We want to see the co-operative concept applied in business and banking. We want to see the black ghetto residents demand that an exploiting landlord or store keeper sell them, at minimal cost, a building or a shop that they will own and improve co-operatively; they can back their demand with a rent strike, or a boycott, and a community so unified behind them that no one else will move into the building or buy at the store. The society we seek to build among black people, then, is not a capitalist one. It is a society in which the spirit of community and humanistic love prevail. The word love is suspect; black expectations of what it might produce have been betrayed too often. But those were expectations of a response from the white community, which failed us. The love we seek to encourage is within the black community, the only American community where men call each other "brother" when they meet. We can build a community of love only where we have the ability and power to do so: among blacks.

(12) As for the white America, perhaps it can stop crying out against "black supremacy," "black nationalism," "racism in reverse," and begin facing reality. The reality is that this nation, from top to bottom, is racist; that racism is not primarily a problem of "human relations" but of an exploitation maintained—either actively or through silence—by the society as a whole. Camus and Sartre have asked, can a man condemn himself? Can whites, particularly liberal whites, condemn themselves? Can they stop blaming us, and blame their own system? Are they capable of the shame which might become a revolutionary emotion?

(13) We have found that they usually cannot condemn themselves, and so we have done it. But the rebuilding of this society, if at all possible, is basically the responsibility of whites—not blacks. We won't fight to save the present society, in Vietnam or anywhere else. We are just going to work, in the way we see fit, and on goals we define, not for civil rights but for all our human rights.

Questions for Discussion and Writing

1. Explain Mr. Carmichael's concept of Black Power.

2. The author suggests several things that liberal whites can do to aid the Negro cause. What are these things? Can you find examples in today's society that some of these things are being done by whites? Can you list other things that are being done in America to aid the Negro?

3. The author sees an ultimate coalition between the poor whites and poor Blacks. What has been the major deterrent to such a coalition? Does the author make this clear in the essay?

4. What is meant by psychological equality? Does the author define it specifically in the essay? How much importance does he attach to it? How does he feel it can best be attained?

5. The author states that "color cannot be forgotten until its weight is recognized and dealt with." Does he indicate in the essay what this recognition involves and how the problem is to be dealt with?

6. Explain Mr. Carmichael's reference to some middle-class Americans as "some sort of Pepsi generation."

7. Are all of the ideas in the essay clearly and logically developed? Support your answer with specific examples.

8. Find out what you can about the Black Panther Party, e.g., organizers, aims and objectives, etc.

Nathan
Wright, Jr.

Nathan Wright, Jr., consultant in education and urbanization is Executive Director of the Department of Urban Work for the Episcopal Diocese of Newark, New Jersey. As Field Secretary for the Congress of Racial Equality (CORE), he succeeded Adam Clayton Powell as Plans Committee Chairman of the 1967 National Conference on Black Power.

Dr. Wright holds several academic degrees, including the doctorate degree in education from Harvard University. He has lectured in urban sociology at New York City Community College and is the author of several books, mainly on religious subjects. In 1967, however, he published *Black Power and Urban Unrest*, a study of economics and the Negro ghetto. Like Carmichael in the preceding essay, he views Black Power as a positive force. He suggests that the Black Power Movement has been more meaningful than the Civil Rights Movement in fostering in black people a sense of pride and dignity in themselves. He also insists, however, that the concept of Black Power, rightly interpreted, does not negate the co-operation and friendship of the white man.

Nathan
Wright, Jr.

The Question

of Power

(1) The present
crossroads or crisis in civil rights—and its possible resolution—must be
associated with the issue of power.

(2) The call on the part of black people for Black Power represents
an unmistakable turnabout in both mood and direction in the area once
appropriately described as civil rights.

(3) There are certain clear differences between the civil rights movement and the impetus toward Black Power. The thrust toward Black Power
does not ask what the black American is due. It seeks inherently to add the
power, the latent and preciously needed potential, of black people for the
enrichment of the life of the nation as a whole.

(4) Black power is not a negative concept. It is a positive, creative
concept, seeking to bring a wanted maturity to our too long adolescent

Reprinted from Nathan Wright, Jr., The Black Power Revolt *(Floyd Barbour, ed.),
by permission of Porter Sargent Publisher. Copyright © 1968 by Porter Sargent Publisher.*

nation's life. To produce growth and a wholesome sense of maturity there must be equitable relationships of power. The gross imbalance between the power of black and white Americans has effectively subverted our democratic goals, blurred the nation's vision of the pathway toward the great destiny of which it dreams, and perverted its moral sense as an apparently all-powerful white America has confronted its seemingly powerless major ethnic minority.

(6) Black Power seeks to bring to the nation's life the saving necessity of equitable and growth-producing power tension and extension.

(7) Vice President Hubert Humphrey recently remarked that in spite of apparent disagreements concerning Black Power among some civil rights leaders, it should be clear to all familiar with American history that Black Power is within the basic American traditions. Black Americans, he asserted, need Black Power to achieve political, civic, and economic goals even as other ethnic groups have used the weight of their ethnic numbers to achieve their goals. In this way America has come thus far toward its own self-realization and fulfillment.

(8) *Black Power reflects the failure of the civil rights movement in at least several significant respects.*

(9) Above all else, black Americans have needed the power which comes from pride in one's own accomplishments. Black people have throughout this nation's history been *dependent* on other people. At first, this was due to necessity. Later it was due to long-standing cultural conditioning.

(10) In the civil rights movement to a not inconsiderable degree the slave mentality of looking to others for direction and support is seen to have been kept in force. Black people manifestly must have the sense of pride and self-respect which can only come through the tradition of self-directed efforts at self-sufficiency. Black organizations and efforts for black self-improvement—as with Jewish organizations led by Jews and Italian organizations, by Italians—must be black led.

(11) Black leadership must be able leadership. But the substitute of white competence for blackness in leadership cannot be said to have a clear advantage. White technical competence in educational matters, for example, may take Negroes much further down the road than black incompetence. But it will have—as the evidence in our inner cities plainly attests—a well-nigh impossible task in taking our youngsters over the bridge at the river or bringing them across the finish line. The ideal that is needed is the kind of black competence which affords pride and holds onto hope in uniquely saving ways. For these precious qualities there can be no effective substitute. We cannot and must not, as black men or white, settle for less, if we are to have the latent potential of our hopeless and increasingly desperate black masses come to its best flower.

(12) Black Power does not negate the value of friendship and co-operation on the part of others. It speaks basically to the role of leadership. The basic American tradition is for each rising ethnic group to devise and execute its own plan for economic, political, and civic freedom and development. So it must be with the black people of our land. They have been the most assisted and the most greatly benighted. The civil rights movement focused upon cooperation and, in a way foreign to the American tradition and to all rising ethnic groups, accepted direction and leadership from outside its ranks. However wise it may be no outside leadership has that crucially significant ingredient of the inner drive and urgency to be free which can come only from one who is a part of the oppressed.

(13) The proof of the civil rights movement pudding has been in its eating. It has been tested severely especially in the decade ending in 1965; and the clear record of its sad legacy after a gloriously executed decade of battle tells its own sad story. We have seen that the black people of America are—as a whole—more benighted than ever in relation to the nation as a whole, and a white America faces a black future in which its rehabilitative and policing costs will stagger our minds and threaten the security of our institutions and our way of life.

(14) Black Power speaks for a new day of candor and integrity. Integration as we have sought to work it out over the past decade and more, has clearly failed. There can be no meaningful integration between unequals. Thus as black men have turned toward an illusive integrationist goal, with white men holding the reins of power, black men have lost both their identity and their self-respect.

(15) No black man needs the presence of a white man to have a sense of worth. Increasingly black men are saying today that if they never saw white men in their lives, their being would not be diminished one bit. Nor is it necessary, as our government statistics seem daily to insist, for black children to have the presence of white children in order to learn as they should.

(16) Where white children are present there is a pervasive sense that one has a future, that one might share in the shaping of the conditions of one's life. Black children, through the impetus toward Black Power, may have by themselves those same horizons. No one seeing life as one dark vast cavern of uncertainty would or could be moved or impelled to learn. But give a child hope, and his life may suddenly come to flower.

(17) The integrationist mood of the civil rights movement has led to what some see as a dead-end street. White people in America overwhelmingly are not quite yet ready for open and honest friendship and brotherhood with black Americans. The integrationist mood of the civil rights movement asked black Americans to play a game of brotherhood where, almost universally, white men have welshed on the rules. If men and

women will not be open and honest and fair and free when their children are of the age of courtship and marriage, how can they ask others to make full and free counter-commitments? In all fairness, black Americans cannot be asked to make emotional commitments to white friendships into which white people have historically built a guarantee of soon or late frustration.

(18) No rising ethnic group in this nation has, on its own, asked for integration. All have asked simply for desegregation. Desegregation involves some integration as a means to an end but not as an end in itself. Desegregation involves the clearing of the decks of all barriers to free choice relationships which do not interfere with the rights of others. It is permissive of growth and is not negative in its implications.

(19) Black men, at this hour in our nation's life, need solidarity. They need pride in what they are. This means pride in blackness. They need the power implicit in their rising from their sitters and their standing on their feet. Black men want desperately to do just this. They want to pull themselves up by their own bootstraps, but where even bootstraps are so often lacking, some substitute must be supplied.

(20) Because the black American's moving into self-sufficiency and pride and self-realization are the only means by which the mounting desperation of black people may be averted, Black Power is the clear self-interest of all white Americans.

(21) White Americans can and must facilitate Black Power by converting their neighbors and by encouraging in many creative ways the solidarity and self-respect which black Americans so sorely need. They can help also in the removal of many specific devices which debilitate black people. Black people are effectively barred from access not only to loans for large business properties, but also to many home ownership loans. Banks are threatened almost daily if they lend to Negroes in a way that breaks the unspoken racist code. Negroes are barred from consideration for many higher echelon civil or public service jobs vital to the well-being of the black and white community by screening committees with prevailing cultural perceptions and by nonobjective oral examinations. White people concerned with the development of Black Power may help to insure that competent black men direct the human resources administrations of our states and shape the Model Cities plans at the local level. What most often appears to be black apathy is in substantial measure a black time-ingrained cynicism at the systematic way in which cards are stacked against black people.

(22) Black power, actively developed, and espoused and facilitated by all, may thus break through the present crisis and inaugurate a new day of hope. Peril may be averted when the powerless command a sense of power to find some semblance of fulfillment.

(23) The current crisis in civil rights came about through an honorable, but faulty intent. Black Power now seeks a better way. It should be our purpose—for the sake of all who comprise and will come to comprise America—to encourage power for growth and for fulfillment on the part of all.

Questions for Discussion and Writing

1. State the central idea of this essay. Compare and/or contrast it with that of Carmichael's "Power and Racism."

2. The author quotes Hubert Humphrey as saying that Black Power is within the American tradition. Explain this statement. Can you think of specific examples in American history that would support this idea?

3. Explain the statement "There can be no meaningful integration among unequals." Do you agree or disagree? Give reasons to support your position.

4. According to the author, what is the basic difference between integration and desegregation? Which does he believe to be more meaningful at present? Which, if either, do you believe to be more meaningful? To whom? In what ways?

5. The author states that Black Power is not a negative but a positive concept. Does he clearly prove this in his essay? How? Do you agree that the Black Power concept as explained here is a positive one? Are you acquainted with other interpretations of the term? Explain.

6. The author concludes that Black Power is "in the clear self-interest of all white Americans." What reason does he give to support this statement? Do you agree? Discuss.

Suggestions
for Further Reading

Baldwin, James, *The Fire Next Time*. New York: The Dial Press, Inc., 1963.

———, *Nobody Knows my Name*. New York: The Dial Press, Inc., 1961.

———, *Notes of a Native Son*. Boston: Beacon Press, Inc., 1955.

Barbour, Floyd (ed.), *Black Power Revolt*. Boston: Porter Sargent Publisher.

Bennett, Lerone, *The Negro Mood*. Chicago: Johnson Publishing Company, 1964.

Butcher, Margaret, *The Negro in American Culture*. New York: Alfred A. Knopf, Inc., 1957.

Carmichael, Stokely, and Charles Hamilton, *Black Power: The Politics of Liberation in America*. New York: Alfred A. Knopf, Inc., 1967.

Cleaver, Eldridge, *Soul on Ice*. New York: McGraw-Hill Book Company, 1968.

Douglass, Frederick, *My Bondage My Freedom*. New York: Miller, Orton and Mulligan, 1855.

DuBois, W. E. B., *Souls of Black Folk*. Chicago: McClurg and Company, 1903.

Ellison, Ralph, *Shadow and Act*. New York: Random House, Inc., 1964.

Epps, Archie (ed.), *The Speeches of Malcolm X at Harvard*. New York: William Morrow and Company, Inc., 1968.

Franklin, John H., and Isidore Starr (eds.), *The Negro in the Twentieth Century America*. New York: Random House, Inc., 1967.

Frazier, E. Franklin, *Black Bourgoisie*. New York: The Free Press of Glencoe, Inc., 1962.

Gayle, Addison (ed.), *Black Expression*. New York: Weybright and Talley, Inc., 1969.

Gloster, Hugh, *Negro Voices in American Fiction*. Chapel Hill, N.C.: University of North Carolina Press, 1948.

Hare, Nathan, *The Black Anglo-Saxons*. New York: Marzani and Munsell, Inc., 1965.

Hill, Herbert (ed.), *Anger and Beyond*. New York: Harper and Row, Publishers, 1966.

Jones, LeRoi, *Blues People: Negro Music in White America*. New York: William Morrow and Company, Inc., 1963.

———, *Home: Social Essays*. New York: William Morrow and Company, Inc., 1966.

King, Martin L., *Strength to Love*. New York: Harper and Row, Publishers, 1963.

———, *Stride Toward Freedom*. New York: Harper and Row, Publishers, 1963.

Locke, Alain, *The Negro and His Music*. Port Washington, N.Y.: Kennikat Press, Inc., 1968.

Lomax, Louis E., *The Negro Revolt*. New York: Harper and Row, Publishers, 1962.

———, *When the Word is Given*. Cleveland, Ohio: The World Publishing Company, 1964.

Meltzer, Milton (ed.), *In Their Own Words: A History of the American Negro*. New York: Thomas Y. Crowell Company, 1964. 3 vols.

Redding, Saunders, *On Being Negro in America*. New York: The Bobbs-Merrill Co., Inc., 1964.

Thurman, Howard, *The Luminous Darkness*. New York: Harper and Row, Publishers, 1965.

Turner, Darwin, *Black American Literature Essays*. Columbus, Ohio: Charles E. Merrill Books, Inc., 1969.

————, *Images of the Negro*. Boston: D. C. Heath and Company, 1965.

Wright, Richard, *White Man Listen*. Garden City, N.Y.: Doubleday and Company, Inc., 1957.

Wright, Nathan, Jr., *Black Power and Urban Unrest. The Creative Possibility*. New York: Hawthorne Books, Inc., 1967